BRITISH AND IRISH AUTHORS

Introductory Critical Studies

H. G. WELLS

H. G. WELLS

JOHN BATCHELOR

Fellow and Tutor in English
New College, Oxford

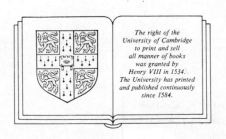

The right of the
University of Cambridge
to print and sell
all manner of books
was granted by
Henry VIII in 1534.
The University has printed
and published continuously
since 1584.

CAMBRIDGE UNIVERSITY PRESS

CAMBRIDGE

LONDON   NEW YORK   NEW ROCHELLE

MELBOURNE   SYDNEY

Published by the Press Syndicate of the University of Cambridge
The Pitt Building, Trumpington Street, Cambridge CB2 1RP
32 East 57th Street, New York, NY 10022, USA
10 Stamford Road, Oakleigh, Melbourne 3166, Australia

© Cambridge University Press 1985

First published 1985

Printed in Great Britain by
Woolnough Bookbinding, Wellingborough

Library of Congress catalogue card number: 84–17440

British Library Cataloguing in Publication Data
Batchelor, John, *1942–*
H. G. Wells. – (British and Irish authors)
1. Wells, H. G. – Criticism and interpretation
1. Title 11. Series
823.'912 PR5777

ISBN 0 521 26026 4 hard covers
ISBN 0 521 27804 x paperback

To Henrietta, William, Clarissa and Leo

Contents

Preface and acknowledgements

Wells was a novelist, a romancer, a prophet, a polemicist and a mass of contradictions; a writer who heralded the future but clung to fixed attitudes from the past. At the turn of the century he predicted the invention of the tank, yet during the Second World War he was still engaged in an essentially Victorian struggle between religion and science. Having established a reputation as a major writer between 1895 and 1910 he secured for himself a second, far more influential, reputation as an educator in the 1920s and 1930s following the success of *The Outline of History*. Yet some of his best novels have never been reprinted and discussion of his writings tends to be focused exclusively on his early work. Wells acted in unconscious complicity with his adversaries; he had a theory of fiction which was coherent and responsible, and which underlies his best work, but he failed to defend it as vigorously as he could have done. This book is a work of advocacy; Wells is a great artist, and those of us who enjoy his work need not feel ashamed of the pleasure that we take in reading him. I am grateful to the Warden and Fellows of New College for a period of sabbatical leave during which I wrote this book, to David Lodge and Tom Shippey for reading my typescript and making a number of helpful suggestions, to Mrs Catherine Stoye, Wells's granddaughter, for checking the Chronology and to Margaret Whitlock and Penny Brown for typing and re-typing the text.

List of abbreviations

In the references the following abbreviations are used:

Atlantic   H. G. Wells, *The Atlantic Edition of the Works of H. G. Wells* (24 vols.). Fisher Unwin, 1924–28.

Autobiography   H. G. Wells, *Experiment in Autobiography: Discoveries and Conclusions of a very Ordinary Brain* (2 vols.). Gollancz, 1935.

Bergonzi   Bernard Bergonzi, *The Early H. G. Wells: A Study of the Scientific Romances*. Manchester University Press, 1961.

Catherine   *The Book of Catherine Wells* (ed. H. G. Wells). Chatto and Windus, 1928.

Dickson   Lovat Dickson, *H. G. Wells: His Turbulent Life and Times*. Macmillan, 1969.

Hammond   J. R. Hammond, *An H. G. Wells Companion*. Macmillan, 1979.

Heritage   *H. G. Wells: The Critical Heritage* (ed. Patrick Parrinder). Routledge, 1972.

Huxley   T. H. Huxley, 'Evolution and Ethics'. Macmillan, 1893.

James/Wells   *Henry James and H. G. Wells: A Record of their Friendship* (ed. Leon Edel and G. N. Ray). Hart-Davis, 1958.

Lodge   David Lodge, 'Tono-Bungay and the Condition of England', *Language of Fiction*. Routledge, 1966.

McConnell   Frank McConnell, *The Science Fiction of H. G. Wells*. Oxford University Press, 1981.

MacKenzies   Norman and Jeanne MacKenzie, *The Time Traveller: A Biography of H. G. Wells*. Weidenfeld and Nicolson, 1973.

Masterman   C. F. G. Masterman, *The Condition of England* [1909] (ed. J. T. Boulton). Methuen, 1960.

Mr Waddy   H. G. Wells, *The Wealth of Mr Waddy* (ed. Harris Wilson). Southern Illinois University Press, 1969.

xi

ABBREVIATIONS

Newell	Kenneth B. Newell, *Structure in Four Novels by H. G. Wells*. Mouton, 1968.
Philmus	*H. G. Wells: Early Writings in Science and Science Fiction* (ed. R. Philmus and D. Y. Hughes). University of California Press, 1975.
Ray	Gordon N. Ray, 'H. G. Wells Tries to be a Novelist', *Edwardians and Late Victorians* (ed. Richard Ellmann). Columbia University Press, 1960.
Ray/West	Gordon N. Ray, *H. G. Wells and Rebecca West*. Macmillan, 1974.
Reade	Winwood Reade, *The Martyrdom of Man* [1872]. Pemberton: The Humanist Library, 1966.
Reed	John R. Reed, *The Natural History of H. G. Wells*. Ohio University Press, 1982.
Romances	H. G. Wells, *The Scientific Romances* (comprises *The Time Machine, The Island of Dr Moreau, The Invisible Man, The War of the Worlds, The First Men in the Moon, In the Days of the Comet, Men Like Gods*; with a preface by H. G. Wells). Victor Gollancz, 1933.
Views	*H. G. Wells: A Collection of Critical Essays* (ed. Bernard Bergonzi: Twentieth Century Views series). Prentice Hall, 1976.
West	Geoffrey West, *H. G. Wells*. Gerald Howe, 1930.
Wilson	*Arnold Bennett and H. G. Wells* (ed. Harris Wilson). Hart-Davis, 1960.

1

The romances of the 1890s:
The Time Machine, *The Island of Dr Moreau*, *The War of the Worlds*

The emergent writer, 1866–1900

Herbert George Wells was born in Bromley, Kent, in 1866, the youngest child of a struggling shopkeeper, Joseph Wells, who had earlier been a gardener and spent as much time as he could picking up small fees as a cricket coach. Wells's mother, Sarah, was a cut above his father socially, being a former lady's maid to Miss Fetherstonhaugh of Up Park, near Petersfield. Her social and religious attitudes had a crucial bearing on Wells's own outlook. He was brought up to hate and fear the working class; his mother was determined that he should be a 'gentleman' and should be kept apart from rough and common boys. Also, she was a strict Protestant with a firm belief in Hell; this faith in an apocalyptic tradition was undoubtedly transmitted to Wells, providing an unconscious pattern which recurs in his prophetic writings. Wells writes about his parents leaving service to set up their 'unsuccessful crockery shop' in terms which suggest that he always knew, as a child, that his parents' situation was hopeless, and at the same time recognised that his own talent was in a way fostered by the circumstances of the parental home. Food was short in the shabby living quarters behind the shop but there was always plenty to read, and as a child Wells read 'everything'. 'Everything' explicitly excluded Scott – Wells was later to say that he had been instinctively repelled, as a child, by the conservatism of Scott's imagination – but included Chaucer, George Eliot, Dickens, Voltaire, Plutarch's *Lives*, Plato's *Republic*, Lucretius, and that 'most entrancing book, *Vathek*!' (Atlantic, 1, p. xii). It seems to have been the violence of Beckford's eighteenth-century oriental extravaganza that attracted him. The narrator of the early, autobiographical, chapters of *Tono-Bungay* recalls his pleasure in a scene in *Vathek* in which the characters are compelled to kick each other: 'That kicking affair! When everybody *had* to kick!' (ch. 1).

In 1877, when Wells was eleven, his father fell off a ladder and injured himself, and the china shop finally failed while he was laid up. Sarah Wells left her husband and went back to Up Park, where Miss Fetherstonhaugh had invited her to work as house-keeper. In this way Up Park became a kind of parental home for Wells and his two elder brothers, and when he was between situations, as he frequently was during his adolescence, he took refuge there. His mother made determined efforts to push him out of the nest. Her ambition was that all her sons should become respectable shopkeepers, preferably drapers, and in spite of the untidiness, ineptitude for figures and self-willed, insubordinate temperament of her youngest son she made many attempts to apprentice him. His first apprentice-ship, to a draper, lasted only a month because he was unable to keep accounts. He was then briefly apprenticed to a chemist. This episode, of little interest in itself, led to one of the most important relationships of his early life, with Horace Byatt, headmaster of Midhurst Grammar School. Wells was sent to the school for a short period to acquire the Latin that a chemist needed. After about six weeks he was uprooted again – his mother had decided that the chemist's shop was unsuitable and insisted that he should be apprenticed to another draper – but Byatt had taken note of his ability, and Wells himself, after this brief taste of good education, knew where he belonged and what he wanted. He spent two frustrating years as an apprentice of Hyde's Drapery Emporium in Southsea – experience that he was to use in *The Wheels of Chance*, *Kipps* and several of the stories – until desperation at the waste of his abilities drove him to break off his apprenticeship. After a further struggle with his mother he went back to Byatt at Midhurst Grammar School, and from there he won a scholarship – part of a national scheme for the training of science teachers – to the Normal School of Science at Kensington (later to become Imperial College). There he enrolled in 1884 as a student under T. H. Huxley, the famous defender and champion of Darwin's theory of evolution.

Wells had rescued himself from his mother's limited lower-middle-class ambitions for him, but he had not yet found him-self; indeed, the next ten years of his life, 1884–94, can be seen as a series of false starts. After a brilliant first year studying biology under Huxley he had to move on to physics, which was badly taught and bored him, and he neglected his studies and devoted his time to student politics and journalism. His politics at this time were the product of emotional revolt rather than informed socialist theory, fed by his reading of Carlyle and Ruskin and by visits to Kelmscott House in Hammersmith, where he met William Morris, Bernard Shaw and other radicals of the day. He was an effective student debater and already saw himself as someone marked out, special, destined to be a prophet. A cartoon he drew of himself in 1886 shows him surrounded by scraps of paper on which are scribbled drawings and captions indicating the possible courses that his future might take: 'How I could save the Nation', 'All about God', 'Secret of the Kosmos', 'Whole Duty of Man' and 'Wells' Design for a new Framework of Society'. The new ideas that he was encountering stirred up in his mind visions which had to be written down; the habits of the creative writer were already becoming established.

He had been writing odds and ends since adolescence, and in 1886 became the first editor of a new student magazine, *The Science Schools Journal*. The papers and short pieces that he wrote for *The Journal* show already the combination of romance, satire and scientific ideas which was to characterise the romances of the 1890s. A paper called 'The Past and Present of the Human Race' contained ideas about human evolution which were to reappear in *The Time Machine*, *The War of the Worlds* and *The First Men in the Moon*; and a story about time travel, 'The Chronic Argonauts', was in effect an early draft of the story which Wells was to work, and re-work, until it was finally revised as *The Time Machine* in 1895. His writing, together with his involvement in student politics, was partly a preparation for a possible alternative career in case he proved an academic failure. In his autobiography Wells recalls that following three years of 'deliberate abstinence' from reading during his student days, at the age of 21 he plunged back into literature with a new purposiveness, and consciously trained himself as a writer. He 'ground out some sonnets' and 'read everything accessible', which included romantic and radical writers as well as popular writers of Gothic and supernatural romance: Shelley, Keats, Heine, Whitman, Lamb, Stevenson, Hawthorne. In a way Wells's student years were typical of the undergraduate careers of wayward writers – from Byron to Auden, one may say – in that he made a marked personal impact on student life, was insubordinate and undisciplined, and was already feeling his way towards his real identity as a writer. He was also falling in love, with his cousin Isabel: a relationship which was to prove another false start.

After completing the course at the Normal School, with

'wilted qualifications', Wells had several teaching posts. The first was at a dismal boys' school in North Wales, which he left after one of the pupils had injured him on the sports field. This injury was to a kidney which was to trouble him for the rest of his life; it may be that he was also suffering from incipient diabetes, although he was not diagnosed as a diabetic until his sixties. The fact was that Wells was never physically fit, and this added to the pressure to make his living from writing; he was simply not suited to the physical strain of teaching.

After finding a second teaching post at a more satisfactory private school (in London) Wells enrolled as an external student for the London B.Sc., in order to improve his teaching qualifications, and at the same time wrote scraps of journalism – quizzes, two-page articles on scientific topics – for the new popular papers, such as *Answers* and *Tit-bits*, which catered for the literate proletarian audience created by the universal elementary education introduced in the 1870s. A better paid job teaching adult students at Briggs' Tutorial College soon offered itself, and in 1890 Wells passed his B.Sc. with first class honours in zoology and got his first publication in a major periodical: an article on the mysteriousness of the physical world called 'The Rediscovery of the Unique', published in 1891 by Frank Harris in *The Fortnightly Review*. By 1891 he felt sufficiently secure to marry his cousin Isabel, and he now saw himself as committed to teaching and to educational writing; his first book-length publication was a textbook for biologists.

In 1892 his life decisively changed direction: he fell in love with one of his students, Elizabeth Catherine Robbins – 'Jane', as Wells was always to call her – and by 1895 he had divorced Isabel and married 'Jane'. By this date, also, circumstances were pushing him away from teaching and into writing: in 1893 and 1894 he had made enough money from his educational writing, and from his journalism for periodicals such as *The Pall Mall Gazette*, *The Pall Mall Budget* and *The National Observer*, to know that he would be able to live entirely on his writing if he chose; a further bout of illness in 1895 made it difficult for him to carry on teaching. The turning point came when W. E. Henley, who had published some of Wells's pieces on time travelling in *The National Observer*, commissioned a serial story on this theme for *The New Review*, which Henley had started (following the closure of *The National Observer*) in January 1895. Wells knew that the time-travelling theme was one on which he could write particu-

4

larly effectively, that it was his 'peculiar treasure' and 'trump card'. Of the serialisation of *The Time Machine* he wrote 'If it does not come off very much I shall know my place for the rest of my career' (MacKenzies, pp. 106–7). It did, of course, 'come off': it was an immense success, and Wells followed it up with such ferocious industry that by the end of 1895 he had *four* books on the market – *Select Conversations with an Uncle*, *The Time Machine*, *The Wonderful Visit*, *The Stolen Bacillus*. He had 'got his name up', he had arrived.

Literary and intellectual background

It has been convincingly argued by Bernard Bergonzi that Wells's romances of the 1890s partake in the decadence and the 'fin de siècle': that in these works Wells can be seen participating in the pessimism, the nihilism, the sense of degeneration and global despair of the 1890s. It is certainly the case that Wells's work before 1900 reflects the cultural and intellectual climate of the last Victorian decade and the powerful, and occasionally terrifying, ideas that were at work in it. For Wells the most important of these ideas came from the advances in biology: Darwin's writings and Huxley's teaching had shown him that man's life-span is infinitesimal in the context of geological time, that man is prey as well as hunter and that he may well be evolving *downwards* – back to the condition of apes – rather than upwards. The fashionable 'transvaluation of all values', as Nietzsche had phrased it, also made its impact on Wells. Nietzsche was being translated into English during the 1890s; Wells may not have read him but was certainly aware of him. Nietzsche's ideas are referred to in *Tono-Bungay*, where Teddy Ponderevo characterises his view of himself as a captain of industry and national leader as his 'Overman Idee' (*sic*: Teddy's pronunciation), and in *The Sleeper Awakes*, where Ostrog proclaims that 'The coming of the Overman is certain and assured'. Wells was aware, also, of Schopenhauer's pessimism (especially as it affected his friend Conrad) and may well have read Max Nordau's 'fin de siècle' denunciations of the nineteenth century, *Degeneration* and *The Malady of the Century*, both of which were available in English in the 1890s.

Nordau's central thesis, that man as a species is irreversibly degenerating, is either reflected as an influence or shared as an intuition in much major literature of the 1890s. It is felt in

Hardy's presentation of 'Father Time', the child who has no will to live and who hangs himself and the younger children in *Jude the Obscure*. It underlies the figure of Kurtz, who 'lacked restraint in the gratification of his various lusts' and has surrendered to 'the fascination of the abomination' in Conrad's *Heart of Darkness*. In *The Island of Dr Moreau* Wells's narrator, Prendick, sees men's lives controlled by a 'blind fate, a vast pitiless mechanism', which seems to 'cut and shape the fabric of existence'. One may compare this with Conrad's letter of 1897 in which he says that the universe is governed by a malign and distant machine: 'It evolved itself [. . .] out of a chaos of scraps of iron and behold! – it knits [. . .]. It knits us in and it knits us out. It has knitted time, space, pain, death, corruption, despair and all the illusions – and nothing matters'.[1] Conrad might have paid more attention to Wells's early romances. He was a friend of Wells and dedicated *The Secret Agent* to him, but he took the view that they differed fundamentally about the future of the race; he felt that Wells saw hope for mankind but did not love it while he, Conrad, loved it but had no hope for it. *The Island of Dr Moreau* might have shown him that there was a time when he and Wells both felt an equally intense despair. Man was alone in an impersonal universe which was itself in a state of irreversible decay. The Second Law of Thermodynamics had taught the Victorians that energy is not 'conserved' but endlessly expended, dissipated, so that the earth and all the planets are steadily cooling and the sun itself will become extinct. This theory of the universe gave Wells *The Time Machine*'s most startling episode: that in which the Traveller moves forward to a future time, thirty million years hence, when the earth is motionless and freezing, the dying sun fills half the sky, and man's remotest descendant has become an amphibious, tentacled horror.

There are many direct literary precedents for Wells's work. He rejected the suggestion that he had learnt from Jules Verne (Verne also rejected it) but it seems clear that the Martian space ships which are fired from a great cannon to land in suburban Surrey in *The War of the Worlds* owe something to Verne's *From Earth to Moon*, much of which concerns the construction of a cannon big enough to fire a manned projectile at the moon. Another precursor is Bulwer Lytton's *The Coming Race*, the first full length novel to take its central theme from Darwin's theory: a subterranean species descended from the frog has developed

6

superhuman powers by natural selection. It seems likely that Wells's underground creatures, the Morlocks and the Selenites, owe something to – or at least are created in the knowledge of – Lytton's romance. The genre of the invasion novel, of which a great many were published in the last twenty years of the century, lies in the background of *The War of the Worlds* and *The War in the Air*; I am thinking particularly of Sir George Chesney's *The Battle of Dorking*, which depends for its effect on the destruction of a familiar Home Counties community by an external aggressor in a way exactly paralleled by the opening chapters of *The War of the Worlds*. In the invasion novel the aggressor was, of course, Germany, except in the case of a maverick work like M. P. Shiel's *The Yellow Danger*, where the aggressor is China. The best of these works is probably Erskine Childers's *The Riddle of the Sands*, with its lovingly detailed attention to the difficulties of navigating small craft through the sandbanks of the North Sea; the oddest is Saki's *When William Came*, in which surrender to the Germans seems to induce in the English nothing but mild upper-class regret. Most of these novels were straightforward propaganda, like William le Queux's *The Invasion*, with a preface by Field Marshal Lord Roberts appealing for more expenditure on armaments. By 1909 the invasion novel was sufficiently distinct as a literary genre to provoke a good frothy satire from the young P. G. Wodehouse, *The Swoop! Or How Clarence Saved England*, in which all the foreign powers invade England simultaneously and are deceived by a wily schoolboy into fighting each other. With *The War of the Worlds* H. G. Wells greatly extends the invasion novel's imaginative range. The aggressor is not The Hun but a monster who represents man evolved out of all recognition; the *future* attacks and destroys the present.

Wells also responds to the utopian tradition; the ideas in Plato, Sir Thomas More and Swift, whom he had read as a child, were recalled and supplemented by the large number of utopian and anti-utopian fictions published in his lifetime. Among the most prominent of these are Edward Bellamy's *Looking Backward*, W. H. Hudson's *The Crystal Age*, William Morris's *News from Nowhere*, Richard Jefferies's *After London* and Samuel Butler's *Erewhon*. Bellamy's novel – famous in its day – is a naive and badly written work which sees the world of the future benignly transformed by the full development of capitalism. Morris's fantasy is the obverse of this. Much better written than

Bellamy's – though almost equally naive – it presents a quasi-medieval dream world in which all the best hopes of communism are fulfilled. Both these books (and *The Crystal Age*) are explicitly challenged in Wells's *The Sleeper Awakes* (revised as *When the Sleeper Wakes*) where the future is seen rather as Bellamy sees it – capitalism triumphant – but with the difference that the result is nightmare, a brutal totalitarianism. Later Wells was to become optimistic about the future, but in the 1890s he saw the social and economic tendencies of his day as anything but hopeful. His imagination had more in common with Butler's *Erewhon*, in which Victorian imperatives are savagely inverted and parodied, and Jefferies's apocalyptic *After London* (in which England is recovering from a cataclysm which seems to anticipate the probable effects of nuclear war) than with the utopias of the optimists.

One may note here Wells's effect on subsequent writers of anti-utopias. Yevgeny Zamyatin's *We*, a projection of a future world state in which freedom is by definition a crime, was written as a direct result of reading and translating Wells, and Orwell's *1984* and Huxley's *Brave New World* would not have been written without the example of *We*; indeed the plots of *1984* and Zamyatin's book are almost identical. Zamyatin remarked of Wells that he 'created a new and entirely original species of literary form', and when considering Wells's place in literary history one is bound to give this claim its due weight.

The sciences – especially biology – philosophy, and the utopias and romances of the period were major influences on Wells, but one should note also that the beginning of his career coincided with the climax of the aesthetic movement. Henley commissioned *The Time Machine* partly because Oscar Wilde had recommended Wells to his attention, 'A Slip under the Microscope' was first published in that notorious organ of aestheticism, *The Yellow Book*, and in an earlier version of *The Time Machine* the Eloi were descendants of 1890s aesthetes, and the Morlocks were the descendants of the aesthetes' natural enemies, the middle-class materialists. In *The Wonderful Visit* Wells sends a Pre-Raphaelite angel, a creature from Italian art, 'polychromatic and gay', to expose the ugliness and absurdity of English society; for a moment he seems to join Wilde, Beardsley, Max Beerbohm and the rest in teasing the bourgeoisie from the standpoint of the *aesthete* rather than from that of the lower-middle-class rebel.

8

The Time Machine

For the first five years of his career as a creative writer Wells worked with extraordinary speed, 'writing away for dear life' to establish himself and to ensure that the success of *The Time Machine* was followed up before interest in his name had had time to fade. From a literary point of view the quality of the work of these years is inevitably uneven, but there are three novels which now stand out as indisputably permanent and major: *The Time Machine*, *The Island of Dr Moreau* and *The War of the Worlds*. *The Time Machine* is a triumph not only because of the simple brilliance of its central idea and the vitality of its exposition, but also because of the technical mastery with which it establishes itself in the reader's mind as credible. The essence of the method is exemplified by 'The Apple', a short story of 1897, in which a young schoolmaster is offered 'The Apple of the Tree of Knowledge' by a stranger on a train. The schoolmaster laconically reflects that 'it was a most extraordinary story to be told in a third-class carriage on a Sussex railway. It was as if the real was a mere veil to the fantastic, and here was the fantastic poking through.'

The easy co-existence of the fantastic and the real, and the trick of making the reader believe that the one is a 'mere veil' to the other, are well established in the early pages of *The Time Machine*. It is in marked contrast to the clumsiness of 'The Chronic Argonauts', Wells's first time-travelling story which was written when he was a student. Here Wells was writing in what he called his 'Babu' – consciously literary – manner, and the reader is repelled by this and muddled by the story's mixture of science and witchcraft: the time traveller, 'Dr Nebogipfel', seems part demon, part alchemist, an uneasily jocular descendant of Mary Shelley's Frankenstein and of Dr Faustus. The half-digested literary romanticism of 'The Chronic Argonauts' is replaced in the first chapter of *The Time Machine* by a tactfully established normality. The Time Traveller is an ordinary, anonymous middle-class person telling his tale to an after-dinner audience which includes the narrator; the feeling of neutrality is helped by the fact that neither the Traveller nor the narrator (nor any of the guests, with the exception of the arbitrarily identified 'Filby') have names. 'The Time Traveller (for so it will be convenient to speak of him) was expounding a recondite matter to us' (ch. 1); he is setting out the theory of time travel. The exposition is not, in fact, entirely plausible; as an instance of an experience of time travel which any normal person might have had, the Traveller says: 'If I am recalling an incident very vividly I go back to the instant of its occurrence.' But this is clearly a fudge: clarity of mind and retentiveness of perception are subjective matters and have nothing to do with the mathematical concept of the 'Fourth Dimension' on which the Traveller's case depends. The reader is diverted from such weaknesses, though, and won over to the argument by the visual 'impressionism', as Bergonzi rightly calls it, with which the Time Machine itself is presented. The small-scale model of the machine, scarcely larger than a small clock, is not described in any detail: it has 'ivory', 'some transparent crystalline substance', a saddle, levers, and transverse bars like handlebars. We may imagine it as a kind of bicycle – cycling was one of Wells's great enthusiasms in the 1890s (*The Wheels of Chance* is based on it), and he saw the bicycle as a revolutionary, democratic form of transport which would initiate social change; it was one of the very few activities in which men and women could enjoy each other's company without chaperones. The machine's resemblance to the liberating, egalitarian bicycle is not spelt out, though; instead, the text diverts the reader's attention from the thing's appearance by compelling him to share the narrator's bewilderment over the question of what happens to it: there are carefully established details about the position of the lamp and the candles in the room, and the placing of the model on an octagonal table. The feeling is of an event which is to be part scientific demonstration and part conjuring trick. The actual disappearance of the model is minutely observed: 'One of the candles on the mantel was blown out, and the little machine suddenly swung round, became indistinct, was seen as a ghost for a second, perhaps, as an eddy of faintly glittering brass and ivory; and it was gone – vanished' (ch. 2).

The Time Traveller then leads his guests down a corridor to see the full-size machine, which he has almost completed. The narrator is struck by a visual effect which gives a moment of romantic strangeness to the otherwise conscientiously neutral way in which the Traveller is presented: 'I remember the flickering light, his queer broad head in silhouette, the dance of the shadows' (ch. 2). For modern readers there is the added strangeness that the inconceivable technological marvel of the Time Machine has been invented by a man whose house is lit by oil lamps and candles. Wells could, of course, have chosen to give the Traveller electric light in 1895, and he is presumably transcribing here a paradox in his own life. In the autobiography he recalls writing the scene in which the Traveller finds his machine removed by the Morlocks and his retreat from the future cut off 'in the luminous circle cast by a shaded paraffin lamp', while his landlady below was audibly complaining about the amount of lamp oil that he used by working so late (Autobiography, pp. 517–19).

The method of the novel is 'heuristic': the reader learns how to read the book by discovering how to ask the right questions, he collaborates with the narrator in the latter's attempt to interpret the experiences 'thrown' at him, so to speak, by the narrative. When the Traveller describes his experiences in the world of 802,701 the reader is in the same position as the narrator who is a member of the after-dinner audience: a framing device identical with that of Conrad's 'Youth', *Heart of Darkness* and *Lord Jim*, in which Marlow reminisces to a small group of friends in a state of post-prandial relaxation. In *The Time Machine* the frame gives the reader a satisfying illusion of narrative density; a feeling that several sequences of discovery and revelation are taking place concurrently. Wells's training as a biologist is in evidence; as though conducting an experiment, the Traveller confronts alternative possible explanations of what he sees and has to opt for the correct one. Initially he interprets the beautiful, diminutive surface people of the future – the Eloi – as descendants of a perfect democratic republic like that of William Morris's *News from Nowhere*. He notes that 'the single house, and possibly even the household, had vanished', and that instead the people eat and sleep in communal palaces: 'the house and the cottage', which form such characteristic features of our English landscape, had disappeared. ' "Communism," said I to myself' (ch. 6). Wells's chapter headings mark the stages in the progress of the Traveller's understanding: the paradisal state in which the Eloi live is stressed in a chapter called 'The Golden Age', and the fact that they are degenerates, 'humanity upon the wane', is recognised in one called 'The Sunset of Mankind'. The chapters headed 'Explanation' and 'The Morlocks' show the Traveller moving from his false reading – that communism has produced a society of beautiful, free, equal and healthy people who have degenerated because they no longer have anything against which to struggle – to the true one, that the future world has declined from the triumph not of communism but of *capitalism*. The Eloi are the descendants of an upper class who have secured the whole surface of the earth for their own exclusive use, leaving the descendants of the industrial proletariat to evolve separately. Wells uses the notion that the working class of the future will live entirely shut away from light and air again in 'A Story of the Days to Come' and in *The Sleeper Awakes*. 'Even now', says the Traveller in *The Time Machine*, in a passage which is rather too obviously an editorial intervention in which Wells the prophet eagerly stresses the plausibility of his projection from present social trends, 'there are existing circumstances to point that way. There is a tendency to utilize underground space for the less ornamental purposes of civilization [he instances urban subways and the London underground railway] . . . Even now, does not an East-end worker live in such artificial conditions as practically to be cut off from the natural surface of the earth?' (ch. 8).

In chapter 9 the Traveller descends one of the ventilation shafts – 'waterless wells', as he has thought them, recalled by Wells from the shafts which ventilated the subterranean kitchens at Up Park – to encounter the Morlocks. Hideous and ferocious though they are he feels a certain identification with them because they are carnivorous, unlike the Eloi who live entirely on fruit. The Traveller himself, when he returns from his journey, is 'starving for a bit of meat', and will not tell his tale until he has got some 'peptone' into his arteries (ch. 3). When he is forced to recognise the central truth about the Morlocks and the Eloi – that their relationship is based on cannibalism, that the Eloi are 'fatted cattle, which the ant-like Morlocks preserved and preyed upon – probably saw to the breeding of', and that they are *eaten* by the Morlocks – the Traveller is torn between troubled identification with the Morlocks, 'these inhuman sons of men', and an attempt to maintain his detachment, to 'look at the thing in a scientific spirit' (ch. 10). The tension set up in the Traveller is shared by the narrator, and the reader, and makes an important, enriching contribution to the experience of reading the tale.

The degeneracy of the Eloi is to be compared with the decadence of high society in the 1890s, and Wells's phrasing may well be inspired by T. H. Huxley's famous lecture, 'Evolution and Ethics' (1893), a fine piece of rhetoric which spoke clearly to the sense of termination and decline which both thrilled and terrified thinking people of the period. Huxley spoke of the degeneracy of ancient Greece: 'The inevitable penalty of over-stimulation, exhaustion, opened the gates of civilization to its great enemy, ennui; the stale and flat weariness where man delights not, nor woman neither.' Wells's Traveller, looking at the ruinous palaces in which the Eloi live, reflects that 'no doubt the exquisite beauty of the buildings I saw was the outcome of the last surgings of the now purposeless energy of mankind'. Peace has brought degeneracy to these people: 'This has ever been the fate of energy in security; it takes to art and to eroticism, and thence comes languor and decay' (ch. 6). The Morlocks, naked, hairy, and compared to apes, rats, ants and spiders in the story's text, relate to another of Huxley's disturbing insights, that, having descended from animals, men can revert to the condition of animals. The conspicuous degeneracy of the Morlocks forces the Traveller to look at the Eloi, whom he has regarded as beings similar to himself (if simpler and more childlike) with fresh eyes. In the ruined museum housed in the green porcelain palace, where the collection of artefacts demonstrates dramatically and tragically the height of civilization from which the Eloi have fallen, the Traveller reflects on the absence of mind in his little Eloi companion, Weena: 'She always seemed to me, I fancy, more human than she was, perhaps because her affection was so human' (ch. 11).

Weena has been greatly disliked by critics of *The Time Machine*. V. S. Pritchett speaks of her relationship with the Traveller as 'faint squirms of idyllic petting'[2] and Bernard Bergonzi finds the relationship embarrassing and unconvincing. But to my mind it adds an enriching and troubling complexity to the Traveller's feelings about the Eloi. Nine episodes of what is, in effect, an earlier draft of *The Time Machine* were published in periodicals in 1894 and 1895 (and are reprinted in Philmus). In these episodes there is greater detachment from the humanity of the future than in the story's final version. The Traveller makes contact with no single figure; there is no Weena, nor anyone like her, and the conventions of the utopian tale are explicitly defied: 'Odd as it may seem, I had no cicerone. In all the narratives of people visiting the future that I have read, some obliging scandalmonger appears at an early stage, and begins to lecture on constitutional and social harmony, and to point out the celebrities' (Philmus, p. 71). In an episode ironically called 'The Refinement of Humanity' the Traveller describes the Eloi as beautiful little creatures which at 'the age of nineteen or twenty' fall into 'an elegant and painless decline' and then 'experience a natural Euthanasia' (p. 74). They seem to be based on 1890s aesthetes: they have flying machines with 'gaily painted wings' (to control such machines would clearly require greater intelligence than the Eloi are allowed, and the machines are wisely dropped from the finished story), and the division between their society and that of the Morlocks is *vertical*, not horizontal: it is not a 'split between working people and rich' but 'between the sombre, mechanically industrious, arithmetical, inartistic type, the type of the Puritan and the American millionaire, and the pleasure loving, witty and graceful type that gives us our clever artists, our actors and writers, some of our gentry, and many an elegant rogue' (p. 86).

It is important that the Traveller's sardonic detachment from the Eloi and Morlocks in the early version is replaced in the finished story by the confused feelings bred in him by Weena; indeed, I would argue that the introduction of Weena effects the change from a succession of coldly brilliant ideas to a persuasive and complex work of fiction. She is a moral touchstone whose presence rebukes the Traveller for his attempt to take refuge from his own distress at the fate that has overtaken mankind: 'I tried a Carlyle-like scorn of this wretched aristocracy-in-decay. But this attitude of mind was impossible. However great their intellectual degradation, the Eloi had kept too much of the human form not to claim my sympathy' (ch. 10). This is an important concession. In the first draft the Traveller insists that mankind in the future will be 'modified beyond human sympathy' (Philmus, p. 89). To forfeit human sympathy creates an obvious difficulty by denying the reader common ground with the narrative, and in the finished story Wells ploughs this difficulty back into the text: the conflict between detachment and sympathy is dramatised first in the Traveller himself, then in the contrast between the Traveller and the narrator. The Traveller feels for the Eloi first protective affection, then detached pity, and for the Morlocks first revulsion and then a kind of compassion: I am thinking of the scene in chapter 12 where he sets fire to the forest and is moved by the 'helplessness and misery' of the Morlocks who are blinded by the glare. At the end of the story the conflict is sharpened by the contrast between the Traveller's attitude to his experiences and that of the narrator. The Traveller brings back from the future 'two strange white flowers' given him by Weena, and the narrator attaches to these flowers a significance that the reader may choose to regard as sentimental: in his view they witness that even when mind and strength have gone, 'gratitude and a mutual tenderness still live on in the heart of man' (epilogue).[3] But the Traveller himself is finally pessimistic about the future of man, seeing 'in the growing pile of civilization only a foolish heaping that must inevitably fall back upon and destroy its makers in the end' (ibid.). The reader is free to set aside the narrator's sentimentality and to be as pessimistic about the future of the race as is the Traveller at his most sceptical. Wells in this way achieves a crafty equivocation at the story's close: feeling and sympathy have been enlisted to ensure the reader's engagement with the story, but perhaps they have been misplaced. It may be that the icy detachment that the Traveller seeks in vain is the only mood appropriate to the contemplation of the future of man.

Wells's pleasure in science as the great liberator is felt at its purest, perhaps, in the Traveller's account of the sensation of time travel:

As I put on pace, night followed day like the flapping of a black wing. The dim suggestion of the laboratory seemed presently to fall away from me, and I saw the sun hopping swiftly across the sky, leaping it every minute. [As he gains speed:] The palpitation of night and day merged into one continuous greyness; the sky took on a wonderful deepness of blue, a splendid luminous colour like that of early twilight; the jerking sun became a streak of fire, a brilliant arch, in space; the moon a fainter fluctuating band; I could see nothing of the stars, save now and then a brighter circle flickering in the blue (ch. 4).

This reminds one of the pleasure that Wells takes in powered flight throughout his work – Bert Smallways's flight by balloon in *The War in the Air*, Bedford's sense of awe and wonder in Cavor's space ship in *The First Men in the Moon*, the Ponderevos' escape in the Lord Roberts β in *Tono-Bungay* – and it communicates the sense of freedom that is present in all the romances at their best. The particularity of the nineteenth-century middle-class urban world is triumphantly blown away and replaced by speed, excitement, escape, the essential concomitants of joy in Wells's early work. And the sense of freedom is swiftly followed by terror. In the year 802,701 – the date itself has been aptly characterised by McConnell as a 'hieroglyph of entropy, a numerical metaphor for a machine about to run down, a process about to play itself out' – the Traveller stops the machine to find himself at the feet of a huge but damaged marble sphinx, a 'diseased' and menacing figure: 'The sightless eyes seemed to watch me; there was the faint shadow of a smile on the lips' (ch. 4). At first we may think that the relation of this sphinx to the world of 802,701 is like that of the Egyptian sphinx to nineteenth-century Europe. It will emerge, of course, that the connection is much more remote than that. From the moment that the Traveller alights from his machine the reader is invited to respond to questions posed by the powerful symbol of the sphinx: who are the people of the future? What is the relationship between the ruinous state of the monuments that surround them and their present condition? What riddle or secret is harboured by this sphinx and what is the menace indicated by its smile and its suggestion of disease? The answers are all related to the Morlocks: the sphinx caps one of the shafts leading down to their subterranean world, and beneath the sphinx, in its pedestal, the Time Machine will be hidden, forcing the Traveller to use nineteenth-century aggression – again showing his common ancestry with the Morlocks – in order to escape back to his own time. The reader collaborates with the Traveller in his unravelling of the story's riddles, and in addition to the brilliance of its original idea the piece gives us the pleasure of a tightly structured text which withholds its significance until the attention is fully engaged. At one point the story becomes self-referential in a startlingly Modernist way: the Traveller compares the difficulties of his situation to the reading of a cryptic text: 'I felt I lacked a clue. I felt – how shall I put it? Suppose you found an inscription, with sentences here and there in excellent plain English, and, interpolated therewith, others made up of words, of letters even, absolutely unknown to you?' (ch. 8).

Freedom brings terror: this romantic paradox is present in all the scientific stories of the 1890s. The individual embarks on an adventure which gives him a sense of power and self-assertion, but which also reminds him of his essential isolation and ignorance. For Wells, the scientist, the innovative man, was always caught in this paradox. He expresses it in a compelling image in an early essay, 'The Rediscovery of the Unique':

Science is a match that man has just got alight. He thought he was in a room – in moments of devotion, a temple – and that his light would be reflected from and display walls inscribed with wonderful secrets and pillars carved with philosophical systems wrought into harmony. It is a curious sensation, now that the preliminary splutter is over and the flame burns up clear, to see his hands lit and just a glimpse of himself and the patch he stands on visible, and around him, in place of all that human comfort and beauty he anticipated – darkness still! (Philmus, pp. 30–1)

But this image – science as a candle-lit point at the centre of a great darkness – is contradicted by another of his early pieces, 'The Universe Rigid', which anticipates the tone of the optimistic, confident Wells of the Edwardian period: 'If you grasped the whole of the present, knew all its tendencies and laws, you would see clearly all the future' (Philmus, p. 93). Both these attitudes to scientific enquiry – the confident and the terrified – are present in *The Time Machine*: the Traveller is fundamentally pessimistic about the future of man but has a continuing drive to *know* which sends him on his last (and presumably fatal) journey. This antithesis contributes a further tension to the story's wealth of resonance and effect.

The Island of Dr Moreau

A similar tension informs and animates *The Island of Dr Moreau*. It is the darkest of the romances, yet Wells clearly enjoyed writing it, and the pessimism of its theme is at odds with the sense of excitement, energy, and pleasure of invention conveyed by the young writer in the act of inventing his fable. It invites comparison and contrast with *The Time Machine*: like the earlier book, it is dominated by the theory of evolution and by the figure of a scientist who has made extraordinary advances. But while the Time Traveller is an adventurer extending man's scope, Moreau is mad and evil. His story is clearly distinct from that of the Time Traveller in that it belongs to the 'abuse of knowledge' tradition which includes the legend of Faust, Mary Shelley's *Frankenstein* and Stevenson's *Dr Jekyll and Mr Hyde*. Darwinism had accelerated the conflict between religion and science which had been part of intellectual life for most of the nineteenth century, and Wells responded with relish and excitement to the challenge that Darwin's theory presented to Christianity. In his preface to the book in the Atlantic Edition he remarked: 'It is a theological grotesque, and the influence of Swift is very apparent in it,' and on the topic of vivisection he added: 'This story was the response of an imaginative mind to the reminder that humanity is but animal rough-hewn to a reasonable shape and in perpetual conflict between instinct and injunction. This story embodies this

17

ideal, but apart from this embodiment it has no allegorical quality. It is written just to give the utmost possible vividness to that conception of men as hewn and confused and tormented beasts' (Atlantic, II, p. ix).

What is odd, though, is that with the sweeping away of Christianity goes a furious outbreak of misanthropy. At the end of the fable Prendick, the narrator, is disgusted by ordinary human beings: 'I see faces keen and bright, others dull or dangerous, others unsteady, insincere; none that have the calm authority of a reasonable soul. I feel as though the animal was surging up through them; that presently the degradation of the Islanders will be played over again on a larger scale' (ch. 22). There is an obvious similarity between this misanthropy and Gulliver's disgust at the resemblance of ordinary citizens to the degraded Yahoos when he returns from his Travels, with the important difference that at the end of *Gulliver's Travels* Swift intends us to recognise that Gulliver is mad, while Prendick has been brought by his experience on the island to perceive a fundamental truth about mankind. Here, as elsewhere in his romances, Wells reverses the direction of his literary model.

Why is Wells in such a bad temper with the human race in this book? The other romances and most of the short stories that use scientific ideas are liberal in tone and implication, reflecting the sense of dignity and acquired freedom that Wells himself gained from his studies of science. Stories like 'The Man Who Could Work Miracles', 'The New Accelerator' and 'The Truth about Pyecraft' have the boisterousness of what Pritchett has called 'Edwardian horseplay' about them (strictly, of course, Pritchett should speak of their *late-Victorian* horseplay) but they are fundamentally good tempered. More sensational stories like 'The Cone', 'The Sea Raiders', 'The Flowering of the Strange Orchid' and 'Under the Knife' still invite the reader to identify with their victims; a normative sense of humanity is still in play. But in *The Island of Dr Moreau* a dark and obsessional aspect of Wells's talent becomes dominant.

Wells himself clearly did not fully understand the impulse that made him write the book. In the preface to the 1933 edition he wrote that it was 'an exercise in youthful blasphemy', and added: 'Now and then, though I rarely admit it, the universe projects itself towards me in a hideous grimace. It grimaced that time, and I did my best to express my vision of the aimless torture in creation' (Romances, p. viii). The 'grimace', the grotesque or distorted facial expression, becomes a leading motif in the story. Details of the characters' faces are carefully noted as moral indicators; negative indicators in every case. Prendick's first encounter with one of Moreau's beast people is with a 'dark face with extraordinary eyes' which he believes at first is a 'nightmare' (ch. 1). Montgomery, Moreau's assistant, is weak and vicious, a disgraced former medical student whose nature is betrayed by his 'drooping nether lip', 'watery-grey eyes' and 'odd' pallor (very odd, considering that he lives on a tropical island). Moreau himself has powerful, heavy features – the stereotyped dictator look – marked by incipient deterioration, 'that odd dropping of the skin above the [eye-]lids that often comes with advancing years' (ch. 6).

Prendick's close attentiveness to physiognomy is a requirement of the narrative method, since the reader collaborates with him in interpreting the nightmare appearance of the creatures on the island. Montgomery's servant, M'ling, has green eyes that shine in the dark and ears covered in fur: at first Prendick believes that M'ling is a man who has been vivisected to produce these weird features, and his terror mounts as he comes to believe that he himself is Moreau's next victim. The reader guesses rather earlier than Prendick that the people on Moreau's island are not *men* at all. The frantic rhetorical questions at the end of chapter 7 seem to be placed deliberately to indicate to the reader that Prendick is interpreting the evidence incorrectly: 'What could it mean? A locked enclosure on a lonely island, a notorious vivisector, and these crippled and distorted men? . . . ' The reader is partially enlightened while Prendick continues totally to misread the situation until chapter 14 in which he learns, of course, that the truth is the opposite of what he imagines and that the deformed men are animals, 'humanized animals – triumphs of vivisection'. At this point the reader becomes detached from Prendick. Prendick has a certain grudging admiration for Moreau, who had been driven to make his extraordinary discoveries by the 'overmastering spell of research' (ch. 7) and feels some affection for Montgomery who twice saves his life. The reader, listening over Prendick's shoulder, so to speak, judges Moreau more harshly. Moreau's transformation of animals into suffering, manlike monsters is an irresponsible and cruel act of 'creation'.

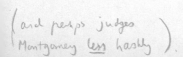
(and perhps judges Montgomery less hastly).

The 'theological grotesque' is deliberately blasphemous and remarkably systematic. The novel makes elaborate parallels between Moreau's created universe and that of the Christian God. Moreau's creatures have a moral system based on perversion of instinct, pugnacity trained into self-sacrifice and repressed sexuality diverted into the impulse to worship. The object of their worship is Moreau himself, the central figure of a myth religion in which he occupies the place of Christ, Moses and God the Father rolled into one. He has given them commandments: 'Not to go on all-Fours; that is the Law. Are we not Men?' and so forth (ch. 15). He has given them a moral system based on fear of retribution and purgatory represented by the 'house of pain', the surgery in which the vivisection is carried out. And he has given them belief in his own omniscience. Prendick suspects that Moreau has 'infected their dwarfed brains with a kind of deification of himself' (ch. 12). The Beast-People turn out to be more human than Moreau has anticipated in that they elaborate on the groundwork that he has given them; part of their religious belief they invent for themselves (just as man does, in Wells's view of history). The Beast-People's 'creed' is an interesting mix of truth and falsehood:

> *His* is the House of Pain
> *His* is the Hand that makes
> *His* is the Hand that wounds
> *His* is the Hand that heals.

These, as attributes of Moreau, are 'real', but the next items are fictitious:

> *His* is the lightning flash
> *His* is the deep salt sea
> *His* are the stars in the sky (ch. 12).

After the deaths of Moreau and Montgomery, Prendick saves himself from the Beast-People by taking further the process of transforming Moreau into the central figure of a mystery religion (his role can be compared with that of St Paul, who is singled out for mockery and abuse much later in Wells's career in *The Happy Turning*, 1945). This religion can be seen, then, as something implanted by Moreau, developed by the Beast-People themselves and now extended by Prendick. Prendick warns the Beast-People that Moreau is not dead, but has undergone resurrection and ascension: ' "He has changed his shape – he has changed his body. [. . .] For a time you will not see him.

He is . . . there" – I pointed upward – "where he can watch you. You cannot see him. But he can see you. Fear the Law" ' (ch. 18). This very direct attack on Christian sensibilities is based on the scathing assumption that faith in the resurrection is based only on *fear*: fear that the dead may become hostile judges looking down and exacting revenge, or, as the Dog-Man thinks, that the disappearance of Moreau may be part of an elaborate trick giving him an excuse to return them to the House of Pain.

The fable forces Christianity to confront the humiliating implications of the Darwinian revolution: that man is no more than a talking animal, that all moral systems are arbitrary and man-made, that the sanctions traditionally endorsing the social order are illusions. The experience of reading *The Island of Dr Moreau* is simultaneously austere and exhilarating: austere because of the uncompromising harshness of its theme, exhilarating because of the inventiveness with which Prendick's terrifying sequence of physical emergencies is communicated to us. Prendick's panic-stricken flight through the jungle, the fire which destroys Moreau's 'house of pain', the way Prendick has to develop the defensive skills of an animal – like Kipling's Mowgli – as the Beast-People, free of Moreau's authority, revert to their animal state: these things are presented with unflagging energy and relish. Material which could easily have been com- pressed to the scale of an effective short tale of horror like 'The Sea Raiders' or 'The Grisly Folk' is extended over some two hundred pages. Wells the iconoclast sweeps away Christianity; Wells the biologist explores further the man-as-animal theme that informed *The Time Machine* and some of the early essays such as 'The Rate of Change in Species' and 'Zoological Retro- gressions'. 'Zoological Retrogressions' seems, like the closing lines of Yeats's 'The Second Coming', to equate the Messiah with a manifestation of apocalyptic violence: 'The Coming Beast must certainly be reckoned in any anticipatory calculations regarding the Coming Man' (Philmus, p. 168). There are no concessions and few positives in *The Island of Dr Moreau*; the reader closes the book feeling as antipathetic to Prendick as he does to Moreau and Montgomery. Its destructive energy pre- sents something of a paradox: the tone suggests that the novel is anti-Christian in a Christian way, as though the Puritan impulse absorbed from his mother's early evangelical teaching were lash- ing him to attack the system with unremitting fury. Indeed, Puritan zeal is the novel's dominant mood.

The War of the Worlds

If *The Time Machine* and *The Island of Dr Moreau* are evolutionary fables, *The War of the Worlds* and *The Invisible Man* are fictions in which Wells is a 'realist of the fantastic'. The phrase comes from a letter that Conrad wrote to Wells congratulating him on the publication of *The Invisible Man*. The novel seems to develop directly from the central idea of *The Island of Dr Moreau* – the abuse of science by a mad scientist – but soon turns into a story about war; in this case a war in which a single suburban terrorist, Griffin, who intends to use his invisibility to make himself into a dictator, takes on the whole of society. Griffin is killed before he gets very far, but the essence of his plan as he describes it to his former fellow-student, Kemp, is one of stark simplicity: he will kill selected victims until he forces first a suburban town, then the whole country, to acknowledge him as ruler. Griffin's will to power is the product of early conditioning; he was a 'shabby, poverty-struck, hemmed-in demonstrator, teaching fools in a provincial college'. He seems, then, at first, to be a figure like Mr Lewisham, from *Love and Mr Lewisham*, who has the gifts of the Time Traveller; a socially disadvantaged figure who uses science to free himself from his circumstances. The reader's sympathies for much of the novel are *for* Griffin and against, for example, the oafish inhabitants of Iping, where his early attempts to gain control are entirely comic in their effect. Half-way through his novel Wells forces it against the grain of our sympathies – and severely damages it, in my view – by turning Griffin into an obvious maniac, raving about a 'Reign of Terror' and the necessity of killing all who disobey him. The best of the novel's inventions are all calculated to enlist the reader's sympathy firmly *with* Griffin by exploring the details and hazards of invisibility; the retina of his eyes and undigested food in his stomach remain visible, he has to be naked and therefore suffers constant cold, he is visible in outline in rain or fog, he makes footprints in snow, he causes hysteria in dogs, and so forth. Further, the reader inevitably responds to the anarchic pleasures – the opportunities for beating the system – that invisibility confers, and is disappointed when Wells turns against the implications of his invention and bends the knee to a conventional morality in which he clearly has no real faith.

Still, since Wells turns *The Invisible Man* – by force, as it were – into a novel about a terrorist, it becomes a 'War' novel and there-

fore belongs with *The War of the Worlds*. In this romance the
Martians invade suburban Surrey, and the conditions of total
war are sprung on an unsuspecting late-Victorian middle class.
In *The Time Machine* an adventurer invades the future; here
creatures from the future – the Martians represent the possible
evolution of man himself – invade the present. They attack the
earth in order to colonise it, and Wells makes an explicit parallel
with the European colonisation of Africa during the late nineteenth century. The Martians, on their cooling planet, see the
earth as a warm, fertile and propitious place populated only by
savages and primitive life:

> We men, the creatures who inhabit this earth, must be to them at least
> as alien and lowly as are the monkeys and lemurs to us. The intellectual
> side of man already admits that life is an incessant struggle for exist-
> ence, and it would seem that this too is the belief of the minds upon
> Mars. Their world is far gone in its cooling, and this world is still
> crowded with life, but crowded only with what they regard as inferior
> animals. To carry warfare sunward is indeed their only escape from the
> destruction that generation after generation creeps upon them.
>
> And before we judge of them too harshly, we must remember what
> ruthless and utter destruction our own species has wrought, not only
> upon animals, such as the vanished bison and the dodo, but upon its
> own inferior races. The Tasmanians, in spite of their human likeness,
> were entirely swept out of existence in a war of extermination waged by
> European immigrants, in the space of fifty years. Are we such apostles
> of mercy as to complain if the Martians warred in the same spirit?
> (ch. 1).

In an early essay, 'Intelligence on Mars', Wells set out ideas
about the possibility of life on Mars which are carried over essentially unchanged into the novel. A 'strange light' was observed
on Mars by a French astronomer who published his observation
in *Nature*, 2 August 1894 (Philmus, p. 175) and Wells uses this
piece of historical particularity as the starting point for his
novel: 'During the opposition of 1894 a great light was seen on
the illuminated part of the disc' (ch. 1). It is perhaps a pity that
he does so, because it ties him to the notion that the Martian
cylinders are shot from a great gun – as is Verne's projectile in
From Earth to Moon – instead of allowing him to invent some more
sophisticated form of propulsion: the 'Cavorite' in *The First Men
in the Moon* is much more intrinsically interesting. But this detail
is typical of Wells's method at its most effective in *The War of the
Worlds*. Verifiable particularities co-exist with terrifying
imaginings.

The impact of the opening chapters of the novel is very like that of Sir George Chesney's *The Battle of Dorking* (1871) in which England is caught unprepared, and unarmed, by a German invasion and has to fight the Germans in the suburban towns of the Home Counties. The conditions of total war, in which the civilian population find themselves in the front line, are anticipated in Chesney's book and it is this shock – defenceless civilians the victims of a ferocious aggressor – that Wells recaptures. The theatre in which he sets the arrival of his Martians is well chosen. It was an area he knew well; Horsell Common, a flat, sandy area with pinewoods, near Woking, where Wells was living as he wrote the novel. In the preface to the Atlantic Edition of his works Wells notes that he was pleased by the prophetic touches in *The War of the Worlds* – 'The reader will be reminded of phases and incidents in the Great War; the use of poison gas' and flight before the tank-like 'War Machines' – and remarks that he relished the power that a writer has over the physical world that surrounds him if he chooses to put it into his novel. He 'would take his bicycle of an afternoon and note the houses and cottages and typical inhabitants and passers-by, to be destroyed after tea by Heat-Ray or smothered in the Red Weed' (Atlantic, II, pp. ix–x). The result is magnificently sustained superimposition of fantasy and closely observed reality. The enormous cylinder, which has a diameter of about thirty yards, is buried in the sand on Horsell Common and has attracted the attention of local people: cyclists, servants, golfers, a butcher and his son on their rounds. A sense of the typical nature of this group is patiently built up so that the modern reader has the incidental pleasure of feeling that an entirely real and representative group from the massive security of late-Victorian England is assembling round the pit. It may seem surprising that they show so little fear of the cylinder, but Wells himself, of course, has created the tradition of terrifying aliens with superhuman powers to which modern readers of science fiction have become accustomed. It is a mark of late-Victorian confidence that these people assume that the creatures in the cylinder will be friendly and recognisably *human*: one of the onlookers immediately – and, it is clear, typically – says of the red-hot cylinder: 'There's a man in it! Men in it! Half roasted to death! Trying to escape!' (ch. 2).

Wells's imagination was always stirred by blood, fires, cataclysm, and this novel could easily overbalance into a torrent of destructive and explosive images. That it does not is a tribute to Wells's use of his 'map' to keep his apocalyptic imagination in check. After the magnificent first appearance of the Martians, octopus-like creatures breathing with difficulty in the earth's heavy atmosphere and dripping saliva from their quivering mouths (this is *almost* gratuitous, since the Martians don't actually need mouths: they feed by blood transfusion and communicate telepathically) the novel is very particular about the spread of their terror from Horsell Common to Woking (which they blast with their Heat-Rays), about the positions in which the cylinders fall (all ten of them fall in the Home Counties and London), and about the distances that the Martians travel in order to destroy the suburban Surrey towns. Wells was indignant over Orson Welles's famous radio adaptation of the novel in the late 1930s which transferred the settings to American cities: for the progression of the novel's effect it is essential that the Martians move out from bases in Surrey and Sussex and form a crescent from which they invade London. The safe domestic English familiarity co-exists with inconceivable – but here amply conceived – terror.

The War of the Worlds has no plot and depends on the careful spacing of its revelations to sustain the reader's interest. Wells abandons the frame narratives that he has used earlier (the narrator who introduces the Traveller in *The Time Machine*, the 'nephew' who 'edits' Prendick's papers in *The Island of Dr Moreau*) in favour of a more fluid and confident narrative technique. In the earlier romances he distances himself from the narrators – the Time Traveller is a remote middle-aged pessimist, Prendick a gentleman of private means with a smattering of biology – but the unnamed narrator of this novel is simply Wells himself, a scientist and writer living in Woking and learning to ride a bicycle at a time of invasion. He is writing some six years after the Martian attack, and the reader is assumed, of course, to have survived the invasion as well: hence asides like 'The planet Mars, I scarcely need remind the reader, revolves about the sun at a mean distance of 140,000,000 miles' (ch. 1) and references to changed conditions – the popular newspapers of the 1890s have disappeared and so has the 'seriocomic periodical *Punch*'. Little else seems to have changed though: there are references to children and tradesmen passing the narrator's house on the Byfleet road, and to the busy multitudes still thronging Fleet Street and the Strand. Beyond that the novel is disappointingly vague about the effects of the invasion: there have been a 'broadening of men's views' and unspecified 'gifts to human science' and that is all.

The narrator has no name, nor has his brother, who is an important secondary narrator – he witnesses the mob panic in London as the Martians invade – nor do the artilleryman and the curate with whom he has long scenes. He speaks the whole of the narrative (the brother's narrative is 'reported') and uses the tone of an eye-witness account composed for a newspaper. This journalistic feel is kept up by the use of chapter headings which read like headlines: 'The Heat-Ray in the Chobham Road', 'The Destruction of Weybridge and Shepperton', 'What Had Happened in Surrey'. 'The Heat-Ray in the Chobham Road' ends with a well controlled account of the arc of the Heat-Ray destroying everything in its path except for people lucky enough to be low on the ground. Trees and buildings catch alight: 'Sparks and burning twigs began to fall into the road, and single leaves like puffs of flame – hats and dresses caught fire. Then came a crying from the common. There were shrieks and shouts, and suddenly a mounted policeman came galloping through the confusion with his hands clasped over his head, screaming' (ch. 6).

The narrator's sense of effective journalism ensures that the impetus and plausibility of the story are maintained, and compels the reader to share his progressive dismay. After the Martians' first attack the narrator is inclined to minimise the nature of the danger. A double perspective is at work since with his six years' retrospect he 'now' knows – and indicates to the reader – that he had underestimated the Martians. This yields an agreeable *frisson* of undisclosed terrors to come: ' "A shell in the pit," said I, "if the worst comes to the worst, will kill them all." [. . .] So some respectable dodo in the Mauritius might have lorded it in his nest, and discussed the arrival of that ship full of pitiless sailors in want of animal food. "We will peck them to death tomorrow, my dear" ' (ch. 7).

The revelations about the Martians' strength are judiciously paced. At first there is optimism among the soldiers and officials dealing with the Martians because the creatures move slowly and with obvious difficulty: the Heat-Ray and the tripods in which they soon begin to tramp over the countryside establish their technological superiority and mobility, and the black poison gas, their second weapon, completes the demonstration of man's helplessness against them (though the Martians are not entirely invulnerable: one of the tripods is shot down near Weybridge and two more are destroyed at sea). Book II of the novel is called 'The Earth Under the Martians' (actually a somewhat misleading heading, since the Martians never get further than the South of England) and begins with the remarkably effective scene in which the narrator and his companion of the moment – a cowardly and hysterical curate – are trapped in a house which is partially destroyed by the landing of the fifth cylinder from Mars. Their hiding place gives them a privileged position from which to observe the Martians assembling their War Machines and also to watch them *feeding*: this unfolds the most chilling of the novel's inventions, that the Martians, who have no stomachs, feed by transfusions of human blood. Wells refers jokily to his own articles on the evolution of man in *The Pall Mall Budget*, December 1893, and notes that the Martians have fulfilled the predictions in those pieces: 'The perfection of mechanical appliances must ultimately supersede limbs, the perfection of chemical devices, digestion – that such organs as hair, external nose, teeth, ears, chin, were no longer essential parts of the human being, and that the tendency of natural selection would lie in the direction of their steady diminution through the coming ages' (bk. II, ch. 2).

The method of feeding contributes to the destruction of the Martians, and the last and best of the novel's surprises is, of course, the revelation that the Martian invasion of earth was doomed from the beginning. In Book II, chapter 8, 'Dead London', the narrator sees an immobile War Machine on Primrose Hill, standing above one of the Martians' pits. He approaches to find it full of the corpses of Martians, 'slain by the putrefactive and disease bacteria against which their systems were unprepared'. *The War of the Worlds* begins as a parody of British imperialism but ends as a celebration, if one may so express it, of Wells's first and leading scientific interest: the theory of evolution.

These germs of disease have taken toll of humanity since the beginning of things – taken toll of our pre-human ancestors since life began here. But by virtue of this natural selection of our kind we have developed resisting-power; to no germs do we succumb without a struggle and to many – those that cause putrefaction in dead matter, for instance – our living frames are altogether immune. But there are no bacteria in Mars, and directly those invaders arrived, directly they drank and fed, our microscopic allies began to work their overthrow (bk. ɪɪ, ch. 8). Humanity is an evolutionary hero; man survives conditions in which the Martians are doomed. At the same time the Martians represent, one must remember, a possible future development of the human animal. The fact that these highly evolved creatures are destroyed by bacteria makes one wonder what would have happened in the world of 802,701 in *The Time Machine*, if the Time Traveller had arrived with a slight cold. Surely the Eloi and the Morlocks – from whose world all disease has long been eradicated – would have been wiped out?

There is an important subsidiary evolutionary theme dramatised by the curate and the artilleryman. A number of the romance's features could well be borrowings from the book of *Revelation*, chapter 9, where a star falls from heaven and opens a bottomless pit, from which emerge monsters bringing death by fire. The curate sees the coming of the Martians as the fulfilment of God's promised vengeance, and gibbers with terror: 'It is just. On me and mine be the punishment laid. We have sinned, we have fallen short'. The artilleryman, by contrast, seems at first to be an evolutionary success, tough, adaptable, and preparing realistically for the probable conditions that will obtain when the Martians have conquered. Through the artilleryman's predictions Wells indicates an alternative novel that could have been written, in which the Martians *farm* mankind (as the Morlocks do the Eloi – the fact that he had already used the essence of this scenario probably dissuaded Wells from making more of it). To the artilleryman most modern Englishmen are fit only to be farmed and fed upon: 'They haven't any spirit in them – no proud dreams and no proud lusts [. . .]. Lives insured and a bit invested for fear of accidents. And on Sundays – fear of the hereafter. As if hell was built for rabbits! Well, the Martians will just be a godsend to these. Nice roomy cages, fattening food, careful breeding, no worry' (bk. ɪɪ, ch. 7). The amenities of the old civilisation, concerts, The Royal Academy, 'nice little feeds at restaurants' will disappear, and the survivors who successfully resist the Martians will be classless, 'able-bodied, clean-minded men', who will live in the London drains in hiding like a breed of 'big savage rat'. They will practise eugenics with 'able-bodied, clean-minded women', and euthanasia against the 'useless and cumbersome and mischievous' (ibid.).

CONCLUSION

How much of this rhetoric does Wells endorse? In some of the other books the artilleryman's attitudes are clearly identifiable with Wells's own; contempt for religion in *The Island of Dr Moreau* and for the decadent upper class in *The Time Machine*, a bullying enthusiasm for eugenics and the rule of the practical man in *Anticipations*, *A Modern Utopia* and *The Food of the Gods*. But in *The War of the Worlds* Wells is firmly, and reassuringly, on the side of normative human values. The artilleryman is shown up as an idle windbag, all talk and no action, and his pre-fascist rhetoric gives way, during his evening drinking and playing cards with the narrator, to a reflective style: 'No longer the energetic regenerator of his species I had encountered in the morning', he lapses into a weak, ruminative and engaging sensuality. It is as though Wells chooses here to laugh at some of his own tendencies: the hectoring, bullying side of his temperament is caricatured and mercifully neutralised by comedy.

The romances of the 1890s: conclusion

Science transformed Wells's life. The discovery of science in his adolescence was also the discovery of freedom:

It must be hard for intelligent people nowadays to realize all that a shabby boy of fifteen could feel as the last rack of a peevish son-crucifying Deity dissolved away into a blue sky, and as the implacable social barriers, as they had seemed, set to keep him in that path into which it had pleased God to call him, weakened down to temporary fences he could see over and presently hope to climb over or push aside (Autobiography, p. 144).

His year of work with Huxley at the Normal School reinforced the sense of freedom, and established the ideas that are reflected in all the romances of the 1890s: that Christianity is nonsense, that man's life is of infinitesimal brevity compared with the age of the earth, that man is the 'culminating ape' and that the evolutionary process is essentially *amoral* and may well be leading to termination, and decadence, rather than to progress.

The romances show a powerful destructive drive. The underfed child of bankrupt and desperate parents had turned himself, at the age of thirty, into a literary success, and one element in almost all his work is the impulse to reorganise the world to suit himself. The socially disadvantaged young man seeing the world from the perspective of a basement kitchen in Bromley and the housekeeper's room at Up Park takes pleasure in showing that

tly fixed order can be blown away by an appropriate
ntelligence and the will. As Mr Polly was to express
world does not please you, *you can change it*. Deter-
ter it at any price, and you can change it altogether'
y of Mr Polly, ch. 9). Each of the romances attacks a new
ie Time Machine exacts revenge for a childhood of basements and ill-feeding: the basement dwellers of the future will
turn on the aristocratic upstairs persons *and eat them*. *The Island of
Dr Moreau*'s corrosive satire sweeps away all religious teaching
and many of the hopes of social progress that optimists of the
period had discovered in Darwinism. In *The Invisible Man* the
attacks are less concentrated and less successful. One of the
targets is suburban middle-class complacency, but others get in
the way: is the novel finally a moral allegory about the abuse of
science or a heroic fable about an outsider who refuses to live by
middle-class standards? It seems open to either interpretation.
In *The War of the Worlds*, by contrast, the targets are clear: late
Victorian Home Counties complacency and pride in Britain's
aggressive imperialism.

Yet if one stands back from these works their collective effect
is not one of angry self-assertiveness but of prodigality. The flow
of ideas is extraordinary, the playfulness and grace of expression
are often irresistibly attractive. Wells is a scientist who wears his
learning lightly. Instead of lingering over the mathematics of
time travel he plunges straight into its imaginative possibilities,
and rather than expound the theory of evolution in any detail he
assumes – reasonably enough – that a reader who has not read a
word of Darwin will still be able to follow the use of the theory in
the evolutionary fables. The pleasure his mind takes in its acts of
creation – the free play of the visualising imagination that
produces such scenes as the last disappearance of the Time
Traveller on his machine, the first Martian laboriously climbing
out of its cylinder, the foliage bursting into life on the moon – is
the pleasure of a temperament which takes science as its *donnée*
but rapidly displays itself as primarily *literary*. And Wells himself, writing about the romances in the 1930s, clearly recognises
this: they are 'exercises of the imagination', 'all fantasies', which
'have to hold the reader to the end by art and illusion and not by
proof and argument' (Romances, p. vii). Wells intends this comment as an apology: these youthful works, he is saying, are not
to be taken as seriously as the realism, prophecy and politics of
his later career. But we are free to take it in the opposite sense:

these early works, to which he devoted the whole of his talent without chaining it to a particular cause, yield the highest kind of literary and imaginative pleasure.

2

The Edwardian achievement, I:
Love and Mr Lewisham, Kipps,
The First Men in the Moon, The War in the Air

Edwardian Wells

The years 1895–1910 are the years in which Wells established himself. The brilliant young innovator who burst on to the literary scene with *The Time Machine* was a world figure by the end of the Edwardian decade. But by this date – 1910 – he was also under attack and less sure of his direction. In 1895, when he was thirty, Wells had been quite clear about where he was going. He was going *up*: his drive was to burst the social and literary barriers, to establish himself in a position of unassailable financial and social advantage. By the age of forty-five he had secured that position; where was he to go next? In the intervening years his need to disentangle himself from constricting situations and impose his will on others had led to his agreement with Jane that they would have an 'open' marriage, to his vain attempt to dominate the Fabian movement and to his self-appointment as apostle of freedom to the nation. In 1910 the problem for Wells was that temperamentally he still had to conquer: but to conquer *what*?

Writing in the 1930s about his second marriage Wells characterised himself as a fighter, and the marriage as his and his wife's 'joint attack upon the world'. He and Jane were sexually incompatible but, as he says, at that early stage of their struggle for 'position and worldly freedom' they were allies rather than lovers (Autobiography, pp. 465, 464). The struggle included a hard professionalism over money. In 1896 he became one of the first clients of J. B. Pinker, the astute literary agent whose list was to include Conrad, James, Bennett and Ford. (Ford Madox Ford published many of his books as Ford Madox Hueffer; he changed his name in 1919. For convenience I shall refer to him as Ford throughout this discussion.)

Wells was early recognised by other writers as a force to be reckoned with: indeed Ford regarded him as already 'The Dean of our profession' in 1896 because of his instant acclaim and rocketing sales (quoted by the MacKenzies, p. 143). In these years Wells was seeking specifically *literary* success. His work as a reviewer of fiction for *The Saturday Review*, 1894–96, gave him a clear sense of the range of quality in contemporary fiction. He knew as well as anyone that much of the commercially successful fiction of the day by figures such as Hall Caine, Marie Corelli and S. R. Crockett was devoid of literary quality, and he ranged himself firmly on the side of the devoted artists: Gissing, George Moore, Stephen Crane, Conrad, Henry James and Ford. His reviews in *The Saturday Review* show him developing a theory of fiction based on realism. He looks for verisimilitude in the characters and for a 'sense of causation' in the plots, and he admired in particular Hardy's *Jude the Obscure* in both these respects. Jude's personality is representative of his class, his tragedy is a direct product of his circumstances. And in particular, in this novel we hear 'the voice of an educated proletarian, speaking more distinctly than it has ever spoken before in English literature' (quoted by Ray, p. 114).

He took issue with artists like Gissing, George Moore and Crane over the question of impersonality: this is an important matter which I shall discuss more fully below in the context of his celebrated quarrel with Henry James (ch. 4, pp. 113–22). Wells was already quite clear, in the 1890s, that the novelist's personality could legitimately express itself in his work. A novel is not obliged to 'show' rather than 'tell', to be written 'as you would a play', and the artistic purity which insists on showing at the expense of telling robs the reader of 'the personality of the author, in order that we may get an enhanced impression of reality' (quoted by Ray, p. 116). Henry James and his followers were to establish a doctrine of 'impersonality' which was followed in (for example) Percy Lubbock's hugely influential *The Craft of Fiction* (1921). This was challenged by E. M. Forster in *Aspects of the Novel* (1927), with his insistence that a novel is a 'repository of the voice' and that we are bound to attend to the 'temperament of the novelist' present in his text; and it was challenged again, more forcefully, when Wayne Booth in *Rhetoric of Fiction* (1961) argued that one is bound to acknowledge the presence of the novelist's values as well as of his dramatised personality (Forster's 'voice'). Wells anticipates these claims. His view of the novel was coherent and intellectually defensible, and one of the tragedies of his later quarrel with Henry James was his failure to defend himself effectively (I shall discuss this below).

Another effect of that celebrated quarrel, and of Wells's own claims in the autobiography (written in the 1930s) that he was a 'journalist' rather than an artist, has been to obscure the fact that at the end of the 1890s Wells belonged firmly with the *artists* and not with the journalists. The group of writers with which Wells was associated were all 'outsiders' in terms of English high society (and in terms of the English literary *haute bourgeoisie*). Wells and Arnold Bennett came from the lower middle class, Conrad, James and Crane were foreigners, Gissing had socially displaced himself by his disastrous marriages. And despite the recognition that these writers enjoyed, none of them approached the sales figures of Hall Caine, Marie Corelli, Conan Doyle and Kipling.

Illness had terminated Wells's career as a teacher, and a second illness (again affecting his kidneys) moved him, in 1898, from the London suburb of Worcester Park to Sandgate, near Folkstone. The theory, which proved correct, was that he would recover if he lived by the sea. The Wellses lives at first in an unsatisfactory rented cottage, and having failed to find a house that suited him Wells resolved to build one. After vexations and delays he moved, in 1900, into Spade House, his 'treasure house by the sea shore' (in the phrase that Ford attributed to Henry James, MacKenzies, p. 177). He was thus brought into physical proximity to his literary friends: Conrad lived at the Pent Farm, quite close to Sandgate, and Ford Madox Ford, a previous tenant of the Pent, lived at Aldington. Henry James, at Rye, was within cycling distance, and in 1899 Stephen Crane, recently famous (after the publication of *The Red Badge of Courage*) and already fatally ill, came to live at Oxted. This constellation of famous names formed a close and intense literary group for a period which was as brief as it was brilliant: with the premature and tragic death of Stephen Crane in 1900 the group's cohesion slackened. With the turn of the century Wells's attention began to be drawn towards politics, and the seeds of his separation from the other members of the group were already sown.

Wells was, as has often been remarked, a 'disentangling' personality.[1] From the moment that he had established secure family life for himself at Spade House the drive to destroy it and escape from it began to make itself felt. Very soon Wells began to lead his sex life outside his marriage. Among the women whom he made (or attempted to make) his mistresses during the Edwardian period were two who were closely linked with both his literary life and with his membership of the Fabian Society. Rosamund Bland was the daughter of Hubert Bland and of E. Nesbit, the writer of children's books, and Amber Reeves was the daughter of the prominent Fabian, Professor Pember Reeves (the Blands were also Fabians). These relationships got Wells into trouble, and the book that he made out of the Amber Reeves affair – *Ann Veronica* – came close to wrecking his literary career. Why did he take these risks? Why, being so firmly established, did he not take his sexual pleasures discreetly – as, ironically, Hubert Bland did – and preserve an orthodox front for his public? The answer is that the drive to disentangle himself from Spade House and all that it stood for was intellectual as well as instinctive. Instinct was undoubtedly an important part of it: since his adolescence he had displayed a strong and primitive biological drive to get up and out of the holes – basements, apprentices' dormitories, dingy London lodgings – in which he found himself. It would be easy to say that although Spade House was the antithesis of these early dwellings in terms of space, light and amenity, the habit of escaping from wherever he happened to be was too strong for him to break. But the drive to throw aside social and moral constraints is part of a coherent intellectual position, worked out in *Anticipations* (1901), *The Discovery of the Future* (1902) and *Mankind in the Making* (1903).

It was the publication of these books that brought Wells to the attention of the Fabians: in 1903 he was approached by Bernard Shaw and Beatrice and Sidney Webb and invited to join the Society. The Fabian Society had started in the 1880s as an intellectual socialist movement which sought to effect political reform by infiltration and persuasion rather than by violence. It had separated from the Liberals in the 1890s and by the Edwardian period its influence was waning and its numbers – about 700 members, overwhelmingly middle class – were too small for it to have a broad political base. By recruiting Wells, Shaw, in particular, hoped to secure for the Society an exciting voice which commanded a wide audience. Shaw had been a friend of Wells since their journalist days in the 1890s; the Webbs did not like Wells personally – Beatrice Webb's observations of him in her diary are decidedly cool, and frequently snobbish – but they were willing to make use of him.

Wells, on the other hand, did not intend to be made use of. From an early stage he decided that the Fabian Society needed to be greatly enlarged, and organised on a quite different footing, if it was to have any national political effectiveness. He set out these views in two aggressive pamphlets, *Faults of the Fabians* and *Reconstruction of the Fabian Society* (1906). In the 1930s Shaw was to admit that Wells was right about the need for the Fabians to reform themselves, but he defeated his own cause by using confrontation rather than persuasion: his aggressiveness antagonised 'The Old Gang', the Blands, the Webbs, Professor Reeves and the Secretary, Pease. As Shaw pointed out to him, his refusal to learn or to observe the procedure of committees was counter-productive; and in spite of Shaw's friendly warnings, Wells allowed himself to be manoeuvred into a situation which was, in effect, a head-on struggle between himself and Shaw. This was a contest in which Shaw was bound to win: he was a practised orator, he was a long-standing member of the Society and, unlike Wells, he knew how to keep his temper. Wells was signally defeated by Shaw's superior debating skills in a meeting of the Society on 14 December 1906. From this date he was effectively out of the Fabian movement, although he retained his formal membership for another two years. He finally resigned from the Society over a small issue: he had been criticised by other Fabians for supporting Churchill – whom Wells personally liked – as a *Liberal* candidate in a by-election, which was seen as treachery to the cause of socialism (MacKenzies, chs. 13 and 14).

The period 1895–1910 may be divided into three phases for Wells. From 1895 to 1900 he consolidates his literary friendships and devotes himself to the art of the novel; from 1900 to 1906 he interests himself in politics and seeks to exert a direct influence on affairs through the Fabian Society; from 1906 to 1910 he uses the novel as a vehicle through which to express his opinions. His own retrospect of the Edwardian period is worth looking at here. Writing in the 1930s about the pressures on his career in what he called his 'Sandgate Period' Wells suppressed the details of his sexual adventures but described clearly the way in which he felt pulled between the values represented by two groups, the writers (especially Conrad, Ford and James) on one side and his new political friends on the other. The division between these two groups represents a conflict of loyalties which was never fully resolved. He veered away from literature towards politics during the Great War and again after the General Strike and in the early 1930s, but he was always a full-time professional writer. It is noticeable that in the autobiography he gives *several* reasons for the drift from literature to politics in the Edwardian period, which suggests strongly that this was a division of his loyalties about which he was neither entirely happy nor entirely clear. But, at the same time, there is no doubt that after 1900 he saw himself as a man of ideas and political influence – a public educator – and that this role informed his writing for the rest of his life.

Love and Mr Lewisham

Love and Mr Lewisham (1900) is the first Wells book that can properly be called a 'novel'. His earlier 'realist' book, *The Wheels of Chance* (1896) is a holiday book: its subtitles, 'A Holiday Adventure' and 'A Bicycling Idyll' indicate its nature clearly enough. Hoopdriver, a draper's assistant, spends a fortnight out on his bicycle touring the South Coast, falls in love with an upper-class girl and, after a series of loosely knit adventures, returns to his work in the draper's shop. The interest of this novel lies in the presence in it of many of Wells's later ideas – about personal liberty, about the class struggle, about the slavery of the retail trade and the relations between the sexes – in an undeveloped and jocular form. Wells himself recognised this; in the preface to the Atlantic Edition, written in the 1920s, he described Hoopdriver as the precursor of the 'thwarted and crippled' personalities of his Edwardian novels, *Love and Mr Lewisham*, *Kipps*, *Ann Veronica* and *The History of Mr Polly*; these four books, he adds, are a distinct group, 'a series of close studies of personality'.

Of *Love and Mr Lewisham* he wrote that it was 'consciously a work of art' which cost him more labour than any of his subsequent novels (Atlantic, VII, p. ix). By Wells's standards it took a long time to write: he was at work on it, in the intervals between other projects, from 1896 to 1899. It was received with coolness by the reviewers (Heritage, pp. 78–84) and Wells's friends were puzzled by it. Arnold Bennett wrote to say that he preferred Wells's scientific romances, and Wells replied in a much quoted letter:

Why the Hell have you joined the conspiracy to restrict me to one particular kind of story? I want to write novels and before God I *will* write novels. They are the proper stuff for my everyday work, a methodical careful distillation of one's thoughts and sentiments and experiences and impressions (Wilson, p. 45).

The tone of this, as of much of the correspondence between Wells and Bennett, is jocular/ferocious, but the point made is quite serious. Wells sought, with *Love and Mr Lewisham*, to create a work of art which was as shapely, controlled, carefully constructed and technically sophisticated as the work of James, Ford, Conrad and George Moore. Wells's temperament naturally impelled him towards discussion novels – even *The Wheels of Chance* contains a high proportion of discursiveness in relation to its length – and in the case of *Love and Mr Lewisham* one can feel that unwonted discipline is present and that the impulse towards discursiveness is being reined in at every turn. The result is a closely organised and economical text. *Love and Mr Lewisham* has many of the Jamesian virtues. It tends to observe a single 'point of view' – Lewisham's – but it also uses an omniscient voice as alternative narrator to place Lewisham in an ironic perspective. It proceeds by 'showing' rather than 'telling', though there are exceptions to this also. The scenes involving Miss Heydinger and Chaffery – Wells's Jamesian 'ficelles', one may say – tend to be discursive rather than dramatic. In the novel's early chapters the omniscient narrator presents Lewisham, an eighteen-year-old schoolmaster at 'Whortley Proprietary School, Sussex' (Midhurst Grammar School) and draws attention to the ironic contrast between Lewisham's view of himself and the view that the average man would be likely to take of him. The narrator identifies himself as a 'male novelist' and the reader can infer that he is middle-aged, prosperous and London based. Lewisham's provincial adolescence is presented by this narrator with a finely judged mixture of distance and compassion. Lewisham making marginal adjustments to his scruffy down-at-heel appearance, and wearing an unnecessary pair of glasses in order to look older than the bigger boys, is presented with well-selected details: he 'brushed his hair with elaboration, and ruffled it picturesquely', he 'inked the elbows of his coat where the stitches were a little white' (ch. 6).

The narrator makes it clear that despite his callowness and self-deception Lewisham has enviable qualities. Although 'downy' he is 'honest' and 'healthy' but his young man's freshness is dulled by his solemn and impossibly ambitious programme of self-education. The 'Schema' for his future stuck on the wall of his lodgings in Whortley predicts that he will take his B.A. from London University in 1892 and his 'Gold Medal' in 1895 (the dramatic date of these first chapters, indicated by the

phrase 'ten years ago', must be about 1888), and will thereafter
go into politics. It is very much the career that Wells would have
envisaged for himself in 1883 when he was about to leave
Midhurst for the Normal School of Science in Kensington.

The adolescent Lewisham is being torn apart. His room indicates that he 'thought little of Love but much on Greatness' (ch.
1), and the tension between his sex drive and his ambition is set
in focus by the pleasing contrast between his heady passion for
Ethel Henderson and the domestic reality of the Frobishers, the
family with whom Ethel Henderson is staying. Lewisham stands
outside the Frobisher's house in the dark, worshipping the only
lit window, which he imagines to be Ethel's. In fact it is her
aunt's: 'Behind the blind, Mrs Frobisher (thirty-eight) was busy
with her curl-papers [. . .]. Outside, Mr Lewisham (eighteen)
stood watching the orange oblong for the best part of half an
hour [. . .]. Then he sighed deeply and returned home in a very
glorious mood indeed' (ch. 3).

The novel neatly reverses the expectations set up by these
opening chapters, which invite the reader to think that
Lewisham's story will resemble the central thread of *Jude the
Obscure*: that Lewisham's appetites will divert him from his
ambitions and destroy him. The novel's action demonstrates
that the ambitions are wholly false and that the way to salvation,
for Lewisham, is to follow his sexual drive: the pattern of the
novel vindicates his sexuality, so to speak, by showing that its
promptings transform him from a self-deluding adolescent into
a competent and self-determining mature male. After their
lyrical 'scandalous ramble' in the country (Wells always writes
about the English countryside with a townsman's nostalgia)
Lewisham and Ethel Henderson lose contact with each other for
some three years. In the earlier chapters Lewisham has been the
subordinate partner in his relationship with Ethel: sexually and
socially inexperienced and dazzled by her attractiveness and air
of 'good society'. In London the relationship is altered, its power
balance has shifted in Lewisham's favour: as a science student
he has a kind of respectability, while Ethel is the accomplice of
her father, Chaffery, the fraudulent medium who is defrauding
the gullible Mr Lagune. Lewisham can now see himself as a
dependable young man protecting a disgraced girl who has been
caught out in a deception. The narrator remarks that this is 'the
cardinal point in their lives'. Lewisham seizes the initiative and
makes a crucial decision: he moves in this speech from the role

of bullied, passive anti-hero to that of hero:

'I don't care where you are, what your people are, nor very much whether you've kept quite clear of this medium humbug. I don't. You will in future. Anyhow. I've had a day and night to think it over. I had to come and try to find you. It's you. I've never forgotten you, never' (ch. 13).

Is he right to be won over by love and to turn his back on 'greatness' in this way? The novel uses its minor characters to point out the choices available to him and the pressures brought to bear on him. If he chooses to ally himself with Miss Heydinger, the plain bluestocking fellow-student, he could have love *and* greatness: she would promote his career, while Ethel is uneducated – as Wells's first wife was – and will certainly obstruct his career. Here one of the differences between Wells and Lewisham makes itself felt. Wells left the dull girl for the bright one: Lewisham gets the dull girl pregnant and sticks by her. The novel's pattern indicates that this course is right for Lewisham, while his own more adventurous behaviour was right for Wells. Wells believed in *industry*: he was proud of his own persistence, his journalist's ability to get 'copy' to publishers and editors on time and the absence of literary crises and agonies of the kind that affected Conrad. Many of Wells's novels juxtapose talented lazy men with persistent effective men: Ewart, the indolent sculptor, is contrasted with George Ponderevo, the vigorous young engineer, in *Tono-Bungay*; Theodore Bulpington, the self-deluding egotist, is contrasted with Teddy Broxted, the scientist and man of the future, in *The Bulpington of Blup*. In *Love and Mr Lewisham* the talented but lazy figure is Chaffery, Ethel's stepfather, and it becomes apparent that Lewisham himself, as he grows from romantic adolescence to aggressive manhood, is the persistent and effective figure.

The scenes with Chaffery are necessary elements in Lewisham's education by life. They teach him moral relativism: a lesson Wells was always eager to teach the world. Lewisham has already become acquainted with moral relativism in an empirical way. In his application for jobs after being sacked from Whortley Proprietary School he is advised by a case-hardened educational agency to lie about his age, his religion, and the subjects that he is qualified to teach. But he clings to the notion that absolute standards of right and wrong exist, and against this Chaffery sets up his persuasive doctrine of dishonesty: 'Honesty is essentially an anarchistic and disintegrating force in society

[. . .]. What is man? Lust and greed tempered by fear and an irrational vanity [. . .]. Life is a struggle for existence, a fight for food. Money is just the lie that mitigates our fury' (ch. 23).

Here again the novel sets up an expectation which is to be reversed. At first it seems that Chaffery's knowingness and amorality are indeed the qualities that are needed to survive in the modern world, but Chaffery's actions and his further speeches cancel this impression. He envies Lewisham's economic struggle in the early days of his penury as a married student – he speaks of 'the spectacle of your vigorous young happiness – you are having a very good time, you know, fighting the world' (ch. 13). And Chaffery's undoubted intelligence is rendered useless, and mischievous, by his dislike of work: 'I am a knave but no fool. The essence of your knave is that he lacks the will, the motive capacity to seek his own greater good.' Wells himself was not lazy, but he is able to enter into the lazy man's conscious self-destructiveness, the luxurious masochist's contempt of virtue, which is often associated with the 'decadent' writers of the 1890s. The highway of virtue is 'windy, hard and austere' but promises 'dry happiness', while the sensualist's 'pleasant by-way' has its 'certain mantrap among the flowers' (ch. 28). That image reminds me of the biological degeneracy of the Eloi, and the ventilation shafts among the riotous vegetation from which the Morlocks emerge at night.

The novel itself represents the opposite of everything Chaffery stands for: the temptations of the easy way – 'lush, my boy, lush, as the poets have it' (Chaffery, ch. 28) – are consistently avoided. Elsewhere Wells does allow himself short cuts. The end of *When the Sleeper Wakes* was 'scamped' when his diseased kidney flared up in 1898: illness propelled him into writing too fast, because by this stage of his career, while an unfinished book was worth nothing a finished book could bring in hundreds of pounds (Autobiography, p. 582). The damaged kidney threatened *Love and Mr Lewisham* as well: Wells recalls that he came near to 'scamping' it, but fortunately the illness prostrated him so completely that he had to put the writing aside and return to it with 'care and elaboration' after an interval of several months (ibid., p. 584). Although the contemporary reviewers neglected the virtues of *Love and Mr Lewisham*, Hubert Bland, writing in 1909, regretted that Wells was no longer the 'artist who gave us *Love and Mr Lewisham*' but was now 'letting his pen wander at large' (Heritage, p. 146). Bland was right to the extent that *Lewisham* is more economical and more concentrated than any of Wells's subsequent books. It has a narrow energy which makes it the most Jamesian of Wells's performances, and it is a pity that James himself did not recognise this. James's response to the novel was curiously obtuse. He admired its 'note of life', 'homely truth' and 'unquenchable fancy', but was unable to recognise its design. For him it was a 'bloody little chunk of life' which was devoid of an '*idea*' or 'subject', 'determined or constituted' (James/Wells, p. 67). The charge is that it is a work of crude realism which is incompletely shaped. This is clearly unjust, and had James read the novel less hastily he would have seen that the 'idea' or 'subject' is set out in the title, where 'Love' and 'Mr Lewisham' are placed in mutual tension, and is sustained throughout the narrative. At the beginning of the action Lewisham is planning his life along certain lines and the antagonist Love is pulling in another direction: by the end of the novel the contest has ended in compromise. Love has wrecked Lewisham's 'Schema', but Lewisham has been transformed from an idealistic adolescent into a mature self-possessed male, the head of a household who fills the 'power-vacuum' at the centre of the novel's world. In common with the other Edwardian novels *Love and Mr Lewisham* presents a social world which is devoid of responsible authorities or moral imperatives. The figures who at first seem authoritative turn out to be inadequate: Bonover, the pompous headmaster; Lagune, wealthy and to that extent 'free', but feeble minded; Miss Heydinger, bossy and invigorating but ultimately pathetic in her infatuation; and then, obviously, Chaffery. Chaffery ought, of course, to be the most powerful figure in the drama. He is certainly the most intelligent, and seems at first to have made the right accommodation with the shoddiness of the modern commercial world: its dishonesty is matched by his moral relativism. But when he leaves Ethel's mother and steals Lagune's money his amorality is exposed as shabby and grotesque, sub- rather than superhuman. Lewisham, at this point in the action, moves, literally and metaphorically, into the roles of husband, father and head of a household that Chaffery had, so to speak, usurped. He and Ethel move into the house in which Mrs Chaffery ekes out a living by letting rooms. On the last page of the novel Lewisham is preparing to 'write' (something Chaffery was always too lazy to do) and Ethel is expecting his baby.

The stages by which sexuality distracts and then strengthens

Lewisham are confidently established. Wells had a strong feeling for the countryside – evinced for example in *The Wheels of Chance*, the early chapters of *Kipps* and the lyrical account of the Potwell Inn in *The History of Mr Polly* – and it is expressed here in chapter 6, 'The Scandalous Ramble'. Lewisham injures his hand getting a piece of blackthorn spray for Ethel – he 'saw with fantastic satisfaction a lengthy scratch flash white on his hand, and turn to red' – and the linked images of blood, blossom and sexuality, return in chapter 29, 'Thorns and Rose Petals'. The Lewishams, now married, are in difficulties with each other. They are desperately short of money, and each of them has a relationship outside the marriage which is concealed from the other: Lewisham receives letters from Miss Heydinger, Ethel has had callow advances from the well-named adolescent poet, Edwin Peak Baynes. After a marital row Lewisham sends roses to Ethel: she thinks they are from the poet and tries to hide them, and when he discovers this Lewisham packs his bags with the intention of leaving her. All marriages have such rows; Wells convinces us that Lewisham's experience here is both poignant and universal. He pricks himself on a rose, 'his finger bled from a thorn, as once it had bled from a blackthorn spray', and, consciously 'inflicting grievous punishment', he prepares to leave. He is prevented by circumstance: the avaricious landlady turns off the gas and he can't see to finish his packing. He returns to the bedroom to find Ethel in a posture which signals surrender: half undressed, and holding one of Lewisham's roses to her face. They are reconciled, and the chapter ends with a wholly successful image expressing metaphorically their sexual union: 'The expiring candle streamed up into a tall flame, flickered, and was suddenly extinguished. The air was heavy with the scent of roses.' Lewisham takes his place in the biological process: 'Natural selection' tells him that 'this way' – the way of paternity and responsibility and manhood – 'is happiness'. It is 'the end of adolescence' and 'the end of empty dreams' (ch. 32). The title of this last chapter is 'The Crowning Victory', and that, surely, is not ironic: by abandoning his austere life-plan and settling down with Ethel and the coming child Lewisham has fallen into his appropriate role.

Kipps

Chaffery describes Lewisham as 'fighting the world'. This is one of the differences between Lewisham and Kipps: Kipps, like

Hoopdriver and Mr Polly, is not a fighter, he is a helpless victim of events. In a sense the subject of *Kipps* was more of a challenge to the novelist than was that of *Love and Mr Lewisham*. Henry James declared that a novelist had to have a reasonably intelligent and articulate central figure as a reflector to communicate all that was in so complex a work of art as a novel had to be. Wells gives himself a reasonably intelligent reflector in Lewisham, but in Kipps he has a central figure who is 'indistinct in his speech, confused in his mind and retreating in his manners' (ch. 2). His point of view therefore will be no help to the novelist: the novel must depend on an omniscient narrator to give us an intelligent mind's perspective on its events. *Kipps* was started in the 1890s, put aside, and then resumed after the publication of *Love and Mr Lewisham*. It was originally conceived as a very big novel, Dickensian in its scale and complication, called *The Wealth of Mr Waddy*. This began with a chapter on 'Mr Waddy's declining years' and how he was adopted by a woman who subsequently became Mrs Chitterlow: and there were the adventures of Helen Walshingham's villainous brother 'as a fugitive in France' (Atlantic, VII, p. ix).

In this novel the English class system was to have been the basis of the comedy: the cantankerous Mr Waddy, saved by Kipps when his wheelchair runs away with him down the cliffs of Folkestone, leaves all his money to Kipps in order to snub his avaricious relations. Much of the novel's first part has survived, and one is bound to be grateful that Wells did not carry out his original intention: the complete novel as originally conceived would have been a limp and sprawling farce, as facetious and superficial as *The Wheels of Chance* and as long as *The World of William Clissold*. The opening scene is boring and predictable slapstick. Old Waddy is introduced swearing at the man pulling his bath chair: the man is stone-deaf and oblivious. Waddy is confined to a bath chair because of an accident in the past: he was struck down by a tricycle and on the same day received the legacy which is the source of his present wealth (*Mr Waddy*, p. 7). Having put *The Wealth of Mr Waddy* on one side Wells used the cycle-accident/legacy connection again – to much better effect – in Kipps's first encounter with Chitterlow. (Kipps is knocked down by Chitterlow on a bicycle: later, Chitterlow puts Kipps in touch with his grandfather's solicitors.)

The Wealth of Mr Waddy is a vulgar work which combines broad farce with crude satire. The representatives of contemporary

England are seen with aggressive hostility and presented in coarse caricature: Chitterlow is grasping, the old Kippses are malignantly myopic, Chester Coote is lecherous, Helen Walshingham is a cold-blooded snob. In short, this early version of *Kipps* is rough and bad tempered. With the published novel the harsh outline of Wells's original intention has become softened, and, further, has been enriched by exploration of the psychologies of (for example) Helen Walshingham and the old Kippses. The editor of *The Wealth of Mr Waddy* unaccountably prefers the slapstick of its opening chapters to the first chapters of *Kipps*, which he finds drab and unimaginative (*Mr Waddy*, p. xxi). I would reverse this judgement, since the first three chapters of *Kipps* seem to me the best in the book. Here Wells is establishing Kipps's identity by giving representative selected episodes from his young life: Kipps's engaging, but limited, temperament and the shabby-genteel environment that has created him are given with absolute authority. After the encounter with Chitterlow in chapter 4 the novel moves into the lighter (and artistically less rich) world of comic action, though it remains, surely, consistently *better* than the equivalent episodes in *The Wealth of Mr Waddy*.

The editor of *Mr Waddy* sees the earlier version of the novel as 'darker' than *Kipps*, and takes the view that in *Kipps* the characters tend to lose their 'depth' and become 'abstractions' (*Mr Waddy*, p. xix). Again, this seems to me totally wrong: Helen Walshingham is surely much *less* 'abstract' – much less a caricature of a grasping snob in reduced circumstances – in *Kipps* than she is in *Mr Waddy*. I would argue that the same is true, in proportion to their significance in the action, of Chester Coote and the old Kippses and Chitterlow: that in each case there are gains in complexity, colour and artistic detachment. If *Mr Waddy* invites comparison with *The Wheels of Chance*, *Kipps* in its final state merits comparison with *Tono-Bungay*, that hugely ambitious, and rich, novel about the Edwardian economic world. And most readers of the novel will pick up the echoes of *Great Expectations* (Kipps's monosyllabic name alone recalls Dickens's Pip), and, more generally, of the many scenes in Dickens in which a child is dismayed and intimidated by the mysteries of the adult world. Kipps 'had come into the care of an aunt and uncle instead of having a father and mother like other little boys', and he has forgotten his mother's face but has a capriciously exact recollection of a dress that she wore with a pattern of flowers and bows. He has an unexplained memory of a scene involving weeping 'in which he was inscrutably moved to join' (bk. 1, ch. 1). Kipps's parents were prevented from marrying by old Mr Waddy, and the weeping was presumably occasioned by the death of Kipps's father, Mr Waddy's unforgiven son, in Australia: a distorted recall, surely, of the Australian Magwitch in *Great Expectations*, who is Pip's adoptive father and Estella's (unacknowledged) true father. For the desperate lower-middle-class gentility of the old Kippses Wells draws on his own childhood at Atlas House, Bromley: 'They [Kipps's uncle and aunt] were always very suspicious about their neighbours and other people generally; they feared the "low" and they hated and despised the "stuck up" and so they "kept themselves *to* themselves" according to the English ideal'. Kipps's absent mother had had 'that fine sense of social distinctions that subsequently played so large a part in Kipps's career', and the first direct consequence of this is that Kipps is sent to an appalling private school, George Garden Woodrow's 'Academy for Young Gentlemen'.[1] The omniscient narrator gives a seemingly effortless, and perfectly judged, aside on the social standing – the extreme social vulnerability, rather – of those for whom such schools catered in Wells's childhood: 'Many of the young gentlemen had parents in "India" and other unverifiable places. Others were the sons of credulous widows, anxious, as Kipps's mother had been, to get something a littler "superior" to board school education as cheaply as possible, and others, again, were sent to demonstrate the dignity of their parents and guardians'. With its social aspirations, its classroom which is no more than an extension to the back of a small suburban house, and its master who tries to teach everything, the school resembles Thomas Morley's 'Bromley Academy' to which Wells had been sent as a child. But Morley was a moderately good teacher, while George Garden Woodrow is utterly worthless. He is pretentious and fraudulent, but for him (as for Chaffery) bleak self-knowledge occasionally breaks through: at times his face expresses 'stagnant amazement, as if he saw before his eyes with pitiless clearness the dishonour and mischief of his being' (bk. 1, ch. 1).

Kipps's holidays from this school represent precious moments of freedom, 'strips of stained-glass window in a dreary waste of scholastic wall' (ch. 1); but for a child of Kipps's class freedom is unattainable. Wells again draws on his own life to show this: the adolescent Kipps is apprenticed to a negligent draper, Shalford, and a furious authorial intervention uses Shalford's abuse of Kipps's young manhood as an object lesson with which to berate the complacency of English society: 'the same national bias towards private enterprise and leaving bad alone' allows impostors like Woodrow and Shalford to cripple young lives. If Kipps 'had been so unfortunate as to have been born a German' he might, observes Wells with bitter irony, 'have been educated in an elaborate and costly special school [. . .] such being their pedagogic way'. Wells sounds as though he is launching into a furious leading article about the state of education in England, but catches himself up – 'why make unpatriotic reflections in a novel?' – and returns to his story. The narrator's rage with Shalford's shop is not shared by Kipps, whose limited intelligence permits him to communicate no more than a numb sense of inarticulate suffering: 'the why and the wherefore was too much for his unfortunate brain'. This brings into prominence the novel's central technical difficulty, that of making Kipps's predicament clear to the reader while to Kipps himself it remains obscure. Wells solves it, here as elsewhere, by introducing a sharper commentator as a subsidiary character: in this case Minton, the fellow-apprentice who puts the situation in a succinct image: 'I tell you we're in a blessed drain-pipe, and we've got to crawl along it until we die'. This stirs Kipps's imagination so that he perceives 'dimly' that the 'great stupid machine of retail trade had caught his life in its wheels' (bk. 1, ch. 2).

Minton, Chitterlow, Masterman and the authorial voice speak directly to the reader's intelligence and to his sense of himself as a competent social being whose point of reference is the metropolis: all Wells's Edwardian novels tacitly assume middle-class London as their cultural norm. But at the same time the confused and inarticulate Kipps retains the reader's interest and affection, and it is a mark of the novel's skill, especially in these early chapters, that it elicits and sustains a double response to Kipps: he is seen both 'from above' as a social victim, and face-to-face as a representative and sympathetic human figure.

During his oppressed adolescence Kipps's sex-drive helps to give him dramatic presence in the reader's mind: 'the development of the sex interest was continuously very interesting to Kipps', and we can respond to that as a universal of young manhood. Also, he is largely blind to his own economic and social impotence, and this naivety is itself both dramatically attractive and universal (it recalls Lewisham's delusions about his future career). Kipps goes to Miss Walshingham's woodwork class and falls in love with her. He does not recognise that he is ill-equipped to compete for her, and the omniscient narrator points out that this ignorance is a form of strength: 'It had not yet come to Kipps to acknowledge any man as his better in his heart of hearts. When one does that the game is played, and one grows old indeed' (bk. 1, ch. 3). In a sense he is a traditional figure in romantic art, a natural man in an artificial social world: when he allows the social world to impose on him he is helpless, when he acts naturally he is freed from it. The resources of Miss Walshingham's gentility are defeated when Kipps cuts his hand in the woodwork class and licks the blood off his wrist: she can do no more than exclaim 'Oh don't'. Nature and the social world are pulling in different directions.

When they pull in the *same* direction Kipps has no escape route left. Paradoxically, the inheritance from his grandfather which ought to offer him freedom instead ensures his bondage, since his money makes him the prey of the Walshinghams. It is important to note, though, that Helen Walshingham is not solely motivated by greed (as she was in the earlier version of the novel). There is genuine physical attraction to Kipps – 'youth calls to youth the wide world through' (bk. 2, ch. 3) – and though the social rewards of marriage to Kipps ('money and opportunity, freedom and London') are, to be sure, uppermost in her mind, she is a creature of mixed motives during their courtship and the ambivalence in her is well developed and sustained.

As it slowly becomes apparent to Kipps that he has been trapped, and as Helen Walshingham's bullying stirs him to muddled rebellion, the novel explores his tangled emotions in well-selected phrases: 'She told him things about his accent; she told him things about his bearing, about his costume and his way of looking at things. She thrust the blade of her intelligence into the tenderest corner of Kipps's secret vanity' (bk. 2, ch. 5). The characterisation of Kipps remains the successful centre of the book. He is unable to see Chester Coote and the Walshinghams for the impostors that they are, but while his limited intelligence enables him to see only that he is in a muddle, his feelings lead him in the right direction, expressed in the diction of lyrical romanticism: 'His heart cried out for Ann, and he saw her as he had seen her at New Romney, sitting amidst the yellow sea-poppies with the sunlight on her face' (bk. 2, ch. 6).

The episodes involving Chitterlow, Sid Pornick and Masterman ask fundamental questions about the position of a rich man in an unjust world. Chitterlow is a shallow entrepreneur, like Bedford in *The First Men in the Moon* (at the beginning of that romance Bedford is out to make quick money by writing a play, and Chitterlow, against all the odds, actually succeeds in doing this) and Edward Ponderevo in *Tono-Bungay*. He persuades Kipps to invest money in his play, *The Pestered Butterfly* (a comic reference to *The Wild Duck*) and after most of Kipps's inheritance has been embezzled and lost by Walshingham, the maverick success of Chitterlow's play makes Kipps almost as rich as he had been before. The function of this seemingly pointless appendix of plot is to demonstrate the mad arbitrariness of the modern capitalist world: to that extent it is like a summary of the themes of *Tono-Bungay*. But it also marks an important difference between *Kipps* and *Tono-Bungay*: the real impediment to happiness for Kipps is not money but the class system, as represented by the Walshinghams' aspirations, Coote's spurious gentility and such episodes as Mrs Bindon Botting's Anagram Tea, Mrs Wace's dinner party and Kipps's miserable solitary dinner at the Royal Grand Hotel. These scenes display Wells's unflagging comic invention and the consistency with which he pursues Kipps's tangled emotions to the point where he undergoes a 'conversion' (in the Royal Grand Hotel sequence) and becomes a 'rebel, an outcast, the hater of everything "stuck-up" ' (bk. 2, ch. 7). His discovery that he hates the upper class into which his money has propelled him enables him to settle happily into the lower-middle-class domesticity of his bookshop and his marriage to Ann Pornick.

The absurdity of bubble capitalism is displayed by Chitterlow: the claims of socialism, expressed by Pornick and Masterman, may seem superfluous since Kipps manifestly finds his appropriate destiny without their aid. But these figures remind one that the story of Kipps's rise, fall and recovery is only part of the novel's concern: it is also, clearly, a discussion novel. Kipps himself is too slow to take in Masterman's political oratory, which flows past him, so to speak, to be absorbed by the reader. Masterman is partly based on the novelist George Gissing. Wells admired Gissing's work and became a close and loyal friend: when Gissing was on his death-bed in France in

December, 1903, Wells left his home to make a (vain but valiant) bid to save him. Gissing's commercial failure as a novelist, his miserable private circumstances and his early death were vivid instances of what society could do to those who would not conform; his story resembles that of another source for Masterman, Hardy's *Jude the Obscure*. Wells's admiration for this novel was unbounded: when he reviewed it in 1896 he remarked that Jude was excluded from Oxford (Hardy's Christminster) partly because the age-limit for entrance scholars was nineteen, and that Jude's story was a 'tremendous indictment' of late-Victorian education.[2]

Wells's reading of *Jude and Obscure* and his memory of Gissing both underly the figure of Masterman, a brilliant, articulate socialist who is dying of tuberculosis. His words echo Minton's image for employment in the retail trade (a drain-pipe in which its victims crawl until they die):

Some of us get out by luck, some by cunning, and crawl on to the grass [. . .]. Most of us don't get out at all. I worked all day, and studied half the night, and here I am [. . .]. These Skunks shut up all the university scholarships at nineteen for fear of men like me (bk. 2, ch. 7).

Masterman's rage is undeniably impressive, poking through the fabric of the novel and demanding independent attention: but the consequent isolation is, in a sense, fatal, since the novel seems to detach itself from Masterman's opinions and leave them resonating in the air. It can be taken as an involuntary demonstration of the inefficacy of bad temper. For Masterman the rich are triumphs of social Darwinism at its ugliest: 'they claw and clutch as though they had nothing!', they keep down the rest of humanity which 'festers and breeds in darkness, darkness those others make by standing in the light' (bk. 2, ch. 7).

Presumably Wells is at least partly in agreement with this, but the novelist in him allows Masterman's initially powerful dramatic presence to dwindle into snarling self-pity. One of the difficulties with Wells's political opinions is that his loyalty to socialism was constantly under pressure from his belief in strong leaders and men of the future – those who have eaten the Food of the Gods – a belief which was to become the basis for his advocacy of an 'open conspiracy' which developed during the war and in the 1920s. The reader who finishes *Kipps* in the belief that he has read an attack on capitalism is bound to concede that it offers no alternative to the system that it appears to attack. Kipps finds security in his bookshop and the action is then

shamelessly rigged (by the introduction of Chitterlow's successful play) to make him a beneficiary of capitalism as well ('wealth
rises like an exhalation all over our little planet and condenses,
or at least some of it does, in the pockets of Kipps' (bk. 3, ch. 4)).
The last part of the novel was written too quickly, as Wells
acknowledged: he called book 3 'a thing of shreds and patches'
(*Mr Waddy*, p. xxii). It reads as though Wells has become
impatient both with dramatisation and with responsible discussion, and has resorted instead to simplistic political rhetoric.
The system is to be condemned, in a vague way, because the
Kippses are unhappy: they are 'little, ill-nourished, ailing,
ignorant children – children who feel pain, who are naughty and
muddled and suffer, and do not understand why' (bk. 3, ch. 2).

Henry James must have decided to overlook such passages
when he praised *Kipps* as 'the first intelligently and consistently
ironic or satiric novel' (James/Wells, p. 105). Irony, alas, is
exactly what is missing from Wells's fits of editorialising por-
tentousness. But many of the things James says about *Kipps* are
valuable: he is right to praise the characterisations of Kipps himself and of Coote and Chitterlow, and to admire the novel's
exploration of the lower-middle class. For him Wells has 'taken
a header straight down into mysterious depths of observation
and knowledge'; the book has 'extraordinary life' and its characters are 'vivid and sharp and *raw*' (ibid.). James's 'raw' is no
doubt double-edged. Kipps could, conceivably, be the hero of a
James novel: a male equivalent of the helpless heiress adrift on
the treacherous waters of polite society. One may entertain, for
a moment, the awesome prospect of *Kipps* re-written in the
manner of *The Wings of the Dove*. But it is unfruitful to pursue at
this point the ways in which Wells and James differed from each
other. The question is, does *Kipps* succeed, artistically, by the
standards that Wells had set himself?

I think the answer is 'yes' if one accepts the notion that the
standards relaxed as the novel grew. The first three chapters
have the same excellences as *Love and Mr Lewisham* has: the
evocation of Kipps's boyhood and adolescence seal the reader
into this remembered world with complete assurance. The
scrupulous realism of these chapters is then drastically dis-
rupted by the change of tone in chapter 4: Chitterlow's advent as
'Fortune' has a noisy facetiousness which becomes part of the
novel's texture. Thenceforth its balance is constantly threatened
by this lazy breeziness of manner. The comedy tends to become

coarse or rushed (the music-box scene in the Royal Grand hotel is decidedly forced), and Wells spoils what could have been one of his best scenes by carelessness. Genteel callers at Kipps's rented house mistake Ann for a servant, and Kipps is bitterly ashamed. This is striking, focusing as it does the unnecessary pain that the class system inflicts on these people, but the pathos of the 'Buttud Toce' (also referred to, confusingly, as 'teacake') which Ann has ordered as a treat and which neither of them can eat because of their quarrel becomes thin through repetition (bk. 2, ch. 2). Even in the early chapters there are small, awkward inconsistencies. Kipps's speech is 'indistinct', short of aspirates, with its mispronunciations rendered phonetically throughout: yet the private academy run by George Garden Woodrow exists precisely to sell gentility to the lower-middle class. It is surely unlikely that Kipps would have left this school with unregenerate working-class speech. Later, as the breeziness becomes dominant, the texture loosens further: the architect who deludes the Kippses into building an absurdly grandiose house begins promisingly and then drops out of sight, while the detailed vexations of house-building – Wells's troubles with the builders of Spade House – are spun out too far. The broad satirical device of the prehistoric 'Labyrinthodon' who looks like Chester Coote, and represents the class-bound world in all its obsolescent arrogance, seems to have come from a different book altogether. While the beginning of *Kipps* is clearly by the artist who wrote *Love and Mr Lewisham*, the end reads like a scrap-book of abandoned jottings for *Tono-Bungay*.

The First Men in the Moon and *The War in the Air*

As a romance, *The First Men in the Moon* (1901) invites comparison with the romances of the 1890s rather than with the near-contemporary *Love and Mr Lewisham*, and to make this comparison is to note immediately a change of attitude. After 1900 Wells became, on balance, optimistic, and his visions of alternative societies were genial rather than nightmarish. *The First Men in the Moon* and *The War of the Worlds* are both stories about evolution, space travel and imperial exploitation, but the tone of *The War of the Worlds* is apocalyptic, the tone of *The First Men in the Moon* verges on the farcical. The *fin de siècle* feeling of his 1890s works has been replaced by a forward-looking buoyancy. Bedford in *The First Men in the Moon* has characteristics in common with other weak, greedy and impatient figures from Wells's Edwardian novels. He has Chitterlow's and Edward Ponderevo's charlatan self-assertiveness and faith in easy money and dubious practices, and he has Mr Polly's temperamental laziness. He has come to Lympne, in Kent, to make quick money by writing a play – there is 'nothing a man can do outside legitimate business transactions that has such opulent possibilities' – but is too indolent to make any progress. Wells envied Shaw's success in the theatre, and one may note here his own attempts at playwriting, the most ambitious of which was *Hoopdriver's Holiday*, a version of *The Wheels of Chance*, written in 1903–4. Like Edward Ponderevo in *Tono-Bungay*, Bedford is an exploiter. His instinct when he lands on the moon is to take possession and colonise, his instinct when he discovers the moon's abundance of gold is to enrich himself. Bedford is an exploiter, Cavor is an innovator and man of science: the contrast between these types is one that Wells was to use many times. It recurs in Edward Ponderevo and his nephew George in *Tono-Bungay*, in Mr Stanley and Capes in *Ann Veronica* and, most strikingly, in Theodore Bulpington and Teddy Broxted in *The Bulpington of Blup*. Cavor is developing an anti-gravitational substance. His motivation is that of the pure researcher: 'He would be made an F.R.S. and his portrait given away as a scientific worthy with *Nature*, and things like that'. Bedford immediately perceives this substance, 'Cavorite', as a potential source of personal advancement: 'a parent company, and daughter companies, applications to the right of us, applications to the left, rings and trusts, privileges and concessions spreading and spreading, until one vast stupendous Cavorite company ran and ruled and world'. The connection with 'Tono-Bungay', the spurious tonic, symbol of Edwardian capitalism, which gives its name to the later novel, becomes explicit: Bedford declares that Cavorite will be 'more universally applicable even than a patent medicine' (ch. 1).

Later Wells was to come down firmly on the side of the dedicated scientist and against the exploiter, but *The First Men in the Moon*, being the detached comedy that it is, holds the balance evenly between them. Cavor's theoretical brilliance is accompanied by total practical incompetence. For the expedition to the moon he provides inadequate clothing, insufficient food and no means of defence. His first experiment with 'Cavorite' is conducted in a similar state of haphazardness which nearly causes the end of the world (this recalls the theme of 'The Man who could Work Miracles'). He fails to guard against an effect of which, in theory, he is fully aware. The air above a square piece of Cavorite is *weightless*, thus causing a 'fountain' or chimney in the upper air which threatens to whip the atmosphere off the world 'as one peels a banana' and fling it 'thousands of miles' into space, destroying all forms of life (ch. 2).

At times the romance reads as though it is another re-working of the Faust motif, following *The Invisible Man* and *The Island of Dr Moreau*. In Bedford's view, the travellers' misadventures on the moon are entirely to be blamed on Cavor's scientific over-reaching. Bedford complains of 'this accursed science' and refers directly to the world which produced the Faust legend: 'The medieval priests and persecutors were right and the Moderns are all wrong.' Science 'offers you gifts. And directly you take them it knocks you to pieces' (ch. 13). But the novel's pattern makes it clear that Bedford is wrong: that his own greed and aggression are as much to blame as Cavor's ambition. Some of their mistakes are made jointly: they lose their spacecraft within a few minutes of landing on the moon because of the pleasure that they take in the sensation of weightlessness. But it is Bedford who insists on eating the intoxicating fungus which causes them to be captured by the moon-people, and Bedford who first resorts to violence. Incidentally, Bedford's imperial dream receives its most grandiose expression during the drunkenness induced by the moon-fungus: 'We must annex this moon', he hiccups, 'This is part of the White Man's Burthen.' The founding of Rhodesia by Salisbury and Cecil Rhodes has inspired him: 'Nempire Caesar never dreamt. B'in all the newspapers. Cavorecia. Bedfordecia' (ch. 11).

As a narrator, Bedford is a figure of some subtlety. He cannot be identified with Wells's own personality (as can, for instance, the scientific journalist who narrates *The War of the Worlds*) but he commands a good deal of the reader's sympathy. For example, he communicates the excitement of his first fight with the Selenites in a way that carries the reader with him. The Selenites' light bodies smash like eggs under his attack: 'I seemed to be wading among those leathery, thin things as a man wades through tall grass, mowing and hitting, first right, then left; smash, smash' (ch. 17). Wells worked hard on this romance – later he picked it out as one of the most 'sedulously polished' of his performances (Atlantic, I, p. x) – and the manipulation of its narrator is evidence of his care. Although Bedford is distanced by his aggression and rapacity, his competence inevitably compels the reader's respect when it is contrasted with Cavor's ineptitude. His relationship with Cavor is at times like Sam Weller's with Pickwick; and just as *The Pickwick Papers* is finally dominated by the figure of Pickwick himself, so *The First Men in the Moon* changes the balance between its two major figures, towards its close, to give Cavor ascendancy.

When, for instance, Bedford sees that the Selenite crowbars are made of gold and plans a second moon-expedition which will ship the gold back to earth, the tone of Cavor's reported reply compels the reader to share Cavor's regret rather than Bedford's jubilation:

He looked at my golden crowbars. [. . .] At last he sighed and spoke. 'It was *I* found the way here, but to find a way isn't always to be master of a way.' (ch. 18)

He recognises that the European powers will inevitably struggle for possession of the moon (as they struggled for possession of Africa in the 1870s and 1880s) and the folly of imperialism will be re-enacted on a larger scale: 'Even of their own planet what have they made but a battle-ground and theatre of infinite folly' (ch. 18).

Cavor's dominance is marked by his seizure, so to speak, of the narrative: the final section of the romance is devoted to his transmissions from the moon so that he becomes, in effect, a second narrator. In the *Strand Magazine* serialisation the transition is marked by a passage which is omitted from the book publication:

Here the story, as we originally received it, ends. But we have just received a most extraordinary communication which certainly gives a curious and unexpected air of conviction to the narrative. If our correspondent is to be believed, Mr Cavor is still in the moon, and he is sending messages to the earth. We hope to be in a position to satisfy the curiosity of our readers in our next issue (*Strand Magazine*, xxi, June 1901, p. 663).

Reading the story in the *Strand Magazine* is a much more 'Edwardian' experience (in the pejorative sense) than reading it as a book: the rather poor illustrations by Claude Shepperson emphasise the jocular elements of the text at the expense of its artistry. Cavor and Bedford are figures from Edwardian clubland, Bedford with an aggressive imperial adventurer's moustache, Cavor plump and untidy in a donnish way. One may note in passing that Wells's descriptions of the Selenites are so inventive and particular that they inspire Shepperson to more interesting drawings, of which the best illustrates Cavor's description of Selenite intellectuals: 'some of the profounder scholars are altogether too great for locomotion, and are carried from place to place in a sort of sedan tub, wabbling jellies of knowledge' (ch. 24). Shepperson's drawing shows a greatly inflated head lolling mournfully over the side of a tin bath-tub as it is carried along by ant-like porters.

Cavor's transmissions from the moon have been disliked as an excrescence or afterthought, but to me they are an essential part of the romance's organisation. They give Cavor the reader's full attention, and they furnish Wells with another context in which to explore the notion of an alternative society. The political works of the period, *Anticipations*, *Mankind in the Making* and *A Modern Utopia* propose hygienic, ordered and centrally controlled communities in which the principle of appropriate specialisation operates at every level. In the Selenite world Wells plays with his utopian ideas and considers some of their limitations and shortcomings. The Selenites are undoubtedly better organised, more intelligent and less aggressive than man, but Cavor feels a repulsion from certain aspects of their society which the reader is certainly invited to share. Some Selenite infants, bred to become manual labourers, are confined in jars 'from which only the forelimbs protrude' and the extended hand is nourished and stimulated while the rest of the body is starved. Horrible, of course: but Cavor finds in it a certain cold-blooded sanity compared with the way in which human society treats its working-class children: 'it is really in the end a far more humane proceeding than our earthly method of leaving children to grow into human beings, and then making machines of them' (ch. 24). The ambivalence intensifies as we learn Cavor's unenviable fate: he is unwise enough to tell the Selenites too much about human aggression and the Selenites are, like Swift's Houyhnhnms, disgusted by what they learn of human nature and human institutions. The transmissions abruptly cease: the novel's final paragraph seeks a tone of tragic elevation:

A blue-lit shadowy dishevelled Cavor struggling in the grip of these insect Selenites, struggling ever more desperately and hopelessly [...] being forced backward step by step out of all speech or sign of his fellows, for evermore into the Unknown – into that silence that has no end (ch. 23).

What, then, are we to make of *The First Men in the Moon*?

Despite its jocularity it can be seen as an anti-imperial fiction which registers its condemnation of imperialism through a 'limited' first-person narrator, whose viewpoint is replaced by that of a more reliable narrative consciousness in the last section. There are some points of contact with Conrad's *Heart of Darkness*, published in *Blackwood's Magazine* in 1899. *Heart of Darkness* is, of course, on one level, an anti-imperialist story – not a 'romance' but a nightmare – spoken by a limited narrator, Marlow, who reflects that the Thames at the time of the Roman invasion was like nineteenth-century Africa, an unexplored region being opened up: 'And this also [. . .] has been one of the dark places of the earth'. The colonial adventurers set out from a civilisation which has itself been colonised: Wells makes precisely the same point. Bedford, newly arrived at Lympne, recalls that it had once been a major Roman port. He thinks of 'the galleys and legions, the captives and officials, the women and traders, the speculators like myself, all the swarm and tumult that came clanking in and out of the harbour. And now just a few lumps of rubble on a grassy slope' (ch. 1).

The essential idea of the romance is a simple one. A community of ant-like creatures in the moon furnishes a commentary on human societies. This Swiftian device provided a framework within which Wells became excited by the beauty and strangeness latent within his subject. His transforming imagination makes the special effects into the most memorable parts of the reader's experience. As the sphere, clad in its Cavorite, crosses the gulf between earth and moon Wells describes the oddities of space travel. These effects, now very familiar to us from the modern science fiction writers of whom he was himself the precursor, were then unprecedented in English. Objects float freely in the sphere and gravitate towards the centre; the moon's brilliance, free of intervening atmosphere, is blinding: a 'scimitar of white dawn with its edge hacked out by notches of darkness, the crescent shore [. . .] out of which peaks and pinnacles came climbing into the blaze of the sun' (ch. 6). The lunar day lasts fourteen earth days, and Wells gives it a complete seasonal cycle within that period. In his description of the stirring of plant life in the lunar dawn Wells anticipates by fifty years the use of stop-frame photography in filming the growth of vegetation. The buds 'swelled and strained and opened with a jerk, thrusting out a coronet of little sharp tips, spreading a whorl of tiny, spiky, browning leaves, that lengthened rapidly, lengthened visibly even as we watched. The movement was slower than any animal's, swifter than any plant's' (ch. 8). As Bedford returns from the moon, having abandoned Cavor and stolen the sphere, he undergoes psychological changes which he describes as irrelevant but which the reader may well see as essential. The inner-directed selfish materialist becomes detached from his own egotism: 'I looked down on Bedford as a trivial, incidental thing with which I chanced to be connected' (ch. 20). I have said that the 'power balance' between the two figures changes so that Cavor dominates the end of the novel: a further, subordinate change has taken place in Bedford himself. He returns to earth more intelligent and sensitive, and therefore better equipped to edit Cavor's transmissions from the moon, than when he left it. The reader's relationship with the narrator shifts and modulates, the experience of reading this romance is in every sense richer than its design might lead one to expect.

Wells likes to attain an aerial perspective from which to view mankind. In this he resembles Willie, the narrator of *In the Days of the Comet* (1906); in the brief introductory chapter of this romance (a chapter headed 'The Man who Wrote in the Tower') Willie looks back, and *down*, on the squalid industrial urban world in which he was born. He records his childhood and young manhood in the Potteries, called by Wells the 'Four Towns'. Presumably he adopts this phrase to distinguish his setting from Bennett's 'Five Towns'. Bennett had published *Anna of the Five Towns* in 1905. He and Wells were, of course, close friends and loyal admirers of each others' work; indeed Wells's relationship with Bennett was the steadiest and most secure of all his literary friendships. Wells had written about the Potteries before, in 'The Cone', a short story written when he was visiting Stoke-on-Trent to convalesce after an illness in 1888 (it was published in a periodical in 1895 and in *The Plattner Story: And Others*, 1897). The setting in which Willie spends his young manhood may owe something to Wells's reading of Bennett, but the personality is obviously that of Wells himself, bright, arrogant and resentful, 'ill clothed, ill fed, ill housed, ill educated and ill trained' (ch. 2).

He looks back on the early twentieth century as a barbaric age preceding the 'change': a comet passing close to the earth has enveloped it in green vapour which has permanently altered human nature for the better: the consequence is an ideal free society which closely resembles the Republic recommended in *Mankind in the Making* and *New Worlds for Old*. *The War in the Air*

(1908) also looks back on a state of disorder which has been replaced by something better: in this case the cataclysm of the war of the title has depopulated the planet and the survivors have set up small, self-sufficient communities. But where Willie in *In the Days of the Comet* closely resembles Wells himself, Bert Smallways, the protagonist of *The War in the Air*, is both representative and distanced: 'a vulgar little creature, the sort of pert, limited soul that the old civilization of the early twentieth century produced by the million' (ch. 3). But although Bert is limited he is not stupid: one commentator on the novel says that he 'remains to the last a typically irreverent Cockney, a Hoopdriver grown none the wiser or less gullible' (Hammond, p. 108), which seems to me quite wrong. At the beginning of the novel, admittedly, Bert has something in common with Hoopdriver, but he is far more like Kipps and Lewisham, rabbit-like adolescents who are changed by life-experience into confident adults. He is the rebellious younger brother of a greengrocer and market gardener at 'Bun Hill' (Bromley) in an England of the near future which has cross-channel monorails and other technical advances, but no reliable powered flight other than airships. When he was writing this Wells believed that the secret of *stability* in aircraft was still far in the future. In his novel this secret is discovered (or stolen) by one Butteridge, a loud-mouthed colonial who alights in a balloon on Dymchurch beach where Bert and his friend Grubb, having abandoned their failed bicycle shop, are trying to eke out a living as beach entertainers, 'Desert Dervishes'. By a sequence of farcical mishaps Bert takes off, alone, in the balloon and is carried across the North Sea to Germany. The experience begins the process of transformation which then is seen working in Bert throughout the novel. His mind begins to enlarge: 'he found himself lifted out of his marvellous modern world' and floating between sea and sky. The authorial voice remarks: 'It was as if Heaven was experimenting with him', which we may take as an indication that Bert has been selected as the biologist's subject, genus *homo*, and that the novelist himself is conducting the experiment. Speaking over Bert's shoulder, the narrator observes that flight is 'like nothing else in human experience. It is one of the supreme things possible to man' (ch. 3). Taking advantage of the balloon's elevation, so to speak, the authorial voice retains its aerial perspective and examines Bert Smallways as a representative of the decay of modern Europe. His mind is full of deposit from the gutter press, 'thinly violent ideas about German competition, about the Yellow Danger, about the Black Peril, about the White Man's Burden'. His inadequacies are direct results of the criminal folly of the nationalist governments of modern Europe which spend on armaments the money that should be 'directed into the channels of physical culture and education' (ch. 4). Elsewhere Wells's editorial passages often threaten to swamp his books – especially in some of the later works like *The Secret Places of the Heart* and *The World of William Clissold* – but here the authorial voice keeps close to Bert and legitimately fills the gaps in his knowledge and puts his adventures into their context. The novelist and the writer of history and political theory in Wells co-operate here. The novelist in him establishes the Bun Hill and the Grubb's Bicycle Shop of Bert's young manhood, and the pleasing and well-selected details of the balloon flight, such as the effect of seeing the balloon's shadow on the clouds, 'a black spot moving with him far below' and occasional moments of danger: 'With an immense and horrifying rustle the balloon brushed against a telephone pole, and for a tense instant he anticipated either an electric explosion or the bursting of the oiled silk, or both'. The writing draws on a reservoir of strong and violent metaphors. Bert ignorantly pulls at the ripping-cord which, fortunately, is fouled by the balloon's fabric: 'but for that little hitch the ripping-cord would have torn the balloon open as though it had been slashed by a sword, and hurled Mr Smallways to eternity at the rate of some thousand feet a second. "No go!" he said, giving it a final tug' (ch. 3). Bert's single-handed fight on Goat Island with the two Germans – the 'bird-faced' officer and Prince Karl Albert – has something of the claustrophobia and vividness of the manhunts (or boyhunts) in Golding's *Lord of the Flies*, and the death of Karl Albert is exhilaratingly garish. Bert uses a new device, an oxygen-containing bullet: 'A great flame spurted from the middle of the Prince, a blinding flare [. . .]. Something hot and wet struck Bert's face. Then through a whirl of blinding smoke and steam he saw limbs and a collapsing burst body fling themselves to earth' (ch. 9).

The historian in Wells sets out the growth of nationalism in modern Europe and the nations' refusal to adapt to modern conditions. Medieval habits of mind have survived into the modern world to its peril: human affairs are inextricably entangled by the old areas of sovereignty and the traditional national prejudices. Wells was consistent about this. Throughout the

1920s and 1930s he would continue to write urging the European nations to abandon their nationalism, to think in terms of the future rather than of the past, and in Hitler he saw the most squalid and petty medieval baron reborn. Here, taking Bert Smallways as his modern man, he broadens out into a huge generalisation: 'All Europe was producing big guns and countless swarms of little Smallways'. Wells himself underestimated *The War in the Air*. Writing in the 1920s he lumped it together with his greatly inferior 'fantasias of possibility', *The World Set Free* and *When the Sleeper Wakes*, but he does, rightly, congratulate himself on his skill as a historian of the future. The book's central idea, that powered flight will transform the nature of warfare, has not been challenged by events. To the modern reader it indeed seems possible that another world war would end in a collapse of civilization and a return to a new primitivism, which is what happens at the end of *The War in the Air*. Bert, now free from the distorting urban class-ridden society of his young manhood, is the sturdy father of a new, healthy race in a post-apocalyptic arcadia. He has greatly changed: he has become a strong, aggressive male, willing to kill his enemies without asking questions in order to protect the semi-feudal community of which he is leader. It has been said that as a novelist Wells's skill lay in the form of realism which can persuade us that an individual's history is representative of larger social forces (Ray, p. 119). Surely this is true of the story of Bert Smallways. There is more to *The War in the Air* than its predictions, interesting though these are. It does not have the sustained excitement and imaginative freedom which are the strengths of the earliest scientific romances, but the success with which it transforms Bert Smallways from oppressed anti-hero into a dominant adult relate to similar patterns in the stories of Lewisham and Kipps, and the interweaving of commentary and imaginative invention relates to *A Modern Utopia*, while its extended scale, and its successful meshing of a particular life-story to a swathe of human history, anticipate Wells's most important single achievement, his 'Condition of England' novel, *Tono-Bungay*.

3

The Edwardian achievement, II:
Tono-Bungay, Ann Veronica
The History of Mr Polly

The Sea Lady, The Food of the Gods, A Modern Utopia

A recent critic of Wells rightly remarks that he was one of the first literary figures of any stature in England to shape himself into a 'Modern' (in the simple historical sense – 'belonging to the Twentieth Century' – rather than in the sense of the literary term 'Modernist'[1]), and that if we recall that he was a Victorian our admiration for his achievement is immediately enhanced (Reed, p. 1). In the Edwardian period a contradiction becomes apparent between his declared objective of universal co-operation and his highly aggressive, individualist nature: 'like a philandering priest, he could work honestly and diligently for the faith he could not keep' (Reed, p. 8). Contradictions are found in all aspects of his life: he was against sexual licence, for instance, despite the licentiousness of his own life, and he was equally ambivalent about the past. Rural England exerts a nostalgic pull which is both attractive and potentially deadly; the past has to be fully understood – and at the same time vigorously resisted – before man can perceive clearly his own future. One of the earliest influences on Wells's thinking was Winwood Reade's *The Martyrdom of Man* (1872), a work which takes the full impact of Darwin's theory and sees man as a partially evolved creature struggling towards an inscrutable future. The prose often shows close resemblances to Wells's own writing:

It is Nature's method to take something which is in itself paltry, repulsive and grotesque, and thence to construct a masterpiece by means of general and gradual laws, those laws themselves being often vile and cruel [. . .]. When we examine the human mind we do not find it perfect and mature, but in a transitional and amphibious condition. We live between two worlds; we soar in the atmosphere; we creep upon the soil; we have the aspiration of creators and the propensities of quadrupeds. There can be but one explanation of this fact. We are passing from the animal into a higher form, and the drama of this planet is in its second act (Reade, p. 316).

Man is a divided animal with multiple identities: the theme is one that Wells was to play on throughout his work, up to and including *The Fate of Homo Sapiens* (1939), *Babes in the Darkling Wood* (1940) and the thesis on 'The Quality of Illusion in the Continuity of the Individual Life' (to abbreviate its title) which he submitted for the London University D.Sc. in 1942. In the decade 1900–10 three works which are towards the 'romance' rather than the 'realist' end of the Wellsian spectrum express three aspects of his identity: *The Sea Lady* advocates sexual freedom while noting, with a detached playfulness that reminds one of *Zuleika Dobson*, that its effects can be fatal; *A Modern Utopia* advocates a hygienic and well-ordered and *aesthetically pleasing* society run by an oligarchy of H. G. Wellses; and *The Food of the Gods* predicts that far-sighted scientists – not Faustian over-reachers, but Nietzschean overmen – will sweep away petty, dirty and disorganised mankind, and replace it with a new race of giants.

The frame of *A Modern Utopia* (1905) has an interesting doubleness. Wells distances himself by having the narrative introduced by a lecturer, whose task it is to present to his audience the ideal state of things on a remote planet that he has inadvertently visited. Yet the lecturer resembles Wells himself as he was becoming – plump, small, with fine blue eyes and a cocky bearing – and the ideals embodied in the utopia are clearly Wells's own. So are the intellectual quarrels. Ruskin, who was frequently a target for Wells's scorn, is attacked here (with William Morris) for his belief that Utopia could exist without machinery: this is the Olympian unworldliness of the 'irresponsible rich'. (Presumably Wells is thinking of Ruskin's famous attack on machine-made – as against handmade – artefacts in 'The Nature of Gothic', from *The Stones of Venice*.) Wells's Utopia has *good* machines. The machines of Edwardian England – and to this extent he agrees with Ruskin – produce ugly objects, but that is the fault of the society for which they provide:

Things made by mankind under modern conditions are ugly primarily because our social organisation is ugly, because we live in an atmosphere of snatch and uncertainty, and do everything in an underbred strenuous manner. This is the misfortune of machinery, and not its fault (ch. 3).

There will be some privacy in Wells's utopia, but since everybody's manners will be aristocratic – nothing 'underbred' about these Utopians, no 'baseness of bearing, grossness of manner' –

the need for privacy will hardly exist. The man of the future may want a home and family, a 'corner definitely his', but 'first and most abundantly' he will want to travel and see the world.

The key concept is set out in chapter 4: Utopia is aristocratic in government as well as in style, run by the Samurai, the 'voluntary noblemen' who have 'taken the world in hand'. In chapter 5 the incompetents are put in their places. Those who are 'indecently dressed, or ragged or dirty' will come under the care of the state, and their breeding will be restricted: the birth of children to 'diseased or inferior' parents will become a very rare 'disaster' (ch. 6). Clearly there is no room here for Hoop-driver, Kipps or Bert Smallways. The state will take responsibility for children: those wishing to become parents must pass state tests of competence before being permitted to marry, but the marriages need not be permanent. The Samurai, based explicitly on the Guardians in Plato's *Republic*, ensure the steady improvement of the race. From their reading of Darwin they know that the history of man is 'a conflict between superior and inferior types' and that 'specific survival rates are of primary significance in the world's development' (ch. 9). In short, *A Modern Utopia* is a bullying work; but it is, at the same time, strikingly optimistic. The prosperous Wells who had built Spade House and was embarking on an open marriage proclaims the coming of a world which is clean, light, hygienic, sexually sane, intelligent, aristocratic and beautiful. Before 1900 Wells had tended to see man as trapped and doomed in the evolutionary process, but from *Anticipations* onwards there is a tendency towards optimism. Among Wells's contemporaries plot tends to express inevitability: accidence and coincidence in the works of Gissing, Conrad, James and Bennett, are plot contrivances which, as a recent critic has put it, 'hem characters in'. For Wells they are 'not steps towards a finality, but doorways opening into freedom and mystery. His plots demonstrate this quality of liberation' (Reed, pp. 172–3). This lends weight to those who argue that Wells is not simply trying to do the same thing as James, Ford and the others, and on the whole doing it badly, but that he is doing something totally different (see the quarrel with Henry James in chapter 4, below). The last page of *The Sea Lady* (1902) suggests that man's experience is drastically limited, and that beyond it are unplumbed possibilities of freedom for the bold mind. The mermaid and Chatteris, her victim, have vanished, and a policeman with a lantern searching the beach finds the wrap that the mermaid discarded before she swam out to sea. He asks 'What do such things mean?' and looks out to sea: 'I picture the interrogation of his lantern going out for a little way, a stain of faint pink curiosity upon the mysterious vast serenity of night' (ch. 8). This is reminiscent of his early essay, 'The Rediscovery of the Unique'; indeed he seems to be quoting, perhaps unconsciously, from his image there of science as a 'match that man has just got alight' to find 'just a glimpse of himself and the patch he stands on visible, and around him, in place of all that human comfort and beauty he anticipated – darkness still' (Philmus, p. 31). *The Sea Lady* reminds man that he is a limited being inhabiting an epistemological wilderness and that sex will destroy him: but to express its themes in this way is altogether too solemn. The somewhat *fin de siècle* subject matter is contradicted – or neutralised – by the playfulness of the treatment. It is a graceful work, which glances at de la Motte Fouqué's *Undine*, Ibsen's *The Lady from the Sea* and (explicitly) at Mrs Humphry Ward's *Marcella*, and has a forceful matriarch who speaks, as Wilde's Lady Bracknell does, lines which suggest that she is putting down a revolution rather than conducting a conversation. Lady Poynting Mallow insists that her nephew marry Miss Doris Thalassia Waters. 'What if she *is* a mermaid! It's no worse than an American silver mine, and not nearly so raw and ill-bred' (ch. 7). Chatteris's friend tries to spell out the difficulties of marriage to a native of the sea:

'He could have a yacht and a diving bell', she suggested, 'if she wanted him to visit her people.' 'They are Pagan demigods, I believe, and live in some mythological way in the Mediterranean.' 'Dear Harry's a Pagan himself – so *that* doesn't matter; and as for being mythological – all good families are' (ibid.).

And so on. It's not as funny as Wilde, but it bowls briskly along and keeps the reader at an agreeable distance from the inherent improbability of the fable: we come to feel that a mermaid in Folkestone is no more outrageous than are the social attitudes expressed by a *grande dame* drawn from well-known literary and dramatic stereotypes. Henry Chatteris hopes for freedom, as do most of Wells's post-Victorian figures, and the fairy-tale neatly traps him so that he is forced to choose between two forms of bondage. If he resists the Lady he will be stifled in a respectable marriage, but to yield to her – as he does – is to be stifled in a more literal sense by drowning. In his conflict Chatteris almost paraphrases the passage from Winwood Reade's *The Martyrdom of*

Man that I have quoted above which speaks of man's 'amphibious' condition, torn between 'creator' and 'quadruped':

'We are matter with minds growing out of ourselves. We reach downward into the beautiful wonderland of matter, and upward to something – ' [. . .] 'Man is a sort of half-way house – he must compromise' (ch. 7).

At this point in the fantasy Chatteris believes that he is opting for the timid, socially determined way: the route to orthodox marriage and sexual restraint. 'Renunciation! That is the life for all of us. We have desires, only to deny them, senses that we all must starve. We can live only as a part of ourselves. Why should *I* be exempt?' (ibid.). But he then turns his back on renunciation – to the reader's awed delight – and the authorial voice leaves open the question whether his drowning is a matter of terror or 'gentle ecstasy' (ch. 8). Burne-Jones's painting, 'In the Depths of the Sea' (1888), which shows a mermaid pulling a sailor down to the sea-bed, seems to ask the same question. Is the mermaid's gioconda smile murderous or lustful?

The Food of the Gods (1904) is hopelessly 'split' between competing ideas. On the one hand it expresses the theme of the abuse of science, as do *The Invisible Man* and *The Island of Dr Moreau*, but the dominant idea, which overwhelms and extinguishes the promising comic possibilities of the romance, is that of the hero or overman who will create a new world. It is a fable expressing the ideas that Wells was later to elaborate into his notion of an 'open conspiracy'. As in so many of Wells's books, the early chapters are by far the best; his mind is fully engaged with the Food itself, its inventors and its effects. The fact that the Food creates giants gives him an opportunity to joke at the appearances of the scientists who have invented it, Redwood and Bensington: 'There is more personal distinction about the mildest mannered actor alive than there is about the entire Royal Society.' (One wonders whether that sentence had any bearing on the Royal Society's reluctance to elect him to a Fellowship in the 1940s.) 'No race of men have such obvious littlenesses' as scientists, represented by some 'queer, shy, misshapen, grey-headed, self-important, little discoverer of great discoveries, ridiculously adorned with the wide ribbon of some order of chivalry' (bk. 1, ch. 1).

Great inventions are made by little men and mishandled by the incompetence of the pure intellectual. Having invented the Food, Bensington – who is clearly temperamentally related to

Cavor from *The First Men in the Moon* – tests it on a farm run by the Skinners, dirty, disorganised old rascals whose disqualifications for the job would be obvious to anyone less unworldly than a great scientist. The Skinners leave the Food lying about; vermin and insects get at it, and this gives rise to remarkable nightmare scenes in which wasps eighteen inches long descend on travellers, and the doctor's buggy is overturned and attacked by rats the size of large dogs. A minor character puts his hand into a pond into which the Food has seeped from a drain, and is attacked by a giant larva: 'Flash! It had buried its fangs deep into his arm – a bizarre shape it was, a foot long and more, brown and jointed like a scorpion' (bk. 1, ch. 5).

The split between the book's sympathies is shown up by a small but significant flaw in its logic. The Food affects everything that consumes it: but as Wells begins to moralise so the Food suddenly, and unaccountably, becomes morally selective. The vain and socially aspiring Doctor Winkles, who pirates the Food for gain, feeds some of it to his youngest child in secret: but the child 'seems to have been as incapable of growth as [. . .] his father was incapable of knowledge' (bk. 1, ch. 4). How could the Food not affect the child if it affects rats and wasps (as well as other children)? Clearly Wells's imagination is changing direction. The Food will be used from this point not to entertain but to teach. The young giants produced by the Food, men and women forty feet high, are to be the architects of a new social order. War is declared on them by standard humanity, and the novel ends with the giants winning a temporary victory and looking forward to a future which they will inevitably dominate.

Structurally the romance is chaotic, and this is compounded by the fact that there is no single figure to whom the reader can relate. Cossar, the intelligent man of action who is the first to realize that the future lies with those who have eaten the Food, seems for a time to be the fore-grounded figure, but he is replaced as narrative centre by the infant Caddles, Mrs Skinner's grandson who has been fed the Food in order to build up his strength. Like a second Gulliver, Caddles looks down at the pygmy world and finds that it cruelly excludes him because of the 'melancholy distinction' of his size. He goes to London in a bemused search for justice and is shot at and killed by the mob and other figures are foregrounded in his place: Redwood's giant son, the three sons of Cossar and back to Redwood himself. One feels, inescapably, that Wells scrambles thus from one narrative centre to another because he is not happy with any of them.

The Food of the Gods is a muddled work of art, but as a fable it presents a key idea to which Wells was to remain loyal for most of his life. Civilisation is to be transformed by a small group of enlightened cultural and educational giants: men like Sanderson, the headmaster of Oundle, whose work was to be praised in fictional form in *Joan and Peter* and in *The Undying Fire*, and directly in *The Story of a Great Schoolmaster* (a biography published in 1925 after Sanderson's death). 'The Open Conspiracy', the idea which dominates *The World of William Clissold* and many of the works of the 1920s and 1930s, was to be a voluntary co-operation of such giants for the re-ordering of the world. With his faith in the capacity of education to transform man, to 'enlarge' him from the 'narrow prison of self' (*The Undying Fire*, ch. 3), went a belief in the efficacy of the individual will. Mr Polly's assertion that 'if the world does not please you *you can change it*' (ch. 9) relates to Wells's personality, to his life, to his dominant beliefs and to his view of literature: literature, for Wells, was part of his process of education – it was itself, as another commentator has put it, 'a means of altering existence' (Reed, p. 188).

Tono-Bungay

Henry James had reservations about the first-person narrator because of the method's 'terrible fluidity of self-revelation' (preface to *The Ambassadors*), but it is the appropriate method for *Tono-Bungay*. George Ponderevo, the strong and firmly characterised narrator of *Tono-Bungay*, is both the central figure of one story and the commentator on another. It can be seen then as two novels: in one the wild career of Edward Ponderevo illustrates the mad arbitrariness and chaotic injustice of the Edwardian economic world, and in the other George Ponderevo, the inner-directed, self-seeking and somewhat cold-blooded nephew, tells his own *Bildungsroman*, the story of his initiation and development. The two are satisfactorily related to each other by George's honest discursive narrative and his vigorously exploring intelligence. The *Kipps* formula, in which a figure who is both stupid and representative illustrates the evils of the modern world, would not do for the more diverse contents of *Tono-Bungay*. Wells was to use limited central figures again – notably Bert Smallways and Mr Polly, and much later, Edward

Albert Tewler in *You Can't be Too Careful* (1941) – but for this novel
he needed an intelligent mind at work reporting the story.

Wells can be said to stand in a symbolic relation to the
Edwardian age much as Oscar Wilde stood in a symbolic
relation to the 1890s, and *Tono-Bungay* is at once the most
'Edwardian' and the most representative of his works. Wells said
of it that he set himself to write a 'spacious' novel which would
give a view of the British social and political system, 'an old and
degenerating system, tried and strained by new inventions and
new ideas and invaded by a growing multitude of mere adventurers'; and he added that he regarded it as the 'finest and most
finished' of his novels 'upon the accepted lines' (Atlantic, XII,
preface). Wells's accepted lines are those of a Victorian tradition, the tradition of the 'Condition of England' novel of the
1840s, and he has also learnt much from C. F. G. Masterman,
who in turn drew on Wells in his own book *The Condition of
England*, which was published in the same year as *Tono-Bungay*.
Masterman read the proofs of *Tono-Bungay* while he was writing
his own book and makes a number of references to it (Masterman, p. xiv, and see pp. 181–2). Masterman – and therefore
Wells – was indebted to Arnold and Ruskin. Masterman used a
quotation from Ruskin as the epigraph to *The Condition of England*
and had edited Ruskin's *A Joy for Ever*, and he was steeped in
Arnold's writings, especially in *Culture and Anarchy*. Ruskin's
belief that before a nation could produce good art it must learn
how to live, and that therefore there is a direct connection
between morality and beauty, and Arnold's precept that all
social questions must be examined objectively (as well as his
passionate belief in education as the source of civilization's
redemption) are represented both in *The Condition of England* and
in *Tono-Bungay*. (There are several detailed parallels: for
example, Masterman's division of society into broad groups –
'The Conqueror', 'The Multitude', 'Prisoners' – closely
resembles Arnold's 'Barbarians', 'Philistines' and 'Populace' in
Culture and Anarchy.) The presence of these great Victorians is felt
throughout *Tono-Bungay*. It is probably not very conscious, since
Wells paid little attention to Arnold and tended to be actively
hostile to Ruskin; yet in *Tono-Bungay* the close attention to the
relationship between housing conditions and civilization, for
instance, could have come directly from Ruskin's work.

This novel also pulls together the ideas that Wells had been
developing in such books as *Anticipations*, *New Worlds for Old* and

Mankind in the Making. New Worlds for Old (1908) sees English society as insane. A visitor from another planet would note a few thousand people housed with conspicuous comfort, several hundreds of thousands housed in buildings 'ill designed and unpleasant to the eye', and the rest crowded into buildings 'evidently too small for a decent life'. In towns, middle-class houses are occupied by 'people for whose needs they were not designed' (ch. 4). The idea of property has run wild and become 'a choking universal weed' and the methods of growing rich include 'the selling of rubbish for money, exemplified by the great patent medicines' (ch. 5). These observations have close connections with *Tono-Bungay*. On the last point one may note that the marketing of the patent medicine in chapter 4 of the novel only slightly exaggerates the style of the patent medicine advertisements in *The Strand Magazine*, where several of Wells's books (including *The First Men in the Moon*) were published in serial form. *Tono-Bungay* probably owes some of its force and assurance, and the confidence with which Wells handles his huge themes, to the fact that he had worked over many of its leading ideas in these earlier books and was therefore at ease with them. *Mankind in the Making* (1903), which focuses on bad education and the lack of any central control of human resources as the causes of society's ills, anticipates *Kipps, The Food of the Gods* and *The History of Mr Polly*. Its account of the nurseries of the future – 'clean, airy, brightly lit, brilliantly adorned' (ch. 3) – compares with the ideal nursery of the young giants in *The Food*. It also anticipates *Tono-Bungay* in its conviction that the old institutions no longer have any validity and that adequate new ones have not appeared to replace them. Man is 'moving forward upon a wide voluminous current' and all human organizations have to be seen as 'provisional' (ch. 1). To hope that man in his *natural* state will correct the evils of the civilisation that he has created is vain romanticism: what is needed is *better* civilisation. Wells has no time for natural man: a dirty savage, 'a nest of parasites within and without; he smells, he rots, he starves' (ch. 3). E. M. Forster identified the growth of the suburbs as a key feature of Edwardian life, but the fact that changes in English society were being reflected in domestic architecture had been noticed much earlier than that. It is a persistent refrain in Ruskin and is important in Morris; *News from Nowhere* creates an imaginary world in which the depressed inhabitants of city suburbs find a better life in hygienic communes dotted about the countryside. Wells pro-

poses something very similar in *Anticipations* (1902). The popu-
lations of the future will live in a kind of extended village: the
city will 'diffuse itself' until it has 'the greenness, the fresh air, of
what is now country' and the old antithesis of town and country
will disappear (ch. 2). His phrase for property in *New Worlds for
Old*, 'a choking universal weed', could be used as a heading for all
the references to Bladesover, the 'Bladesover System' and its
effect on national life, in *Tono-Bungay*.

The country house is a favourite setting for novelists; a potent
image of the national identity and the traditions that sustain it
from *Mansfield Park* to such Edwardian novels as H. O. Sturgis's
Belchamber and Galsworthy's *The Country House*. The convention
had been treated satirically by Peacock – especially in *Headlong
Hall* – and by W. H. Mallock in *The New Republic* (Wells was to
follow these satires explicitly in *Boon* (1915)). In *Tono-Bungay*,
instead of satirising the convention Wells may be said to
demolish it: born within it, his central figure as he develops
learns passionately to reject it. At first Bladesover seems secure
and serene. 'The unavoidable suggestion of that wide park and
that fair large house, dominating church, village and the
country-side, was that they represented the thing that mattered
supremely in the world' (bk. 1, ch. 1). But the sceptical young
George knows by intuition what the adult George will know for
a fact: that this ostensible order is already obsolescent. The
relationship between the country house and the landscape is
caught in what Forster, describing another country house
(Penge in *Maurice*), refers to as the immobility which precedes
decay. Wells expresses this immobility in a justly celebrated
passage:

It is like an early day in a fine October. The hand of change rests on it
all, unfelt, unseen; resting for a while, as it were half reluctantly, before
it grips and ends the thing for ever. One frost and the whole face of
things will be bare, links snap, patience ends, our fine foliage of pre-
tences lie glowing in the mire (bk. 1, ch. 1).

The historic accumulation of wealth, land and power in the
hands of the few accounts for the present appearance of market
towns like Wimblehurst (Midhurst, Sussex) where Edward
Ponderevo first sets up as a chemist, and lies behind the present
condition of London. The London suburbs consist of mid-
Victorian houses built for middle-class people who wish to ape
the manners of Bladesover. The pretentious dignity of these
houses combined with their glaring deficiencies – dark base-

ments for the servants, inadequate sanitation – prompt a paragraph of fine indignation which is characteristic both of Wells and of George Ponderevo, and which relates Bladesover as the symbolic shell of obsolete authority to diseased and festering London, the hideous secondary product of that authority. The suburban house in which Edward and Aunt Susan live, after bankruptcy has forced them out of their Wimblehurst shop, has probably never been lived in by the middle-class people for which it was designed and is now divided into inconvenient tenements, 'wasteful of labour and devoid of beauty'. It is a 'natural growth', part of the 'system to which Bladesover is the key' (bk. 1, ch. 3).

In what sense is Bladesover the 'key' to the senior Ponderevos' misery? In two senses: private ownership of land has made for congestion, and the dignity of the country house has dictated the life-style towards which the lower classes aspire. The country house *creates* 'that snobbishness which is the distinctive quality of English thought. Everybody who is not actually in the shadow of a Bladesover is as it were perpetually seeking after lost orientations' (bk. 1, ch. 1). Uncle Teddy's snobbishness steadily expands with his income. He rents the Elizabethan Lady Grove and turns himself into a (burlesque) country squire; then, like Galsworthy's Soames in *The Man of Property* (1906; Wells certainly knew this book and may have been referring to it) plans to build a modern palace, Crest Hill (Soames's house is called 'Robin Hill') which will express his millionaire status.

On close examination the connections that Wells sees between Bladesover and the condition of England can be shown to be artificial. Pretension to gentility and land-starvation may account *in part* for the ugliness and discomfort of the late-Victorian suburbs that he condemns, but the immediate reason for their growth was, obviously, the huge economic expansion of the period. In short the 'key' to the spread of London is to be found not in the country house tradition but in the same burgeoning of capitalism that underlies Teddy Ponderevo's meteoric rise and fall.

Perhaps Wells gives the country house its artificial importance in this way out of affection. George Ponderevo is engaged throughout the novel in a quest for certainties in a shabby and confused world. Bladesover does have the merit of offering one system of certainties, the value of which George acknowledges in the very process of outgrowing them:

The Bladesover system has at least done one good thing for England, it has abolished the peasant habit of mind. If many of us still live and breathe pantry and housekeeper's room, we are quit of the dream of living by economising parasitically on hens and pigs [. . .]. About that park there were some elements of a liberal education; there was a great space of greensward not given over to manure and grubbing; there was mystery, there was matter for the imagination (bk. 1, ch. 1).

In the 'prig' novels (especially *The Research Magnificent*) Wells was to look forward to a new aristocracy which would save the world from its confusion, and here, where he praises Bladesover for the aristocratic education that it conferred on the house-keeper's son, he anticipates that idea.

George Ponderevo's quest is both moral and intellectual. He shares with many protagonists of late-Victorian and Edwardian literature the need for an external moral imperative in a world which has lost its faith. Evangelical Christianity was, of course, forced on Wells as a child, and for him as for many writers the phrases and habits of mind of that persuasion lingered long after the doctrine had been repudiated. Religious imagery abounds in this novel. As he collaborates with Uncle Teddy on the market-ing of 'Tono-Bungay', George regards the patent medicine as an inherently worthless substance to which symbolic value has become attached. He expresses his job in a deliberate echo of the phrase used in the catechism to define the word 'sacrament' (an 'outward and visible sign of inward and spiritual grace'): his duty is to 'give Tono-Bungay substance and an outward and visible bottle'. Ewart the sculptor, George's dissolute friend, rec-ognises that Tono-Bungay is a placebo which replaces Christianity for 'little clerks and jaded women and over-worked people' (bk. 2, ch. 3). The point is emphasised when Ewart designs a chalice for Teddy Ponderevo to donate to a church (one of Teddy's social aspirations is to play the munificent patron of the arts). Sex is the only religion that Ewart recognises so he decorates his design with angels modelled on the prosti-tute with whom he lives. He then fails to deliver the chalice, and Teddy exclaims that the congregation to whom it is promised will 'begin to want the blasted thing!' and complains that it 'isn't Business'. George protests that 'It's art [. . .] and religion' (bk. 2, ch. 2). Ewart consciously (and maliciously) debases the cur-rency of religious art; Teddy Ponderevo unconsciously debases the currency of religious language and in this, it is clear, he is typical of his age. George is reasonably well qualified to condemn Teddy's unconscious blasphemy; he has no respect for religion but he retains, as did Wells himself, elements of the religious outlook. As he disentangles himself from his unhappy marriage to Marion (based on Wells's first marriage) he reflects on his spiritual condition in terms that are consistent with what we know of his personality but which at the same time speak directly to the typical muddled, and intelligent, Edwardian reader in his spiritual desert: 'I had what the old theologians call a "conviction of sin". I sought salvation.' And he adds, as though to vindicate this choice of phrase: 'Names and forms don't, I think, matter very much, the real need is something that we can hold and that holds one'(bk. 2, ch. 4). Marriage will not fulfil that need; nor will the aristocratic tradition enshrined in the countryside; nor, obviously, will received Christianity in any of its forms. Early in the novel George encounters, and resists, the religious views of his appalling cousin, Nicodemus Frapp (Wells has a fine fund of grotesque names for the supporting casts of his novels). George has no father, and like Lewisham and Kipps he encounters potential father figures who are incompetents or impostors (Uncle Teddy among them). Nicodemus Frapp is a baker who takes George on as an apprentice, 'a bent, slow-moving, unwilling, dark man' who alleviates the hopeless dinginess of his life by a form of worship which is no more than a channelling of resentment. Frapp and his wife drink 'imaginary draughts of blood' and console themselves with the belief that those who enjoy worldly success are predestined to damnation, a 'serving out and "showing up" of the lucky, the bold, and the cheerful' (bk. 1, ch. 2).

For much of his story George is torn between his need for moral clarity and his reluctant recognition that the world he lives in is one of obstinate moral relativity. As his marriage collapses he reflects on the 'irresoluble complexity of reality, of things and relations alike. Nothing is simple. Every wrong done has a certain justice in it, and every good deed has dregs of evil' (bk. 2, ch. 4). The co-ordinating theme of the novel is that the institutions which have traditionally shaped men's lives are discredited, and that the intelligent, responsible seeker – George – finds nothing to replace them. He goes to London seeking a 'larger world' and is dismayed by the city's resistance to him. 'I thought I was destined to do something definite to a world that had a definite purpose', and this intention is based on an illusion, the 'constant error of youth to overestimate the Will in things.' As a young man he believes that the disorder of London is the result of a malignant intention, whereas at the time of writing he knows that 'London was a witless old giantess of a town, too slack to keep herself clean' (bk. 1, ch. 3).

That Bladesover must be the key to London is George's persistent refrain. The London museums are extensions of the collections of curios at Bladesover, and the public libraries are descendants of the Bladesover library. Both sprang 'from the elegant leisure of the gentleman of taste' (bk. 2, ch. 1). This is historically true: one may recall, for example, the fact that Uffizi, the 'offices' of the Medici, gave the word 'gallery' – the office corridor – to the world. But that Bladesover is a key – that there can *be* a key – to England's disorder as a whole is an illusion, and it is an illusion that persists in the mind of George Ponderevo and of the novelist himself. But a sympathetic reader of the novel may well find that this does not matter. Wells is a better poet than he is an analyst in *Tono-Bungay*, and the novel's imagery confounds George's quest by suggesting that there is *no* order, that decay and disease are universal and that the world is in irreversible decline. George Ponderevo undertakes a desperate expedition to 'Mordet Island' in search of 'Quap', a radioactive material which, it is hoped, will retrieve Uncle Teddy from financial disaster. For George this experience is as disorienting as Marlow's journey up the Congo in Conrad's *Heart of Darkness*; just as Marlow becomes 'psychologically interesting' under stress, so George loses his moral balance and gratuitously murders a native of Mordet Island because of the (remote) possibility that the man would report his theft of the Quap.

It has been pointed out that this cancerous stuff is symbolically related to the earlier account of London and that the Mordet Island expedition is not an excrescence but is integral to the novel's structure (Lodge, pp. 235–8). The Quap provides Wells with a new way of expressing entropy, the notion that the universe is dying, which dominates the end of *The Time Machine*. The Quap is radioactive matter which behaves like cancer, 'creeps and lives as a disease lives by destroying'. Its behaviour may indicate the way the world will end, by ultimate 'eating away and dry-rotting and dispersal', and George adds this to the other possible cataclysms that Wells himself had used in some of his romances: 'the ideas of the suffocating comet, the dark body out of space, the burning out of the sun, the distorted orbit' (bk. 3, ch. 4). I have referred to Marlow's disorienting experience in *Heart of Darkness*: Conrad's presence is felt throughout the Quap episode. The Captain of the *Maud-Mary*, in which the expedition sails, a Roumanian Jew who likes to be thought a 'gentleman of good family' and has learnt English out of a book, owes his exotic appearance, his excitable temperament, his inefficiency and his weird pronunciations of English to Wells's observation of Conrad's personality. It may seem a curiously spiteful portrait, but Wells did find Conrad's self-pity, conscious superiority and financial incompetence extremely irritating. Mordet Island has the exoticism of a Conrad setting, and the scenes in which the crew pump out, and finally abandon, the sinking *Maud-Mary* as its cargo of Quap corrodes its timbers, recall the *Judea* being destroyed by its cargo of smouldering coal in Conrad's 'Youth'. But more important than these details is the change in George as narrator; the confident chronicler of Edwardian London now finds that he is confronting the unknowable, as does Conrad's Marlow, and Edwardian optimism gives way to what looks like a resurgence of 1890s pessimism.

George soon recovers from the effect of the Quap episode largely because he has already found in his experiments in powered flight an appropriate channel for his intelligence and energy. Science promises a 'key' and is still promising it at the end of the novel; George is convinced that there is such a thing as scientific truth and that it is attainable: scientific truth 'is the remotest of mistresses, she hides in strange places, she is attained by tortuous and laborious roads, but *she is always there*! Win to her and she will not fail you; she is yours and mankind's for ever' (bk. 3, ch. 3). His faith in order has survived the Mordet Island ordeal, and he is still asserting it in the final chapter where he takes his latest invention, the X^2 destroyer, on a test voyage down the Thames. A river journey metaphorically represents the writer's and the reader's mind moving through the text, as in *Heart of Darkness*: 'that rush down the river became mysteriously connected with this book' writes George. The difference is that in Conrad's story the movement is from mouth to source, from the familiar to the inscrutable, while George's journey outward, from the city to the open sea, is marked by a progress from complexity to simplicity. In this journey he displays a confidently synthesising state of mind. The modern world is sham and display, and the former strengths and simplicities of England have become engulfed by this new meretriciousness just as the Tower of London, which he passes as he moves downstream, the 'neat little sunlit ancient Tower', is dwarfed by Tower Bridge, the 'vulgarest, most typical exploit of modern England' (bk. 4, ch. 3). The river journey enables George to perceive 'a sort of unity' fusing 'things that have hitherto been utterly alien and remote. [. . .] As I passed down the Thames I seemed in a new and parallel manner to be passing all England in review. I saw it then as I had wanted my readers to see it' (ibid.).

The masters of form in this period, Conrad, Ford and Henry James, propose the following position: the novelist must be in complete control of his art since it is impossible to secure complete knowledge of life. George Ponderevo, as narrator of this novel, says the opposite. His experiences have given him as full a knowledge of life as is available to modern man, but he cannot claim any mastery of literary form. It is an attractive strategy since it persuades the reader not to look for Jamesian cohesion in the structure and legitimises the novel's eclecticism. At the same time, though, there *is*, finally, cohesion in the technique: we emerge with a sense of a consistently dramatised narrator who has kept up a disarming and persuasive commentary on his method. From the beginning he makes it clear that he is unable to follow existing literary conventions:

I've read an average share of novels and made some starts before this beginning, and I've found the restraints and rules of the art (as I made them out) impossible for me. I like to write, I am keenly interested in writing, but it is not my technique (bk. 1, ch. 1).

The novel will be large in its ambition and open-ended in its structure, and the method will be one which in Jamesian terms squanders its effects and forces its intentions on the reader with what may seem an exposed innocence: 'What I'm really trying to render is nothing more nor less than Life – as one man has found it' (bk. 1, ch. 1). As we have seen, George's quest for certainty leads him to challenge the claims to legitimacy of a number of people and institutions: among them Bladesover, the Frapps' Christianity, Beatrice Normandy's offer of passionate fulfilment (her affair with George is one of the novel's sub-plots), Lady Grove and its attendant village (Duffield) and Crest Hill's expression of Edwardian aspirations. He comes to rest on a faith in hidden 'scientific truth' which is still sustaining him on the novel's last page. But an important part of George's function is to provide the frame for the story of his Uncle Teddy. In terms of dramatic organisation this novel resembles *Love and Mr Lewisham* and *Kipps* in that there is a power vacuum at its centre. Uncle Teddy, as the impostor who fills this vacuum, represents Edwardian commercial life: even his name could be taken as an unflattering tribute to the monarch, as could his fatness and lechery. He is a sly, dishonest anti-hero who finds that the social order allows him to adopt the posture of a hero. He plays Nietzschean overman, Napoleon and religious prophet (Tono-Bungay gives people 'Faith', he declares). We are torn between condemning Teddy and admiring him. In the early, Wimble-hurst chapters, he represents freedom and excitement for young George (and Aunt Susan, the most sympathetic figure in the novel, gives George the love that his own mother has withheld). But as he makes money so Teddy begins to look vulgar: a fat man offering disingenuous proposals 'round the end of his cigar' and looking 'energetic and knowing and luxurious and most unexpectedly a little bounder' (bk. 2, ch. 2). George knows, of course, that the Tono-Bungay project is inherently dishonest, and he agrees to join Teddy because he is under multiple pressures: from Marion, who will not marry him until he has a sufficient income; from Aunt Susan, who convinces him that Tono-Bungay represents the only chance that she and Teddy have of escaping from their dingy lives in London; and from Teddy's insidious flattery. It is a dramatic necessity that Teddy should forfeit the reader's sympathy as his story unfolds. His life-style becomes ludicrously vain, he wounds Aunt Susan by taking the appalling lady novelist Mrs Scrymgeour as his mistress, and he displays small-minded vindictiveness when he expresses a wish to go back to Wimblehurst and triumph person-ally over his former enemies there. He has to be developed in this way so that he can be seen to deserve the punishments in store for him: bankruptcy, the threat of imprisonment, death from pneumonia following the flight from England in George's latest air-ship, the Lord Roberts β.

With the death of Teddy the over-reacher is punished, the bubble has burst, and that particular story has closed, leaving the reader with lingering regret for Teddy's human frailty and (especially) for Aunt Susan's suffering. George's framing narra-tive ends with the movement from river into open sea (charac-teristic of much of Arnold's poetry, and another pointer to the presence of Arnold's work in the book). This resolves nothing, and instead of giving a sense of closure leaves us with the opposite sense of expansion and opening out. For George as narrator the threads in the story have merged just as the tributaries of the Thames converge and mingle their waters. He stands back from his own narrative, this 'big pile of manuscript', and remarks that its title ought properly to have been *Waste* (the title used by Harley Granville-Barker for his play of 1907). And indeed, when one looks at the lives of Aunt Susan, who is left widowed, childless and alone, and of the Hon. Beatrice Normandy, one can see his point. Beatrice belongs to the tradition of Dickens's Estella and Thackeray's Becky Sharp: as a child she is enchanting, a flirtatious 'sweet imp' sitting on a wall (bk. 1, ch. 1). (An immature, upper-class girl sitting on a wall with a forbidden garden beyond it appears again in *The History of Mr Polly*: perhaps some such memory had a special place in Wells's own emotional history.) As she and George become adult they change places socially: George moves up from the servants' hall to become a successful businessman and engineer, while Beatrice becomes the mistress of Lord Carnaby. Unfortunately she also deteriorates into that favourite Victorian dramatic cliché, the Fallen Woman, and speaks lines distressingly akin to those of Pinero's Mrs Tanqueray: 'A woman when she's spoiled, is *spoiled*. She's dirty in grain. She's done' (bk. 4, ch. 2).

But although George at the end of the narrative says that his theme is 'waste' the tone throughout has been that of buoyancy and achievement. From the beginning he has stressed that his subject is change, flux, the absence of fixity; he has been struck by 'a transverse force' and carried above the Edwardian world by the trajectory of his uncle's flight, 'astraddle on Tono-Bungay' as though on a rocket (bk. 1, ch. 1). This and many other images of flight prepare the reader for actual flight in the Lord Roberts β whereby George tries to save Teddy from justice. I said earlier that *Tono-Bungay* can be seen as two novels, and the sense of doubleness experienced by the reader is present right to the end: Teddy seems energetic and self-determining but is shown to be a helpless victim of economic forces, while George himself, who takes science as his mistress, masters the elements – both air and sea – and in the novel's last scene, as the inventor of a destroyer which he is willing to sell to a foreign power if the

British Government is too myopic to buy it, he is well on the way to becoming in reality the 'overman' or 'Napoleon' that Teddy liked to imagine himself.

Ann Veronica and The History of Mr Polly

In the 1920s Wells wrote that *Ann Veronica* belongs 'to that earlier group of the author's novels in which the whole book centres upon a single personality' – Hoopdriver, Lewisham, Kipps – rather than to the 'more broadly conceived' type of novel that began with *Tono-Bungay*. The novel was to have been much longer than as it now stands: it was planned, as *Kipps* was originally planned, as a Victorian three-decker, but it 'became unsatisfactory technically' and 'ran to monologue', so Wells brought it to an abrupt end with Ann Veronica's elopement. He has much to say about the book's reception in England: it was attacked with 'hysterical animosity' and was universally misunderstood; the reviewers ignored Ann Veronica's intelligence and concentrated on her morals. Wells reviles their stupidity; the criticism of fiction has still to rise above the level 'at which the villain is hissed and the "nice" characters applauded' (Atlantic, XIII, p. ix). He joins Hardy, George Moore, Wilde and less distinguished figures like Grant Allen in his assault on the sexual philistinism of the British.

Yet *Ann Veronica* clearly *intends* to provoke, and to issue an open challenge. In part it is a defence of Wells's own sexual behaviour, since his affair with Amber Reeves furnishes the basis for the relationship between Capes and Ann Veronica. It is also an entirely serious feminist novel and incorporates the ideas about the family in the coming socialist state that Wells had been developing in *Anticipations*, *The Discovery of the Future*, *Mankind in the Making*, *A Modern Utopia*, *New Worlds for Old* and, especially, *Socialism and the Family* (1906). This last work asserts that the male-dominated family unit will be replaced by a situation in which the socialist state, not the parent, is responsible for children. The adult male head of the family, who under the Victorian system virtually enjoyed private ownership of women and children, is to be deposed and replaced by the state. At the moment the male has 'a vexatious power of jealous restriction and interference upon his wife and children. The educated girl resents the proposed loss of her freedom' (part 1). The pamphlet's most provocative feature is its declaration that Free Love is already 'open to any solvent person' strong enough to live in defiance of the conventions, since the restraints operating in society are pure 'restraints of opinion', that would be 'as powerful tomorrow if legal marriage was altogether abolished' (part 2).

Although Wells despised it, there is no doubt that Grant Allen's *The British Barbarians* (1893) anticipates leading ideas about sexual freedom in Wells's own work.[2] In Grant Allen's fantasy a man from the twenty-fifth century falls in love with a married woman, and in a fit of jealousy her husband 'kills' the visitor, who returns to his own time. The woman then shoots herself and the reader is to suppose that the lovers are reunited in the utopia of the future. Jealous husbands in *In the Days of the Comet* (1906) and the possessive males in *Ann Veronica* are Wells's barbarians, people whose responses to life are primitive, instinctive and aggressive (and tribal). *A Modern Utopia* (1905) distinguishes firmly between the barbarism of modern so-called civilization and the civility and sexual liberalism that will characterise a well-run state. A similar situation prevails at the end of *In the Days of the Comet* when the 'Great Change' effected by the comet passing near the earth has freed individuals from their egotism. The narrator remarks that 'the old-time men and women went apart in couples, into defensive little houses, like beasts into little pits', and that this possessive coupling in the world before the Change is something that 'we who float upon a sea of love' in the new sexual utopia find 'hard to understand' (bk. 3, ch. 3). The characters in this romance (Willie, Verrall, Nettie and Anna) are insubstantial figures, and there is an obvious danger that those in *Ann Veronica* will be just as uninteresting, mere lay-figures illustrating a political and sexual thesis. That they are not – that Ann Veronica, her father, Capes, Manning and Ramage are all distinct and vigorously drawn individuals – is testimony to Wells's command of the 'ancient art of the story-teller'.[3]

Sexual freedom is its leading theme, but it is also, in a way, another 'Condition of England' novel, a *Tono-Bungay* seen from a different angle (they were published in the same year, 1909). Born in the stifling suburbs, Ann Veronica seeks freedom in London, but finds instead a new form of imprisonment because she is a woman. She knows nothing at all about adult sexual behaviour, and assumes that she can move into, and dominate, a man's world as does Shaw's Vivie Warren in *Mrs Warren's Profession*. 'The figure of Vivien, hard, capable, successful, and bullying, [. . .] appealed to her. She saw herself very much in Vivie's position'. She is deflected from this view of herself by a predatory middle-aged man who follows her. He is 'indistinguishably about her father's age'. She comes to see that many of the women she encounters sell themselves for a living: in Piccadilly a woman, 'altogether beautiful and fine,' turns out as she gets closer to be tawdry and painted; she is being followed by a man, and Ann Veronica's intuition tells her that 'the woman knew the man was there' (ch. 5). Wells is still referring to Shaw's play. Mrs Warren's profession is, of course, the oldest profession. Ann Veronica has overlooked the fact that Vivie Warren owes her independence to the education which is paid for by Mrs Warren's earnings as a prostitute. This encounter in Piccadilly reminds the reader of that fact, and it is underlined when Ann Veronica gets into debt (to pay for her biology course) to Ramage, and then discovers that he expects sexual favours in return.

What are the strengths and weaknesses of *Ann Veronica*? Its strength lies in the characterisation of Ann Veronica herself, this intelligent girl brought up by a limited and unimaginative father to be a 'young lady' in that part of the Edwardian world which still lived by Victorian assumptions. Higher education for women had been a reality since the 1860s, but her father tries to withhold it from her: he 'had met and argued with a Somerville girl at a friend's dinner-table, and he thought that sort of thing unsexed a woman' (ch. 1). Ann Veronica is allowed to study biology at the 'Tredgold's Women's College' but not, as she wishes, at Imperial College, where 'Russell' (probably an Edwardian equivalent of Wells's beloved Huxley) taught, because her father dislikes what he has heard about Russell's religious views. A girl kept in sexual ignorance by a late-Victorian patriarch and then exposed to the study of biology is bound to have a conflicting set of ideas about the world she lives in, and Wells exploits the comic possibilities of this conflict. Ann Veronica pays a stiflingly genteel 'call' in the company of her aunt, and speculates on the contents of her aunt's mind. It seems to consist of locked rooms, possibly empty, into which most of the important topics – sex, religion, politics, money, crime – can never enter.She reflects on her aunt's biological heredity (presumably Darwin's *Descent of Man* is in Wells's mind at this point). Her aunt's ancestral past contains 'all sorts of scandalous things,' such as 'fire and slaughterings, exogamy, marriage by capture, corroborees, cannibalism'. She has a pleasing vision of Miss Stanley's ancestresses dancing 'through a brief and stirring life in the woady buff' (ch. 2).

The early chapters convey very clearly Ann Veronica's need to escape from the 'wrappered' life of the suburbs, those nasty developments of 'little red-and-white rough-cast villas' which are like 'a bright fungoid growth in the ditch'. She is 'wildly discontented and eager for freedom and life' (ch. 1). Her friends the Widgetts, Bohemian allies against the suburban calm, do much to unwrapper her. She is due to accompany them to a fancy-dress ball and her father prevents her from leaving the house by brute force: Widgett values and Stanley values are brought into open conflict. As a direct result of this she rebels and goes to make her fortune in London, where a number of landladies take her for a prostitute, and some of the men to whom she offers herself as a secretary reject her 'with the utmost civility and admiration and terror' (ch. 7). The word 'terror' reminds us of the personality of Wells, middle-aged man of the world, pointing out the differences between the way Ann Veronica sees herself – independent, forceful and sexually neutral – and the way the male-dominated world sees her, as a pretty and vulnerable sex-object. The one person who gives her tangible help is the one she understands least: Ramage, her father's neighbour, whom Mr Stanley 'admired and detested in almost equal measure' (ch. 1) and whose 'protuberant eyes' signal clearly to the reader – though not to her – his sexual motivation in being kind to her. There are some extremely successful scenes in which she is involved in direct physical conflict with men. She attempts to leave her father's house in order to go to the Fadden Ball, and they struggle for possession of the front door key (ch. 4), and she violently resists Ramage's attempt to make love to her in the *cabinet particulier* to which he takes her after the performance of *Tristan and Isolde* (ch. 9). The latter scene is outstandingly successful. Full of her passion for Capes, Ann Veronica has been artlessly discussing love in a way that Ramage imagines is designed to lead him on, so that when he forces her to kiss him their mutual misunderstanding is complete:

They were both astonished at the other's strength. Perhaps Ramage was the more astonished. Ann Veronica had been an ardent hockey player and had had a course of ju-jitsu in the high school. Her defence ceased rapidly to be in any sense ladylike, and became vigorous and effective; a strand of black hair that had escaped its hairpins came athwart Ramage's eyes, and then the knuckles of a small but very hardly clenched fist had thrust itself with extreme effectiveness and painfulness under his jawbone and ear. 'Let go!' said Ann Veronica through her teeth, strenuously inflicting agony, and he cried out sharply and let go and receded a pace.

'*Now*!' said Ann Veronica. 'Why did you dare to do that?' (ch. 9).

Ann Veronica displays a beguiling mixture of courage, innocence and emotional confusion. Her interaction with the novel's male impostors – her father, Ramage, and the intolerable Manning – elicits some of Wells's best comic invention and most fresh and energised writing, and her conflicting motives are presented with complete authority. She allows herself to become engaged to marry Manning knowing all along that she loves Capes, and the reader's attention and sympathy remain fully engaged. To be married will be to become part of a work of art, 'the pampered Queen of Fortune, the crown of a good man's love' (ch. 13). And with Capes she seeks to keep the relationship temperate and detached while the novel's prose ironically displays her overwhelming physical attraction to him. Capes examines her 'microtome sections of the developing salamander' in the laboratory, and at the same time she unwillingly notes his physical beauty: 'All over his cheeks was a fine golden down of delicate hairs [. . .]. She became aware of the modelling of his ear, of the muscles of his neck and the textures of the hair that came off his brow, the soft minute curve of eyelid [. . .]; acutely beautiful things' (ch. 8). The pain and anger with which she reacts when she thinks Capes is 'putting down' women is entirely consistent with the passion that she feels for him. Science is 'supremely relevant' after the wrappered life of the suburbs in which sex was smothered in mystery (her sister had cried at her wedding: 'Perhaps marriage hurt?' thinks Ann Veronica): it is her training as a scientist, we feel, that enables her to cut through the wrappers and express her sexuality. Capes tells her that since his separation from his wife his sexual life has been 'vicious' in an unglamorous way (presumably we are to understand that he resorts to prostitutes) and Ann Veronica replies in terms which are, for the Edwardian period, strikingly direct: 'I want you. I want you to be my lover' (ch. 14).

These are the best parts of the novel. While Ann Veronica with her strength and her attractive mixture of honesty and confusion is fighting the world, the reader is entirely with her. But as she begins to win the fight the writing flags. The suffragette episode, for example, in which she deliberately gets herself arrested following a raid on the House of Commons, is decidedly thin and second-hand. The suffragette leader, Kitty Brett – 'about as capable of intelligent argument as a runaway steam-roller' – is treated with the same myopic hostility that is extended to the ludicrous figure of Miss Miniver, heralding the 'Insurrection of Women!', and wanting Ann Veronica to tell her 'all that happened, one sister woman to another'. Miss Miniver is an unredeemed figure of fun, 'a wild light in her eye, and her straight hair was out demonstrating and suffragetting upon some independent notions of its own'. Are these really the words of a man whom modern feminists have embraced as one of their own persuasion? Miss Miniver's ludicrous confusion of mind – 'the Higher Thought, the Simple Life, Socialism, Humanitarianism, it was all the same really' – seems designed to allay the fears of conservative males: 'she mentioned, with a familiar respect, Christ and Buddha and Shelley and Nietzsche and Plato. Pioneers all of them'. And it is she who takes Ann Veronica to a Fabian meeting, thus discrediting that organis-ation also: Ann Veronica in the Essex Hall 'heard and saw the giant leaders of the Fabian Society who are remaking the world; Bernard Shaw and Toomer and Dr Tumpany and Wilkins the author' (Wilkins is Wells himself) (ch. 7).

Once Capes and Ann Veronica have struck out for their free-dom and decided to live together the novel sags dismayingly. The dialogue between the two figures becomes self-congratulatory and portentous, the comic energy vanishes and the prose preaches at us directly and tediously. Capes's story loses its direction, and seems, among other things, to betray the essential 'relevance' of science that had been proclaimed earlier in the novel. In the epilogue, in which Capes and Ann Veronica, now married, have invited Miss Stanley and Ann Veronica's father to dinner, the reader learns with some astonishment that Capes has turned his back on science and is making his fortune as a playwright, under the pen-name of Thomas More. He is thus explicitly identified with the literary architect of utopias (and therefore with Wells himself). The transformation of Capes from scientist into playwright needs much more preparation to make it plausible than it is in fact given in the text. The idea that one can make a fortune as a playwright has appeared in Wells's novels before, of course: as a joke in *The First Men in the Moon* (it is clear that Bedford never even begins to write his play) and as a fantasy in *Kipps* (Chitterlow's runaway success with *The Pestered Butterfly* restores Kipps's fortunes). Here the idea is offered 'for real', so to speak, but I, at least, find it hard to believe. And indeed the whole of this epilogue suggests that Wells has become bored by this novel and is using a well-tried formula to round it off; there is something very *déjà vu* about the final paragraphs in which Ann Veronica is expecting a baby, and the sense that the race will continue is evoked (as it is at the end of *Love and Mr Lewisham* and *Kipps*) to give the novel a sense of cadence.

In chapter 6 Ann Veronica's brother, Roddy, says that a girl has 'got to take the world as it is, and the only possible trade for a girl that isn't sweated is to get hold of a man and make him do it for her'. Surely the plot of the novel proves that Roddy is right; Ann Veronica *can* only survive by having men defend her and work for her – the things that enable her to defy her father are first Ramage's money and then marriage to Capes. Wells's feminism is heavily qualified by his realism: Ann Veronica may win a measure of sexual freedom but it is quite clear that economic independence is denied her.

The History of Mr Polly is often regarded as less serious, less strenuously representative of Wells's thinking, than *Tono-Bungay* and *Ann Veronica*. *Tono-Bungay* addresses itself to the whole state of modern England, *Ann Veronica* makes radical proposals about the status of women. *Mr Polly* seems by contrast to be a genial comedy which is neither innovative nor taxing; a return, ostensibly, to Wells's talents as a Dickensian entertainer. It must be the most widely read of all Wells's novels, the one that is put into the hands of schoolchildren before *Kipps* and *Tono-Bungay*, probably before *The Time Machine* and *The War of the Worlds*. So is the verdict correct? Is it a well-constructed piece of entertainment and comic invention, or is there more to it than that?

My answer would be that *The History of Mr Polly* has as much to say about society and the condition of man as the more obviously political novels of the period and that it is as utopian as *A Modern Utopia*. Wells speaks of himself as a legislator and a historian of the future, and that predisposes his readers to assume that, when he is legislating, his alternatives to the society in which we are compelled to live will be found in a future or an imaginary world. But the utopia in *The History of Mr Polly* is located in the past, a past which is rural and arcadian. Precursors of this arcadia can be found in Stevenson's *Virginibus Puerisque* and Morris's *News from Nowhere* and *The Dream of John*

Ball; and Edward Thomas's *The South Country*, Kipling's Sussex stories and George Sturt's *Memoirs of a Surrey Labourer* are contemporary works which show a familial likeness to it. In short, Wells does something typically, centrally Edwardian when he invokes a tradition of rural England as a corrective to the misery of lower-middle-class urban life, and as the repository of national virtues.

The past is a womb. The Potwell Inn lies in a river valley which resembles the peaceful, safe core of the Thames-side setting in *The Wind in the Willows*. At the heart of Kenneth Grahame's romance is a passionately retrogressive fantasy in which Rat and Mole enjoy a timeless and privileged life. They are Edwardian clubmen freed, by the transformation into animals, from the pressures of the economic and social world that have made them prosperous. On the 'frontier', the outer perimeter, of this world is a social order which contains policemen, law-courts and prisons, all comically distorted by the childlike perspective of the romance's centre but still threatening. The Potwell Inn in Wells's novel is a similarly central place. The comfortable bulk of the plump woman (who in due course becomes, with precisely observed comic delicacy, the 'fat' woman), and the steady flow of the Thames 'broad and shining to its destiny' on an evening 'serenely luminous' contribute to the reader's sense of security:

It was as if everything lay securely within a great, warm, friendly globe of crystal sky. It was as safe and enclosed and fearless as a child that has still to be born. It was an evening full of a quality of tranquil, unqualified assurance. Mr. Polly's mind was filled with the persuasion that indeed all things whatsoever must needs be satisfying and complete. It was incredible that life had ever done more than seem to jar, that there could be any shadow in life save such velvet softnesses as made the setting for that silent swan, or any murmur but the ripple of the water as it swirled round the chained and gently swaying punt (ch. 10).

As well as the prose works that I referred to above this relates to another literary tradition, that of Arnold's *The Scholar-Gipsy*, which shows the Gipsy responding to the river-valley's promise of ease and a good state of mind. Indeed, the last phrase of the Wells paragraph seems to contain a verbal echo of Arnold's poem, where the Gipsy is surprised 'trailing in the cool stream thy fingers wet, / As the punt's rope chops round'. Wells probably got his knowledge of Arnold from his friend Masterman, whose *The Condition of England* is Arnoldian in structure and feeling. Masterman's chapter on 'The Countryside' deplores the decay and disappearance of rural England in a tone echoed in Galsworthy, George Sturt and, especially, in Forster's *Howards End*. The little farmhouse which gives that novel its name is the fragile symbol of a national identity which is being eroded by the spread of the London suburbs, encroaching like 'red rust'. 'Logically', Forster writes, the beautiful places which sustain individuality have 'no right to be alive', and one's only hope for them is in 'the weakness of logic' (ch. 44). Arnold, similarly, fears that the dominant Victorian forces will contaminate and destroy the fragile tradition that the Scholar-Gipsy represents: 'fly our paths, our feverish contact fly! / For strong the infection of our mental strife'. Forster and Masterman, like Arnold, see the values for which the English rural tradition stands as so vulnerable that they can survive only by avoiding contemporary pressures.

Wells is more robust. In the self-assertive figures of some of the earlier works – Bedford, Chitterlow, Butteridge, Teddy Ponderevo – he has shown weak figures pretending to be strong. In *Mr Polly* he does the opposite, he characterises a retiring, ineffectual little man who under the pressure of exigency finds in himself an unexpected reserve of strength; and this strength is universal, we all have it within us. In the Great Fishbourne Fire scene Wells restates, in a way, the central discovery of the romantic movement: that if a man follows his intuitions and is obedient to his impulses he can win freedom for himself. Arnold's custodian of the 'spark from heaven' – which I take to be 'imagination' as bequeathed to the Victorians by the romantics – has to retreat from the 'strange disease of modern life'. Mr Polly, by contrast, pushes against the obstructiveness of the social and economic world and finds that his will can prevail:

When a man has once broken through the paper walls of everyday circumstance, those unsubstantial walls that hold so many of us securely prisoned from the cradle to the grave, he has made a discovery. If the world does not please you, *you can change it*. Determine to alter it at any price, and you can change it altogether (ch. 9).

Mr Polly is first seen as a victim, horribly constricted by the traps into which he has blundered: his marriage to Miriam whom he has found 'utterly loathsome for fifteen years' and his dingy, unprofitable shop. He sets out to kill himself, 'and it seemed to him now that life had never begun for him, never!' He recognises that he has been culpably passive, 'submitted to things, blundered into things' and had failed to fight and take risks for 'the things he thought beautiful and the things he desired' (ch. 8). The past, as I have said, is invoked as the alternative to, and the consolation for, this trapped condition. From his solitary childhood Polly has attached himself to the past: to its literature, which he reads with disordered enthusiasm (Shakespeare, 'Bocashieu','Rabooloose'), and to its art and architecture. In Canterbury he imagines himself as one of Ruskin's medieval craftsmen (Wells doesn't name Ruskin in his text, but 'The Nature of Gothic' is obviously the source for this idea): 'There was a blood affinity between Mr Polly and the Gothic; in the Middle Ages he would, no doubt, have sat upon a scaffolding and carved out penetrating and none-too-flattering portraits of church dignitaries upon the capitals'. Living in Canterbury inspires him to read Chaucer, and he comes across what the reader recognises as the prototype of the plump woman at the Potwell Inn: 'He appreciated the wife of Bath very keenly. He would have liked to have known that woman'. It becomes clear that he is a comic novelist manqué; anarchic phrase-making is one of the pleasures of his inner life. While being inter-viewed for a job he invents descriptions of his prospective employer: the 'insubordinate phrasemaker' within him 'would be proffering such combinations as "Chubby Chops", or "Chubby Charmer", for the gentleman, very much as a hat sales-man proffers hats'. And like many writers he is fundamentally lazy; he 'dreamt always of picturesque and mellow things, and had an instinctive hatred of the strenuous life'. The literary and Gothic pasts that attract him offer no more than temporary escapes from his uncongenial circumstances into fantasy, but rural England offers a 'real' alternative to his trapped condition because its traditions are so strong that the novel can present them, plausibly, as though they are not 'past' at all. This is in marked contrast with other writers about rural England: Master-man declares that it is hastening into decay because the peasants have been divorced from the land, and Sturt in *Memoirs of a Surrey Labourer* and Thomas in *The South Country* both record desolation. Perhaps it is easier for Wells to believe in rural con-tinuity than it is for these writers because he knows rural England less well than they do; his view of it is essentially suburban.

As an apprentice Polly finds that his 'rare Sundays and hol-idays' shine 'like diamonds among pebbles' because he is able to walk inland from Port Burdock, into the Kentish countryside with its hop-gardens and oast-crowned farms, 'clean roads and red sandpits and pines, and gorse and heather'. There is no ironic perspective on any of this: utopia and reality, past and present have merged, so to speak, in a strong and simple evocation of an ideal:

There is no country like the English countryside for those who have learned to love it; its firm yet gentle lines of hill and dale, its ordered confusion of features, its deer parks and downland, its castles and stately houses, its hamlets and old churches, its farms and ricks and great barns and ancient trees, its pools and ponds and shining threads of rivers, its flower-starred hedgerows, its orchards and woodland patches, its village greens and kindly inns (ch. 1).

In *Tono-Bungay* George Ponderevo had praised Bladesover for giving him a 'non-peasant' view of life, and this is an emphatically non-peasant view of the landscape. Kipling at his most patriotic could not be more assured. In *Tono-Bungay* Teddy Ponderevo, as the new tenant of Lady Grove, intimidated the Vicar of Duffield (the village of which Lady Grove is the Great House) by his wish to 'Buck-Up the country' and his remark that it needs 'Light railways,' and 'wire fencing – machinery – all that.' The Vicar's response is interesting. His face 'betrayed dismay. Perhaps he was thinking of his country walks amidst the hawthorns and honeysuckle.' Uncle Teddy blunders on: ' "There's great things," said my uncle, "to be done on Mod'un lines with Village Jam and Pickles – boiled in the country" ' (bk. 3, ch. 2). There is no doubt that at this point the novel's sympathies are with the Vicar and against Teddy. The debility of Archie Garvell (who, like all 'modern upper-class England' is soft, and 'claims credit for things demonstrably half done' (bk. 1, ch. 1)), of the former inhabitants of Lady Grove (an old Catholic family who had 'died out in it, century by century' (bk. 3, ch. 2)), and of the Vicar himself, may be mocked: but the landscape which is inescapably identified with these upper-class people is valued for its beauty and its amenity. This sets up a pleasing tension in *Tono-Bungay* which is never resolved, and which enables the reader to enjoy sudden shifts of perspective such as the one quoted above in which Teddy's vulgarity is judged on the Vicar's own terms.

The arcadian sympathies in *The History of Mr Polly* do not, then, represent so much a departure from *Tono-Bungay* as a natural extension of one theme in that book. Polly is the heir to an unobtrusive rural England which continues, and remains delightful, despite the rise and fall of plutocrats and the resulting rapid changes in the ownership of great estates. The comic and romantic, arcadian and utopian elements of *The History of Mr Polly* unite in the figure of Polly himself. This ill-educated and abused figure of the opening chapters, his indigestion[4] and the 'huge cloud of insolvency' that hangs over him blighting his life, has within him the conviction that there is 'interest and happiness in the world,' a conviction which is like 'a creature which has been beaten about the head and left for dead but still lives'. His appalling education, compared to a surgical operation conducted by a butcher-boy and a left-handed clerk, has left his 'nice little curiosities and willingness of a child' in a 'jumbled and thwarted condition' (ch. 1). His pleasure in literature, landscape and the Gothic is accompanied by an underdeveloped, childlike emotional life. As a teenager he has no girl-friends, and the strongest affection in his life is for 'Parsons', a fellow-apprentice at Port Burdock: he 'had grown up with a tattered and dissipated affectionateness that was becoming wildly shy' (ch. 4). His one heterosexual passion is his totally deluded affection for the wicked schoolgirl who sits on a wall and torments him, surveying him 'much as an exceptionally intelligent cat might survey a new sort of dog' (ch. 5).

When Polly becomes a tramp the novel idealises him. Elsewhere Wells was harshly realistic about low-life figures in rural settings. The rustics at his school in Midhurst were sly, cruel, stupid and dirty-minded, and the tramps in *The Invisible Man* and *The War of the Worlds* and the incompetent farm manager and his wife in *The Food of the Gods* are dirty and dishonest. Here, by contrast, Mr Polly becomes 'a leisurely and dusty tramp, plump equatorially and slightly bald'. This life gives him good health for the first time in many years, living in the open, eating sparingly and walking all day. His experiences are picturesque and delightful: a vole plops into the river, a cow looms up out of a misty field like a boat floating on a magic lake, a memorable sunset near Maidstone makes the hills look 'exactly as he had seen mountains painted in pictures' (ch. 9). When he befriends the plump woman and learns that the Potwell Inn is threatened by Uncle Jim the tone becomes farcical as well as arcadian, and he wins the fight with Uncle Jim really rather too easily. Uncle Jim is, after all, a highly experienced combatant and criminal while Polly, judging from his incompetent wrestle with his neighbour Rusper on the pavement outside their adjoining shops in Fishbourne earlier in the action, is no fighter at all.

As well as being arcadian and utopian, comic and romantic, *Mr Polly* is rather consciously a 'Condition of England' novel. It is the 'history' not only of Polly himself but also of the doomed commercial lower-middle class from which he escapes. As in all his novels after *Love and Mr Lewisham* Wells interweaves a good deal of commentary with his dramatisation. Some of the commentary here is put into the writings of the gentleman who sits at ease in the Climax Club and writes a commentary on the condition of the small shopkeeper. Wells distances himself from this 'gifted if unpleasant contemporary', but his argument is obviously one with which Wells agrees, reflecting as it does his views on his own parents and their class:

A great proportion of the lower middle class should properly be assigned to the unemployed and the unemployable [...]. A great proportion of small shopkeepers, for example, are people who have, through the inefficiency that comes from inadequate training and sheer aimlessness, or through improvements in machinery or the drift of trade, been thrown out of employment, and who set up in needless shops as a method of eking out the savings upon which they count (ch. 7).

All the elements that I have described above – comic, romantic, utopian, farcical and 'Condition of England' – are brought together in the Great Fishbourne Fire chapter, which, with its physical emergencies, farcical invention and high sensory excitement is surely one of the best sustained performances in the whole of Wells's output. It seems to me that this chapter alone could put *Mr Polly* among the handful of major works, by any novelist, to survive from the Edwardian decade. Polly determines to kill himself and at the same time plans to set fire to the shop in order that Miriam should benefit from his insurance. But his body, of course, revolts against his intentions. He prepares to cut his throat with his razor: 'He drew the blade lightly under one ear. "Lord!" but it stung like a nettle!'. In accordance with his plan he upsets the oil-lamp, but again the plan is subverted by his instincts. Perhaps recalling Wells's mother's threats about the fires of Hell, and certainly recalling the miserable Nicodemus Frapp who urges George Ponderevo to take a look at the bakehouse fire when he has dared to deny the existence of God (in *Tono-Bungay*), the flames on the stairs of his shop admonish Polly: 'A thin, tall, red flame came up [. . .] and stood still, quite still, as it seemed, and looked at him. It was a strange-looking flame, a flattish, salmon colour, redly streaked. It was so queer and quiet-mannered that the sight of it held Mr Polly agape'. Then Polly's trousers catch light and he is impelled, of course, to confound his own design by saving himself: 'He had nerved himself for throat-cutting, but this was fire!' A whole row of more or less bankrupt shops is engulfed in the flames, each shopkeeper in turn fervently hoping that the fire will reach him so that he can collect the insurance money and kick himself free of debt. Wells derives much simple visual enjoyment from the fire: 'Mr Polly's establishment looked more like a house afire than most houses on fire contrive to look from start to finish. Every window showed eager, flickering flames, and flames like serpents' tongues were licking out of three large holes in the roof'. A farce, of an elementary kind, is appropriately played out against this brightly coloured backdrop, as Mr Polly struggles to get Rumbold's deaf old mother-in-law from the adjoining house over the roof-tops to safety. ' "You sit here ten minutes," shouted Mr Polly, "and you'll pop like a roast chestnut. Don't understand me? *Roast Chestnut!* ROAST CHESTNUT! POP! There ought to be a limit to deafness." ' The maddening old woman stops to wave her handkerchief to the crowd assembled below, but Polly finally gets her down. He is now a man of will and self-determination, transformed from a passive victim to an aggress-ive agent by his own botched suicide attempt. He descends with Mr Rumbold's mother-in-law 'into the world again out of the conflagration he had lit to be his funeral-pyre, moist, excited, and tremendously alive, amidst a tempest of applause' (ch. 8). I think we may take it that the applause is Wells's own, for the artistic success of this episode, and it is richly deserved.

4

The decade of struggle:
Mr Britling Sees it Through, Boon,
'prig' novels and discussion novels

'Sparring and punching', 1910–20

In 1910 Wells had a new and unpleasant experience; he was unable to find a publisher for a new novel. The novel was *The New Machiavelli*; the writing had overlapped with that of *Mr Polly* and the text was complete by 1910. It was a new kind of novel, a 'large and outspoken' book about politics (MacKenzies, p. 268). Macmillan, Heinemann, and Chapman and Hall were all reluctant to take it, partly because of the scandal surrounding *Ann Veronica* but partly, also, because of the risk of libel; the novel contains clearly identifiable portraits of Arthur Balfour and, especially, Beatrice and Sidney Webb. It was finally accepted by a new publisher, John Lane (through Macmillan's agency) and was serialised in *The English Review* in 1911.

Since 1900 Wells had been torn between art and his 'messianic' view of himself, his quest for a purpose in life to express in his writings. This tension was fruitful in *Tono-Bungay*, but from *The New Machiavalli* onwards it damages his work. This novel and the subsequent so-called 'prig' novels are marked by absence of humour, hasty composition and a solipsistic conviction that the central figure in each of them is exclusively possessed of truth and righteousness. The novels become moves or gambits in Wells's struggle to shore up his failing prestige; these were the years during which the former admirers of his fiction came to see him as largely a spent force. One such admirer, Walter Lippmann, reviewing *The Wife of Sir Isaac Harman* (1914), expresses clearly the disappointment that Wells's readers now felt: 'Where formerly each book had been a fresh adventure and a new conquest, these later ones seem like creations from an arm-chair which cost little and give little' (Heritage, p. 220). There has been 'an evident slackening of effort,' a 'too great fluency of style, an increase of mannerism, a tendency to large rhetoric,' and 'plots which creak along by accident' (ibid., p. 221).

The tide has turned against Wells in 1909, the year in which St Loe Strachey (who had praised *The War of the Worlds* in 1898) led the campaign against the morals of *Ann Veronica* with a review in *The Spectator* headed 'A Poisonous Book' (ibid., pp. 169–72). *The History of Mr Polly*, published the following year, received only a luke-warm response from the reviewers; the one exception was H. L. Mencken, writing in the American periodical *Smart Set*, who recognised that Mr Polly is the subject of Wells's lively scientific curiosity, a badly adapted animal whose 'history' is largely the history of his stomach (ibid., p. 179). In the main the reviewers tended to see *Mr Polly* as a re-working, in a slighter and more playful vein, of the material of *Kipps*.

The *New Machiavelli* (1911) may be seen as a counter-attack; Wells abandons the Kipps and Mr Polly figures and insists that the new work should be seen as a novel of ideas. Some reviews gave respectful attention to the discussion novel as a new form, but an ominous, and important, review in *Nation* compared Wells's present standing as a novelist unfavourably with that of Arnold Bennett. Wells and Bennett were old friends, and Bennett himself had written one of the most laudatory, and accurate, reviews of *Tono-Bungay* (ibid., pp. 154–6) and remained a loyal supporter of Wells throughout his life. Nevertheless, it must have been bitter for Wells to read that Bennett was now regarded as 'the foremost of our contemporary exponents of representation' (p. 195); Wells had lost his Edwardian pre-eminence and the power-relationship between the two friends within the literary world had shifted in Bennett's favour. Worse was to follow. Despite Wells's reiterated claim that his novels of ideas were different in kind from his earlier works, reviewers continued to pick, with intensifying animus, on the books' weaknesses *as realism*. Alfred Orage (with whom Wells had quarrelled) wrote in *The New Age* that *The Passionate Friends* (1913) was 'as loose and incontinent a production both in style and ideas as could well be produced by an habitual writer', that Wells's 'passion' was no more than promiscuity and that his characters were devoid of charm, virtue or conviction (ibid., pp. 214–15). Wells spoke of himself as 'sparring and punching' in his relationship with James and the 'prig' novels can be seen as retaliatory punches in an increasingly hostile climate of opinion: blows directed both against the reviewers' resistance and against the sense that other novelists were (as he wrote to James in 1915) 'coming over' him (James/Wells, p. 264). The Great

War restored some of his lost ground: *Mr Britling Sees it Through* struck the mood of the time (1916) and was a huge commercial success, especially in America (where it earned, as Wells records in his autobiography, over £20,000). Also it was received respectfully by the reviewers; but the recovery did not last. For the editor of *The Times Literary Supplement* to ask Virginia Woolf to review Wells's *Joan and Peter* (1918) might be regarded as an act of cruelty to both parties. She hated the book, she made mincemeat of it, and it is hard to disagree with her (Heritage, pp. 244–7); Wells himself, though, obstinately insisted until the end of his life on describing it as one of his finest pieces of work.

He left Sandgate at the end of the Edwardian decade to live in Church Row, Hampstead. The move can be seen partly as a reaction to his affair with Amber Reeves (documented in *Ann Veronica* and in *The New Machiavelli*) and partly as an attempt to regain his sense of artistic direction. In 1914–15 his anxieties about his standing as a writer disturbed his judgement, and he pulled together many jottings on literary figures and, specifically, on his resentment of other people's literary distinction into what he was later to call his 'waste paper basket' of a book, *Boon* (1915). *Boon* is famous for its cruel treatment of Henry James, but the assault on James is only one aspect of its ill-temper; Wells had plainly lost his balance. His biographers believe that he was acknowledging, in *Boon*, that he had been forced to choose between art and 'evangelism' (the role of political commentator and prophet) and that part of him knew that he was making the wrong choice (MacKenzies, p. 292). Anthony West, Wells's son by Rebecca West, thought that in the late thirties Wells at last recognised that he ought to have devoted himself to art and was in agony because he was now too old to make good his neglect; in works like *The Croquet Player* 'he had returned to the real source of what could have been his strength too late' (Views, p. 23).

This decade was frustrating for Wells in other directions also. His political opinions were sought – for example, he wrote a series of articles for the *Daily Mail*, many of which were collected in *An Englishman Looks at the World* (1914) – but they were not sought by the people he really wanted to impress. In 1913 Shaw and the Webbs founded *The New Statesman* as a socialist version of the *Spectator* and did not ask Wells to contribute; his vanity was severely wounded (MacKenzies, p. 288). Meanwhile in his private life there were more women and more house-moving. He disliked Hampstead almost from the moment that he got there, and in 1912 moved to the Rectory at Little Easton, near Dunmow in Essex, which he rented from the celebrated Lady Warwick, Edward VII's former mistress. He enlarged the house and renamed it 'Easton Glebe', and here he played the role of happy father of a growing family and took on some of the manners of an hospitable and unconventional country gentleman. At the same time he had a succession of love affairs, most of them with his wife's full knowledge and connivance. A relationship with Elizabeth von Arnim, whose *Elizabeth and her German Garden* had been an Edwardian best-seller, was followed by his ten-year 'marriage' to Rebecca West.

'Rebecca West' – Cicily Fairfield – came from a family of gentry on the decline, and one can see in her affair with Wells an attraction of opposites. When they first met, in 1912, she was a brilliant and penniless upper-class girl of twenty, he was an enormously successful middle-class man of forty-six. The immediate cause of the meeting was Rebecca West's hostile review of *Marriage* in the feminist paper, *The Freewoman*, 19 September 1912 (MacKenzies, p. 283). It may seem an odd beginning for a passionate relationship, but Wells was surely attracted by the fact that Rebecca West shared his conviction that the novel could properly be used as a vehicle for political discussion, and he was piqued and intrigued by the fact that while others denounced him for his sexual explicitness Rebecca West said that he was essentially *prudish*. She wrote:

Of course, he is the Old Maid among novelists; even the sex obsession that lay clotted on *Ann Veronica* and *The New Machiavelli* like cold white sauce was merely Old Maid's mania, the reaction towards the flesh of a mind too long absorbed in airships and colloids (Heritage, p. 203).

They fell in love early in 1913 and a year later their only child, Anthony, was born. In his book on their relationship Gordon N. Ray remarks that at the beginning the balance of power was firmly in Wells's favour. He was a celebrated and secure public figure, she was a young journalist just beginning to make a name for herself. When the relationship ended in 1923 the balance was shifting towards Rebecca. She was establishing herself as a novelist and literary journalist while he was a sick and ageing man who was widely regarded as having done his best work. Wells himself seems partially to recognise this in a letter to Rebecca written in 1934: 'You have a richness. I am simplicity. That is why I came off artistically from the beginning and got slovenly later and why you had to begin with such a spate of undisciplined imagination [. . .] before you got to the MASTERY of [your present work]' (quoted in Ray/West, p. 191). One should note here that Gordon N. Ray's book needs to be considered in the light of Anthony West's new biography (1984) of his father. Anthony West suggests that the 'marriage' between Wells and Rebecca West was largely a fiction invented by Rebecca West; that she was more predator than prey, and that during these years she saw much less of Wells than she would have liked. The biographers' belief that Wells spent several days a week with her, and weekends with his wife, during these years is based on her own testimony and may well be wrong. Anthony West also suggests that major difficulties between his parents were created by Wells's relationship with Margaret Sanger, the American feminist and campaigner for birth control, whom he met in 1920. Margaret Sanger married, in 1921, an oil tycoon, J. Noah H. Slee, who was twenty years older than herself. The biographers refer to her friendship with Wells and remark that he 'found enormous pleasure in her company', but they do not say that the relationship was a sexual one (MacKenzies, p. 33).

By 1914 Wells was supporting two households, and, *pace* Anthony West, he must have been to some extent torn between the claims of Rebecca West and her baby and the lavish and hospitable life-style that he had generated at Easton Glebe (which he records affectionately in *Mr Britling Sees it Through*). It may well be that the declaration of war on 4 August 1914 came as a relief from this complex situation, diverting his attentions and aggressions outward to the national enemy. Certainly he threw himself into war journalism with a jingoism for which he was fiercely criticised by Shaw, Vernon Lee and other friends, and of which he himself came to be ashamed. The title of the article he wrote on the day that war was declared, 'The War That Will End War', became a national slogan (MacKenzies, p. 298). With the passage of time Wells came to share the national disillusionment with the war, and this is reflected in *Mr Britling Sees it Through* (the title turned out to be inept and untimely; as he wrote the book Wells believed that the war could not continue beyond 1916, the year of *Mr Britling*'s publication). In the last two years of the war his response to it took two directions: a weird and embarrassing religiosity, expressed in *God the Invisible King* and *The Soul of a Bishop* (both 1917), and a call for the reconstruction of society after the war to base itself on educational reform.

Wells wanted the war to provoke revolution: in 1917, in Russia, it did just that, and Wells welcomed the Bolsheviks' success. He was still applauding them in *Russia in the Shadows*, published in 1920, and it took him a long time to move to the position that he held during the Second World War, that communism and fascism were both equally detestable (MacKenzies, p. 315). The books such as *The Research Magnificent* (1915) and *Joan and Peter* (1918), which take educational revolution in the new world as their theme, suffer, like the other 'prig' novels, from the solipsistic conviction that only one point of view is possible. They lack humour and dramatic tension, although the last of them, *The Undying Fire* (1919), if read not as a novel but as a Socratic dialogue, does have its own odd and lofty impressiveness.

The New Machiavelli, *Marriage*, 'prig' novels and discussion novels

The New Machiavelli retains many of the qualities of observation, energy and comedy of Wells's major Edwardian novels, especially in its earlier chapters. Late-Victorian 'Bromstead' (the Bromley of his childhood) is polluted and made hideous by suburban sprawl, 'parallelograms of untidy road' and uninhabitable 'raw' houses. The 'Ravensbrook' (the Ravensbourne, Bromley's river) becomes full of 'old iron, rusty cans, abandoned boots and the like'. Dick Remington's parents are clearly Wells's own parents, somewhat elevated socially. His father is an incompetent schoolmaster and also an incompetent gardener. Wells's hatred of gardening as peasant 'grubbing', expressed in *Tono-Bungay*, is connected, presumably, with the fact that his own father had been employed as a gardener before he set up as a shopkeeper. The father in this novel is driven by his garden to ecstasies of rage. There is a fine scene in which he attacks his lettuces which have 'shot' and gone to seed: 'He had the hoe in both hands and slogged. Great swipes he made, and at each stroke he said "Take that!" '. The gardening kills him: 'I and my mother returned from church to find my father dead. He had been pruning the grape-vine' (bk. 1, ch. 2). This may seem as abrupt and arbitrary as the many sudden deaths in Forster's comedies, but it is of course based on a childhood memory: it recalls Wells's father falling off his ladder and breaking his leg, and the consequent bankruptcy of his shop in Bromley.

Remington's father is frustrated, intelligent and humorous,

like Joe Wells, and his mother is narrow and bigoted like Sarah Wells. (H. G. Wells often treated his mother with considerable hostility in his writings.) Mrs Remington is rigidly conventional, her attitude to church-going a concentration of all that Wells found horrible in the Victorians. Her ideal would have been 'she in a poke bonnet and a large flounced crinoline, all mauve and magenta and starched under a little lace-trimmed parasol, and he in a tall silk hat and peg-top trousers and a roll-collar coat, and looking rather like the Prince Consort – white angels almost visibly raining benedictions on their amiable progress' (bk. 1, ch. 3).

All the 'prig' novels begin well but then lose their energy. Wells's personal circumstances are partly to blame: he was writing and living at a hectic pace and the novels tended to be written in the time left over from his journalism and travels. Also, in this period he is like a composer writing too many variations on a single theme: the theme itself is a good one, but in the variations the invention grows thin. In *The New Machiavelli* all the artistic virtue is in the first few chapters. After the murderous attack on the lettuces –'the air was thick with flying fragments of abortive salad [. . .]. It was the French Revolution of that cold tyranny, the vindictive overthrow of the pampered vegetable aristocrat' – the father speaks a monologue which recalls the theme of *Love and Mr Lewisham*, in which the quest for greatness is frustrated by the intractability of circumstances. Mr Remington senior contemplates his own wasted talents and misdirected life: he reflects that if he had gone to a university, had any sort of sound training, and 'hadn't slipped into the haphazard places that came easiest,' he might have escaped from Bromstead. Just as Lewisham, in the earlier novel, tries to propel himself towards success with the aid of his 'Schema', Remington urges his son to 'make a good Plan and stick to it,' and warns him that the world of late Victorian small-town businessmen is no place for a man of imagination:

'You stick to a plan. Don't wait for any one to show you the way. Nobody will. There isn't a way till you make one. Get education, get a good education. Fight your way to the top. It's your only chance. I've watched you. You'll do no good at digging and property minding. There isn't a neighbour in Bromstead won't be able to skin you at such-like games. You and I are the brainy unstable kind, topside or nothing [. . .] *Live*, Dick!' (bk. 1, ch. 2).

These objectives, to make a good plan, get a good education, and *live*, underpin all the 'prig' novels. They had been present in Wells's Edwardian novels but the emphasis has now changed. In the Edwardian period, for Wells as for his contemporaries, to '*Live*' had been a paramount duty; in the next decade to Plan and to Educate take priority.[1] After the death of Dick Remington's father the novel's energy becomes intermittent, though there is a good comic portrait of Uncle Minter, the Victorian Primitive from Staffordshire, and indeed in the whole of the Potteries sequence the writing is vigorously engaged. Wells has clearly been reading Bennett carefully and seeks to beat him at his own game in his description of the Minter house at Newcastle-under-Lyme, its vulgar prosperity emphasised by the fact that each bedroom has its own bathroom 'equipped with the porcelain-baths and fittings my uncle manufactured'. Uncle Minter, maker of lavatory pans, presides over a landscape which is a brutal expression of Victorian capitalism:

Social and economical relations were simple and manifest [. . .]. You can see here the works, the pot-bank or the ironworks or whatnot, and here close at hand the congested, meanly housed workers, and at a little distance a small middle-class quarter, and again remoter, the big house of the employer (bk. 2, ch. 1).

Uncle Minter himself is the Old Man of the Tribe from Wells's writings about evolution: 'About as much civilized, about as much tamed to the ideas of collective action and mutual consideration as a Central African negro' (ibid.). The evolutionary and geological images used to represent institutions in the earlier novels – the Labyrinthodon in *Kipps* standing for obsolete class attitudes, the 'Quap' in *Tono-Bungay* representing in its decay the diseased state of modern societies – are caught up again in this novel. The British Empire is an 'early vertebrated monster' with a backbone which has 'anchylosed', and in a passage which the modern reader may well find extraordinary Wells expresses his *hope* for a war with Germany: 'Since I love England as much as I detest her present lethargy of soul, I pray for a chastening war' (bk. 3, ch. 3). It is the language of evolutionary theory that allows him to say this so easily: to think of war as the necessary extermination of monsters ripe for extinction makes it acceptable. Again, it is evolutionary theory that allows Wells to advocate a new aristocracy while at the same time continuing to think of himself as a socialist. The giants in *The Food of the Gods* and the sighted man in 'The Country of the Blind' represent the future's leaders, and in *The New Machiavelli* Remington

looks forward to the possibility of 'co-ordinating the will of the
finer individuals, by habit and literature, into a broad common
aim. We must have an aristocracy – not of privilege, but of
understanding and purpose – or mankind will fail'. Educational
reform is an indispensable precondition of these objectives:
'Our civilization needs, and almost consciously needs, a culture
of fine creative minds, and all the necessary tolerances, open-
nesses, and considerations that march with that.' That is 'the
Most Vital Thing'.

Unfortunately, as Remington's exposition of his theory
unfolds, the novel's dramatic interest steadily dwindles so that
the reader is left with a stark choice: he must either attend to
Remington's political ideas or close the book. The expression of
these ideas is a matter not so much of argument as of increasingly dogmatic emphasis: 'Good teaching [. . .] is better than
good conduct'; Germany has better education than England
because she has 'attended sedulously to her collective mind for
sixty pregnant years' while in England 'almost universally we
have the wrong men in our places of responsibility and the right
men in no place at all'; England needs 'State Help for Mothers';
war with Germany will do no harm, 'better blunder than
paralysis, better fire and sword than futility' (bk. 3, ch. 3). The
plot, such as it is, consists of Remington testing the existing
political options and finding them inferior to his own schemes.
The Fabian movement has some ideas of which he approves but
is rendered futile by its parochial organisation (he includes brisk
and hostile caricatures of Beatrice and Sydney Webb as 'Oscar
and Altiora Bailey') and the Liberal party is over-cautious and
constrained by meaningless codes of decorum. Remington
abandons conventional politics and deliberately destroys his
political career by leaving his wife and eloping with Isabel Rivers
to Italy: a reflection of Wells's affair with Amber Reeves (who
had also appeared as Ann Veronica) and his break with the
Fabians. As the novel's title indicates, Remington is like
Machiavelli; he turns his back on power and writes a testament
– the novel – which will guide others towards the proper uses of
power.

In the next 'prig' novel, *Marriage*, Trafford, Remington's successor as the exponent of Wells's ideas, defies the conventions in
a more original manner: he and his wife Marjorie refresh their
marriage by eloping with each other, so to speak, to Labrador,
where they find a primitive and challenging life which is a wel-

come contrast to the staleness of civilized middle-class England. *Marriage* has some absurd features, as this summary perhaps indicates, but it also has some very good ones. The Pope family is established in the early chapters with Wells's characteristic narrative confidence. Marjorie Pope's father, the carriage-maker, is a socially elevated version of Uncle Minter from the previous novel, and he also has much in common with Ann Veronica's father. Marjorie, like Ann Veronica herself, is beautiful, wilful and incompetent with money. Because of this incompetence she is in danger of making a mercenary marriage to Will Magnet, the successful humorist, when a Shavian *deus ex machina* – young Professor Trafford – falls into the Popes' garden in a disabled aeroplane. I describe this as Shavian because it closely resembles the descent of Lina Szczepanowska and Joey Percival into the Tarleton's greenhouse in Shaw's *Misalliance* (Shaw's play was first performed in 1909: the 'Misalliance' of the title is, of course, another marriage, and Lina, like Trafford, is a liberating force in the convention-bound middle-class milieu into which she has crash-landed).

Trafford in the aeroplane crashes into the Popes' garden while the family are playing croquet, thus juxtaposing symbols which are polarised in Wells's imagination: powered flight is associated with science, courage and freedom: croquet with genteel aggression and the pointless diversions of the stupid rich, associations which were to be fully developed later in *The Croquet Player* (1936). There is again a sense of a 'spokesman' who cannot be contradicted. Until the appearance of Trafford this role is taken by the narrative voice, which comments vigorously on Mr Pope's tyrannical selfishness, Lady Plessington's toothy bossiness, Mr Magnet's sexual inadequacy and compensating vanity, and the deficiencies of Marjorie's education. Her school-mistresses and dons are criminally reticent:

The young need particularly to be told truthfully and fully all that we know of three fundamental things; the first of which is God, the next their duty towards their neighbours in the matter of work and money, and the third Sex (bk. 1, ch. 2).

The dominance of the central figure – the narrator or Trafford – is undoubtedly a flaw, and Henry James objected to another feature of the novel's construction – the fact that we are not given the details of the three hours during which Trafford and Marjorie fall in love with each other in a country lane. But here I think James's judgement is quite wrong, since Trafford's attractions are obvious. He stands for the intellectual liberty that science offers, and at the same time he is young (26; surprisingly young for a 'Professor') and sexually appealing. And the other males in the novel are conspicuously unappetising: Magnet, Margaret's official suitor, is plump, balding and nearly forty, and Uncle Hubert, the Oxford don, is half-starved and bullied by his wife. Marjorie feels an admiration for this woman which is entirely naturalistic: she would like to emulate Aunt Plessington's 'loud authoritative rudeness' (bk. 1, ch. 2) just as Ann Veronica sought to model herself on Shaw's Vivie Warren. Marjorie's interior consciousness is very well done. She has an entirely convincing sexual dream, based on the excitement of Trafford's flight in the aeroplane, anxiety over her unpaid bills at 'Oxbridge' (it is a puzzling detail that she studies at 'Oxbridge' while Uncle Hubert teaches at 'Oxford') and the threatened marriage to the repulsive Magnet. In her dream she flies an aeroplane 'with a curious uneasy feeling that in a minute or so she would be unable any longer to manage the machine' and then 'the engine refused to work until her bills were paid, and she began to fall, and fall, and fall towards Mr Magnet. She tried frantically to pay her bills. She was falling down the fronts of skyscrapers and precipices – and Mr Magnet was waiting for her below with a quiet kindly smile that grew wider and wider and wider . . . ' (bk. 1, ch. 3).

When he grouped the 'prig' novels together Wells defined a prig as someone elected by himself to lead the world (Dickson, p. 211). One can see that Trafford in *Marriage*, Stratton in *The Passionate Friends*, Benham in *The Research Magnificent* and Oswald Sydenham and Peter Stubland in *Joan and Peter* are all such figures. Benham in *The Research Magnificent* is the character of whom the word 'prig' is first used, but in the 1920s Wells was to write, somewhat confusingly, that Benham was the last of his characters who have 'eaten the Food of the Gods and whose lives are tragically disorganised by that fermenting stuff', and that the publication of this novel in 1915 closed the phase of novels about 'new wine in old bottles', books that turn on a man asking 'what shall he do with his life' (a phase which started with *The New Machiavelli* (Atlantic, XIX, Preface)). And in addition to this classification Wells was to speak of a larger group of 'experiments in [an] ampler form' which included *Tono-Bungay*, *The New Machiavelli*, *The Research Magnificent*, *Joan and Peter* and *The World of William Clissold*: novels which have a 'wider intention' than those which develop the 'narrative interest of an incident, a situation or a simple relationship' (Atlantic, XXIII, p. x). And he suggests yet another grouping when he distinguishes between two kinds of discussion novel: those which are largely dialogue – *The Soul of a Bishop, The Secret Places of the Heart* and *The Undying Fire* – and the 'palatial' discussion novels like *Joan and Peter* (Atlantic, XXV, Preface). There is something nervously *ad hoc* about these interchangeable groupings, as though Wells longed to cover the naked failure of *Joan and Peter* – one of his most ambitious and least successful books – with *some* kind of intellectual or artistic justification, and tries several but finds that none of them quite fit.

For the reader, *The Passionate Friends* (1913), is a remarkably flat experience, and *The Wife of Sir Isaac Harman* (1914) follows it as a welcome relief. Though one is bound to ask one question: what was the source of Wells's anti-semitism? Was it general, or was there one particular Jew who was annoying him during this period? *Marriage* contains the cowardly Sir Rupert Solomonson, 'manifestly a Jew, a square-rigged Jew (you have remarked of course that there are square-rigged Jews, whose noses are within bounds, and fore-and-aft Jews, whose noses aren't)'. In *The Wife of Sir Isaac Harman* the fact that Harman is a grasping, sneaking, socially inept and sexually insufficient Jew who is both a bully and a coward, is of course crucial; he is one of the most repulsive husbands in fiction since Henry James's Osmond, and if the novel were written with anything approaching James's care it could have been a striking work of art. As it is, it shows the usual haste and inattentiveness but begins well, and has throughout sparks of liveliness which suggest a revival of interest in the craft of writing which has been attributed, probably rightly, to the influence of Rebecca West (Dickson, p. 223). Harman himself is viewed with so much hostility that he remains an outline figure, but his wife and her lover, Brumley, are carefully drawn and there are some good comic details. Mr Brumley and Lady Beach-Mandarin set out to call on Lady Harman: 'They ran over the ghost of Swinburne, at the foot of Putney Hill – or, perhaps, it was only the rhythm of the engine changed for a moment' (ch. 3). Following the triad of novels which deal with sexual jealousy and express objections to the 'existing stereotyped marriage formula' (*Marriage, The Wife of Sir Isaac Harman*, and *The Passionate Friends*) (Atlantic, XVIII, Preface), Wells returns to the most explicitly 'priggish' of his novels in *The Research Magnificent*, 1915. William Benham is the son of a schoolmaster who sets out to understand and put right the confusion of the world. His ideas take further the hopes for a new aristocracy expressed by Remington in *The New Machiavelli*. He is contrasted with his friend Prothero, who becomes a Cambridge don (Wells likes his characters to come in pairs, each illustrating a point of view). Benham's belief in aristocracy is formed at school when he defies a master who threatens to beat him: 'The beginning of all aristocracy is the subjugation of fear' (Prelude). Prothero derides this ideal. You cannot have aristocracy, he claims, because 'all men are ridiculous' (ch. 1). Intelligent enough to see clearly the choice that he is making, Prothero deliberately opts for a life of cynical sensuality (he is not unlike Kipps's friend Chaffery at a higher social level). Wells's own early ambitions had been academic, of course, and as a don manqué he held decided views on the intellectual life and its responsibilities. Prothero declares that an intellectual must:

Hold his chin up or else he becomes – even as these dons we see about us – a thing that talks appointments, a toady, a port-wine bibber, a mass of detail, a conscious maker of neat sayings, a growing belly under a dwindling brain. Their gladness is drink or gratified vanity or gratified malice, their sorrow is indigestion or – old maid's melancholy. They are the lords of the world who will not take the sceptre (ch. 1).

(The attack on the irresponsibility of dons is developed later, with scathing assurance, in *The Camford Visitation* (1937)). Prothero remarks that an intellectual is 'either a prince or a Greek slave'. He has chosen a form of slavery: Benham chooses to be a prince. It is curious, given the advocacy of sexual freedom in the earlier works, that in this book a condition of the princely role is *celibacy*. Benham's marriage to Amanda, whom he hopes will be like the women Guardians who are both the 'friends' and the 'mates' of men in Plato's *Republic* (ch. 3), ends in failure because she is fundamentally conventional in outlook. She wants a smart house in London where she can play the hostess (and spend Benham's money: Wells's novels increasingly stress the extravagance and wastefulness of women). Benham concludes that in order to pursue his work he must leave her. He 'was making up his mind to be a prig', which means cultivating the 'cold uningratiating virtues' and becoming 'so concentrated and specialised in interest as to be a trifle inhuman, so resolved as to be rather rhetorical and forced' (ch. 6). And he abandons his marriage, describing it as 'the end of my adolescence', in order to devote himself to his campaign for a new aristocracy which will create an 'open conspiracy'; this phrase heralds a dominant theme of Wells's works of the 1920s and 30s. With the publication of *God the Invisible King* (1917) Wells's friends thought that he had lost his reason; he seems here to have abandoned politics and to proclaim instead a new religion at work in the world. God is a finite being, as limited as man, struggling against evil. But as one reads the book one comes to see that this religion in fact has much in common with the Open Conspiracy: God will work in society as the open conspirators will, and his presence will make itself apparent as crystals become visible in a solution. The 'new understanding' will have no church and no orthodoxy: 'simply it grows clear' ('Envoy'). For Dr Scrope in *The Soul of a Bishop* (1917) religious truth is less simple. 'Princhester' is an industrial town like Lincoln or Durham which has grown round an ancient cathedral church. The landscape suggests the Potteries, which had already appeared in 'The Cone', *In the Days of the Comet* and *The New Machiavelli*. The Bishop is a divided man: his dual consciousness recalls early stories on this theme such as 'The Remarkable case of Davidson's Eyes' and 'Mr Skelmersdale in Fairyland' and anticipates deranged figures who believe themselves to live in two worlds such as Albert Edward Preemby (who believes himself to be Sargon King of Kings) in *Christina Alberta's Father* (1925) and Arnold Blettsworthy in *Mr Blettsworthy on Rampole Island* (1928). He is an insomniac who goes through the Christian observances by day and disbelieves in them at night, experiencing a 'distressful alternation between nights of lucid doubt and days of dull acquiescence'. The doubts have been brought into prominence by the war. What is the church doing in the war? The answer seems to be nothing: it is an essentially Victorian institution reconstructed from the decorative remnants of traditions that nobody understands, 'prayers and litanies composed in Byzantine and medieval times'. As in earlier writings, Wells welcomes the war because although it is 'black and evil' it has forced people to recognise 'the epic quality of history'. It drives home what Darwin had already taught, that the ascendancy of civilised man is no more than a passing phase in the history of the world: 'The flimsy roof under which we had been living our lives of comedy fell and shattered the floor under our feet; we saw the stars above and the abyss below' (ch. 3). The changes had been coming since the death of Queen Victoria: her death was 'as if some compact and dignified paper-weight had been lifted from people's ideas, and as if at once they had begun to blow about anyhow' (ch. 2).

The Undying Fire (1919) combines the virtues of the 'prig' novels and the divided consciousness novels. Using the book of Job as his model allows Wells to drop the devices of the realist novel and compose instead a fabric of dialogue and exposition which has its own odd coherence. Job Huss, the headmaster of a school, experiences an agony of religious doubt brought on by a series of adversities; he then recovers and asserts what is in effect a more crisp and considered version of the philosophy of education that we have heard before from Remington and Benham. Education 'is the greatest of all human tasks' and is designed to free man from his egotism: 'What is a man without instruction? [. . .] A greedy egotism, a clutching desire, a thing of lusts and fears'; whereas 'a man instructed is a man enlarged from that narrow prison of self into participation in an undying life, that began we know not when, that grows above and beyond the greatness of the stars' (ch. 3).

Mr Britling Sees it Through

Mr Britling Sees it Through (1916) is a much more 'central' work than the 'prig' novels and the mystical writings that I have been discussing, and one reason for its centrality is its autobiographical content: it could equally have been called '*Mr Wells Stands Up to It*'. Britling, like Wells, is a successful writer with a somewhat cool marriage enlivened by sexual adventures outside, and his house, Matching's Easy, is closely based on Easton Glebe. 'Lady Homartyn' in the novel is based on Lady Warwick, Wells's neighbour and landlady, and 'Heinrich' is based on Karl Büttow, the German tutor that the Wellses had engaged for their sons. (There are two little boys who match Gyp and Frank Wells). This novel then moves beyond its sources: the most important member of Britling's family, Hugh, the son of his first marriage who is killed in the war is not based on a particular person. It is as though having recorded the home that he loved as the setting for his story, Wells found that his imagination produced a stronger reality: the treatment of Hugh's young life and death is extraordinarily moving and persuasive.

In my discussion of the major Edwardian novels (ch. 3, above) I noted the conservatism of Wells's imagination when he is dealing with landscape: the atavistic pull of the country house in

Tono-Bungay and the triumph of arcadia at the Potwell Inn in *The History of Mr Polly*. The opening chapters of *Mr Britling* invite us to respond nostalgically to the landscape but at the same time the novel introduces a corrective viewpoint in the figure of the American onlooker, Direck, who detects artifice, and therefore weakness, in the charm of its timbered cottages and grassy lanes: 'It wasn't like any reality he had ever seen. It was like travelling in literature'. Britling has a converted barn which is used for games and dances, and Direck seizes upon it as a symptom of the debility of modern England: 'That barn isn't a barn any longer, and [. . .] the farmyard isn't a farmyard'. Like the rest of the countryside, it gives false signals: 'It looks and feels more like the traditional Old England than anyone could possibly have believed, and [. . .] in reality it is less like the traditional Old England than anyone would ever possibly have imagined' (bk. 1, ch. 1). This challenges Britling/Wells's patriotism. For all its absurdity he likes the eclecticism of England, the interweaving of historical forces that have made it what it is, and wants to defend it as 'the amiable summation of a grotesque assembly of faults'. Having been a radical critic of England himself, he has now become accepting: for him 'England was "here". Essex was the county he knew' (bk. 1, ch. 2). This may be seen partly as the *arriviste*'s naive pleasure in his attractive house and his upper-class neighbourhood. Certainly Wells was not above such pleasures: there is transparent snobbery in the satisfaction Britling takes in his intimacy with the great when he introduces Direck to Lady Homartyn (Lady Warwick). And if Wells/Britling is smug about his grand neighbours he is also dismayingly complacent over his treatment of his wife. Edith Britling's failure to please her husband is entirely her fault, it would appear. 'Temperamentally they were incompatible', 'In all things she was defensive. She never came out,' and she is sexually unresponsive: 'she thwarted him and disappointed him, while he filled her with dumb inexplicable distress'. So the marriage has now cooled to 'real habitual affection and much mutual help', and Britling is free to take his sexual pleasures elsewhere (with the spiteful Mrs Harrowdean, for example). Being 'fastidious' and 'rather unenterprising' Edith doesn't need to be loved, and finds fulfilment in her children and her house and garden. The fact that Britling doesn't love her is entirely *her fault*, it would seem. She never dreamt that she had 'hurt' his heart, and that after its first 'urgent, tumultuous, incomprehensible search for her it had hidden itself bitterly away . . . ' (bk. 1, ch. 4). By attributing to Edith such stupidity and emotional torpor Wells/Britling seeks to exonerate his own self-centred behaviour: it is totally unjust, and the fact that it is so clearly based on Wells's marriage to Jane makes one wonder – again – about Wells's lack of moral balance, his ruthless selfishness and his emotional obtuseness.

Written with more detachment, this novel would be a study of a figure whose self-centredness verges on the brutal, but by tricking Mr Britling out with comic attributes – his odd clothes and general untidiness, the games he invents, the rather heavily conscious unconventionality of his household's manners, his hair-raising inability to drive his car – Wells works hard to enlist the reader's sympathy. Personally, I withhold my sympathy until Hugh Britling is killed in the war. Thereafter the characterisation of Mr Britling becomes complex and sympathetic and the writing is energised and engaged. Mr Britling's strongest affections are for his children: 'it is only through our children that we are able to achieve disinterested love, real love' (bk. 1, ch. 5). And his love for Hugh, the son of his first wife, has an 'intimate emotional hold' on him because Hugh is intelligent and thoughtful (as his mother was) while his 'very jolly little step-brothers' are – as the novel does not shrink from pointing out – average and dull, like poor Edith. (One really does wonder what Frank, Gyp and Jane Wells thought about these three portraits.) After Hugh's death Britling finds no consolation in his wife and his other children and in the young people around him: 'Loneliness struck him like a blow. He had dependants, he had cares. He had never a soul to whom he might weep . . . ' He goes out into his garden at night 'and suddenly his boy was all about him'. Grief takes the form of denial, as it does so often in bereavement; the dead child is still alive, 'playing, climbing the cedars, twisting miraculously about the lawn on a bicycle, discoursing gravely upon his future, lying on the grass, breathing very hard and drawing preposterous caricatures'. The last paragraph of this chapter has striking technical virtues:

He went into the far corner of the hockey paddock, and there he moved about for a while and then stood for a long time holding the fence with both hands and staring blankly into the darkness. At last he turned away, and went stumbling and blundering towards the rose-garden. A spray of creeper tore his face and distressed him. He made his way to the seat in the arbour, and sat down and whispered a little to himself, and then became very still with his arm upon the back of the seat and his head upon his arm (bk. 2, ch. 4).

The spray of creeper recalls the symbolic placing of the black-thorn and the rose in *Love and Mr Lewisham*, which accompany key moments of emotional recognition in the lives of the characters; and beyond that this paragraph shows an admirable, and untypical, under-explicitness. By suppressing any comment it leaves the reader to *see* the anguish expressed in Britling's actions. And if it is like *Love and Mr Lewisham* in its economy and restraint it is also reminiscent of another precursor, the spirits of the dead children in a garden in Kipling's 'They'. Wells makes many references to Kipling in the course of this novel and it may well be that that distinguished story has contributed to his effect here.

Mr Britling Sees it Through is 'a study of the English spirit at war' and its title was chosen in 1915 'under the persuasion that the war would end in about a year's time': indeed in the Atlantic Edition Wells shortened the title to *Mr Britling* (Atlantic, xxii, Preface). It is 'essentially the history of the opening and of the realisation of the Great War as it happened to one small group of people in Essex, and more particularly as it happens to one human brain' (bk. 2, ch. 1). The design might well have led Wells to write it in the first person, but the novel greatly benefits from his decision *not* to do this. In *Tono-Bungay* the first person works because of the doubleness of the content – the stories of George and of Teddy are successfully knit together by the fact that the protagonist of one is also the narrator of both. If Britling were himself the narrator of this novel his egotism would, surely, swamp the novel and bore the reader well before the story is saved, in dramatic terms, by the death of Hugh at the end of book 2. And the use of an omniscient narrator enables the reader to share, for example, Direck's perspective: when Britling praises England's go-as-you-please backwardness and good temper the reader can endorse Direck's view that what the country needs is more efficiency. The omniscient narrator can also remind the reader that the differences between the months immediately preceding the war and the dramatic present (1915–16) represents a huge historical change. The upper-middle class of 1914 took the war first as an incredible, distant event (Wells notes that there was more anxiety about civil war in Ireland than about German aggression): 'War had not been a reality in the daily life of England for more than a thousand years. The mental habit of the nation for fifty generations was against its emotional recognition. The English were the spoiled children of peace' (bk. 2, ch. 1). On the declaration of war in August 1914 the conflict is seen as a magnificent patriotic challenge: then as a tiresome and increasingly uncontrollable threat: then as a source of stark personal disaster. The shape of the novel fits these three stages, and the titles of its three books express the impact of experience on the unpreparedness of the English: 'Matching's Easy at Ease', 'Matching's Easy at War', 'The Testament of Matching's Easy'.

Part of the interest of the characterisation of Mr Britling lies in the depressions to which he is subject: the 'lump sums of bitter sorrow' in which he pays for 'his general cheerful activity' (bk. 1, ch. 4). These give a welcome and attractive dualism to his personality. He responds to the declaration of war with a burst of furious activity which produces his pamphlet called 'And Now War Ends'. (This pamphlet represents Wells's own little book, *The War That Will End War* (1914), of which he later became ashamed.) The dangerous absurdity of his euphoria is thrown into relief by the eccentric notions of Aunt Wilshire, in whom the war provokes a 'peculiar exaltation'. Her belief is that the Kaiser is intent on war because Queen Victoria prevented him spoiling a carpet at Windsor Castle when he was eight (bk. 2, ch. 1); the reader comes to see that Aunt Wilshire is no more ignorant and mistaken in her reading of the war than is Britling himself. A painful division develops within him as his illusions about England are challenged by the politician-rigged state's mismanagement of the the war. Evidence is provided by Hugh's fresh, intelligent and scathing letters from the trenches, which form a distinct literary artefact within the novel. His anecdotes – about the soldier who sees himself as 'private Ortheris' from Kipling's *Soldiers Three*, for example, who is cured of his mock heroism by a humiliating sexual rebuff and then shows real heroism when he is horribly killed – keep the letters earthy and witty, while at the same time their cumulative effect is to force Mr Britling to see 'what indeed all along he had been seeing more and more clearly. The war, even by the standards of adventure and conquest, had long since become a monstrous absurdity' (bk. 2, ch. 4).

In Hugh's letters Wells imitates a young man's honest and vigorous irreverence very effectively, and this sensitivity to style and tone is still present in the extended postscript in which Mr Britling attempts to write a letter to the parents of Heinrich, the tutor, who has also been killed. Writing as a bereaved father to the bereaved parents of an enemy soldier is potentially a cliché situation and Britling's letter is lamentably heavy-handed: '*Your boy* [. . .] *dreamt constantly of such a world peace as this that I have foreshadowed; he was more generous than his country* [. . .]. *My youngster too was full of a kindred and yet larger dream, the dream of human science, which knows neither king nor country nor race* . . . ' (bk. 3, ch. 2). But mercifully Britling/Wells senses the clumsiness of this and feels ashamed of its idealism and dogmatism (a shame which is sadly missing from the similar passages of exhortation and confident political utterance in the 'prig' novels): 'Never had it been so plain to him that he was a weak, silly, ill-informed, and hasty-minded writer'. He re-reads his letter and recognises its inappropriateness. 'It was like the disquisition of a debating society. He was distressed by a fancy of an old German couple, spectacled and peering, puzzled by his letter. Perhaps they would be obscurely hurt by his perplexing generalisations. Why, they would ask, should this Englishman preach to them?' (bk. 3, ch. 2).

Boon and the quarrel with Henry James

The difference between James and Wells has been expressed thus: James is an artist 'who is devoted wholly to fathoming and re-creating human experience' and Wells is a writer 'unconcerned with aesthetic matters for whom literature is merely one way of communicating and advancing his ideas' (James/Wells, p. 39). The assumption behind this is that the quarrel ended in a victory for James, and indeed this is the common opinion. My own view is that Wells had a coherent and intellectually defensible theory of the novel which he could have pressed much more vigorously and aggressively, and that he was outwitted by the patrician dignity and elaborate courtesy of his adversary. Wells mistook politeness for agreement, and friendliness – for there can be no doubt that James did, at a personal level, feel friendly towards Wells – for professional esteem. So that when James, after a series of cordial letters about Wells's novels then attacked him (and Bennett) in a two-part essay on 'The Younger Generation', Wells felt that the old man had behaved treacherously towards him and took his revenge by adding to *Boon* the section called 'Of Art, of Literature, of Mr Henry James' which includes a direct attack on James and a malicious – but effective – parody of his writing. Wells's mistake was that he had read James's letters about his novels superficially; the *tone* may be friendly but the content is frequently damning. On reading *The New Machiavelli* James complained to Wells that he disliked the first-person technique, and Wells promised that he would not use it again: 'This shall be the last of my gushing Hari-Karis' (James/Wells, p. 130). But within two years he *had* used it again, in *The Passionate Friends* (1913), a 'prig' novel in which a Wells figure called Stratton advocates the 'Open Conspiracy'. By anybody's standards *The Passionate Friends* is a solemn and boring book, and James's letter about it is masterly. Fulsome but meaningless flattery is followed by harsh and incisive rebuke, and if Wells had read the letter with attention he could not possibly have mistaken it for praise. James says that he finds Wells 'perverse' and 'unconscious' and notes his inability to handle the novel's form with any degree of artistic responsibility. The narrative method denies any 'perspective' (detachment from the narrator's consciousness), the form has neither 'beauty' nor 'authenticity', and the relationship between Stratton and the heroine (Lady Mary Justin), given in 'foreshortened, impressionising *report*' (instead of being properly dramatised), carries no conviction. In short, James is saying that the novel is a resounding flop; but his rather empty remarks about 'high intensity' and 'rich and roaring impressionism' seem to have persuaded Wells that James had actually liked the book, whereas the fact was that James liked *him* (ibid., pp. 172–7).

Indeed, throughout the correspondence James makes it clear that he is responding to Wells's *personality*, as expressed in the novels, rather than to the novels as works of art. Of *Marriage* James wrote that he listened to the narrating voice and disregarded the dramatised persons: 'I live with you and in you and (almost cannibal-like) *on* you, on you H.G.W., to the sacrifice of your Marjories and your Traffords, and whoever may be of their company' (ibid., pp. 166–7). And Wells knew, perhaps instinctively rather than consciously, that James's purpose was to educate him: to take his raw talent and turn him into a real novelist. Wells was elected to the Academic Committee of the Royal Society in 1912, but declined to serve, despite the pressure that James (and Sir Edmund Gosse) tried to exert. In his letter of refusal Wells expresses himself in terms which do clearly indicate that he feared being put into the position of an apprentice to James, and also that for him this refusal was a way of emphasising his distance from the masters of form. He says politely that he regrets not being more closely associated with James – 'I do look up to, and admire and feel proud of my connexion with your beautiful fine abundant mind – I like to be about with you and in the same boat with you' – but he believes that writers should be 'anarchic': 'better the wild rush of Boomster and the Quack than the cold politeness of the established thing' (ibid., pp. 159, 160). James may well have felt that there was some personal application in the phrase 'cold politeness'. After Wells's refusal James wrote to Gosse about him to say 'He has cut loose from literature clearly – practically altogether; he will still do a lot of writing probably – but it won't be *that*' (ibid., p. 164n.). So if Wells's purpose in this was to widen the gap between James's view of writing and his own, he was successful.

In his essay 'The Contemporary Novel' (1911), Wells says: 'I was a professional critic of novels long before I wrote them', as though to stress his qualifications for writing a theoretical defence of his own kind of art. He draws attention to the fact that he, Wells, was the first reviewer to recognise Conrad (and indeed, to be able to claim to have 'discovered' Conrad is something to boast about).[2] He is establishing his authority to speak: 'When a man has focussed so much of his life upon the novel, it is not reasonable to expect him to take too modest or apologetic a view of it' (ibid., p. 131). But he goes on to make a claim which is manifestly wrong; namely, that the Victorians thought of the novel as 'relaxation' for the 'Weary Giant', the exhausted paterfamilias resting at the end of the day. One has only to think of Dickens and George Eliot and Charlotte Brontë, or of Disraeli, Mrs Gaskell and Kingsley, to reply immediately that that is nonsense: that it was clearly recognised from the 1840s onwards that the novel was a vehicle of moral judgement and social education. Wells really cannot claim as his own the discovery that the novel is an 'important and necessary' moral force in civilisation. His caricature of the Victorian reader as a 'weary giant' is simply wrong, and his declaration that the 'weary giant theory of the novel' ruled British criticism 'up to the period of the Boer War' is totally out of touch with the realities of literary history: is, indeed, the opposite of the truth (ibid.). But this introduction, distorting though it is, brings him to one of his real targets: James's irritating nagging about form. 'If the novel is to be recognised as something more than a relaxation,' he declares, 'it was also, I think, to be kept from the restrictions imposed upon it by the fierce pedantries of those who would impose a general form for it'. The error of these fierce pedants is that of treating the novel 'as though its form was as well-defined as the sonnet'. Wells makes the reasonable objection that while the short story must make a 'single, vivid effect' because it can be read at a sitting, the novel cannot be so read and therefore can, and should, be 'discursive', not a single interest, but a woven tapestry of interests': 'It is an error to think that the novel, like the story, aims at a single, concentrated impression.' The novelist is a moralist: the novel has 'inseparable moral consequences' because it leaves impressions of 'acts judged and made attractive or unattractive'. The time is one of conflict and revolution, and the novel must participate in these things. The reason for the historical distortion in the early part of the essay becomes clear: Wells needed to persuade himself of the monolithically resistant nature of Victorian life, where the reader 'judged a novel by the convictions that had been built up in him by his training and his priest or his pastor', in order to emphasise his perception of the present as a time of striking instability: 'We live [. . .] in a period of adventurous and insurgent thought, in an intellectual spring unprecedented in the world's history. There is an enormous criticism going on of the faiths upon which men's lives and associations are based, and of every standard and rule of conduct. And it is inevitable that the novel [. . .] should reflect and co-operate in the atmosphere and uncertainties and changing variety of this seething and creative time'. The modern novel is to be 'a study of the association and inter-reaction of individualised human beings inspired by diversified motives, ruled by traditions, and swayed by the suggestions of a complex intellectual atmosphere' (ibid., pp. 134–48). In this radically simplified view of the modern literary situation Wells is able to represent as pedantic and restrictive James's notion that there is one, and only one, art of the novel. The essay ends with a threat: 'We are going to appeal to the young and the hopeful and the curious, against the established, the dignified, and defensive' (ibid., p. 156).

'The Contemporary Novel' adopts a tone of measured detachment while *Boon* is aggressively insulting, but on the theory of the novel the two works are saying more or less the same thing. 'Of Art, of Literature, of Mr Henry James' (from *Boon*) again argues that the novel must be allowed to be discursive and cannot be expected to have unity; the novel is not a picture, and cannot be apprehended as a whole. James's fundamental error is that 'he wants a novel to be simply and completely *done*, he demands homogeneity . . . Why should a book have that? For a picture it's reasonable, because you see it all at once' (*Boon*, ch. 4). To achieve his unity James in his own work has sinned against 'Life', clearing his characters of political or religious convictions, of 'lusts or whims', dreams or passions, so that the people in his books are like rabbits gutted for the table. The only human motives left in his novels are 'a certain avidity and an entirely superficial curiosity' and these unreal people participate in plots which the Jamesian passion for unity makes equally unreal:

It is like a church lit but without a congregation to distract you, with every light and line focused on the high altar. And on the altar, very reverently placed, intensely there, is a dead kitten, an egg-shell, a bit of string (ibid.).

The style is as artificial as the characterisation and the plotting, and is made endurable only by its 'copious wit' and the ingenuity of its metaphors. The manner is so elaborate and the content is so small that reading a James novel is like watching 'a magnificent but painful hippopotamus resolved at any cost, even at the cost of its dignity, upon picking up a pea which has got into a corner of its den. Most things, it insists, are beyond it, but it can, at any rate, modestly, and with an artistic singleness of mind, pick up that pea . . . ' (ibid.).

As if this were not enough, Wells went on in *Boon* to write a brief parody of a James novel, 'The Spoils of Mr Blandish', in which a fastidious gentleman buys the perfect house, fills it with antiques, and then discovers that it contains a smugglers' hoard of old brandy. He arranges to sell the brandy but is too late: his butler, Mutimer, has drunk it all by the time a purchaser has been found. The treatment is undeniably funny and refers to recognisable features of *The Spoils of Poynton*, *The Ambassadors* and *The Wings of the Dove*. Mr Blandish is James himself seen as a patrician dilettante who is devoid of normal human drives:[3]

He didn't marry, he didn't go upon adventures; lust, avarice, ambition, all these things that as Milton says are to be got 'not without dust and heat', were not for him [. . .]. He had independent means, he could live freely and delicately and charmingly, he could travel and meet and be delighted by all the best sorts of people in the best sorts of places (*Boon*, ch. 4).

Wells's behaviour on the publication of *Boon* was really very odd.

It ought to have been obvious to him that the attack on James was so murderous that their relationship could not survive: yet he left a copy of the book for James at his club. Possibly he hoped that James would take the attack on himself as a necessary part of Wells's defence of his own work, and would pay full attention to the self-negating comic frame of the book: would take *Boon* as both serious and unserious simultaneously. James was, of course, bitterly offended by *Boon* and wrote Wells a letter terminating their friendship. 'It is difficult of course for a writer to put himself *fully* in the place of another writer who finds him extraordinarily futile and void, and who is moved to publish that to the world', says James with dignity. Wells tried to retrieve the situation by saying that *Boon* was a 'waste-paper basket' and that the attack on James had not really been meant. James replied that that defence was 'the reverse of felicitous' since a waste-paper basket was for material that one did not intend to publish. In this exchange James was victorious: he was very much hurt, but retained his self-control and took the opportunity to restate his beliefs about the novel. Wells's diversity, he held, was a squandering of talent and he, James, had remained faithful to a view of fictional form which is not spendthrift. Wells had written: 'To you literature like painting is an end, to me literature like architecture is a means, it has a use'. James incisively attacked this. Wells's distinction between a 'form that is (like) painting and a form that is (like) architecture' was 'null and void'; 'There is no sense in which architecture is aesthetically "for use" that doesn't leave any other art whatever exactly as much so' (James/Wells, pp. 261–7). I take it that the key word of this sentence is 'aesthetically'. In so far as it is ' "aesthetically" for use' – in so far as it is *an art* – architecture is subject to the same tests, and open to the same criticisms and modes of judgement, as any other art. Art and life are mutually dependent.

I have no view of life and literature, I maintain, other than that our form of the latter in especial is admirable exactly by its range and variety, its plasticity and liberality, its fairly living on the sincere and shifting experience of the individual practitioner (ibid., p. 266).

Literature is 'relevant' to life in a degree 'that leaves everything else behind':

It is art that *makes* life, makes interest, makes importance, for our consideration and application of these things, and I know of no substitute whatever for the force and beauty of its process (ibid., p. 267).

James seems modestly to say that the connection between art

and life is obvious: but the first and the second of these two state-
ments from his last letter to Wells shows a shift taking place:
from being *equal* with 'life', art moves to the *dominant* position.
James's will was just as strong as Wells's, and his prejudices
were more fixed. There *is* an unexamined assumption, in James,
that unity is by definition a virtue, and if Wells had chosen to
continue, in the correspondence that followed *Boon*, to attack
James on that particular point, the contest between the two
would look more even: it might, indeed, have ended in victory for
Wells.

In the 1930s Wells reconsidered his quarrel with James while
writing his autobiography and set out what was potentially a better defence of his own practice than that contained in 'The Contemporary Novel' in 1911:

Throughout the broad smooth flow of nineteenth century life [. . .] The
Novel in English was produced in an atmosphere of security for the
entertainment of secure people who like to feel established and safe for
good. Its standards were established within that apparently permanent
frame and the criticism of it began to be irritated and perplexed when,
through a new instability, the splintering frame began to get into the
picture.

I suppose for a time I was the outstanding instance among writers of
fiction in English of the frame getting into the picture (Autobiography,
II, pp. 494–5).

Literary history is again being over-simplified – the atmosphere
of security and the apparently permanent frame were clearly not
constant features of nineteenth-century life – but when the
metaphor changes and the frame ceases to refer to the structure,
or moral system, supporting society and refers instead to the
'container', so to speak, of a work of art, part of which splinters
and becomes involved with the work's subject, then one has a
wholly appropriate image for Wells's own practice. Wells goes
on to say of Trafford, in *Marriage*, that he is 'a scientific intelligence caught in the meshes of love' (p. 497), but then turns away
from this potentially fruitful idea to defend the discussion novel
('conflicts and changes of ideas' within the brain) against the
claims of the dramatic or 'established' novel. What one would
like, at this point, is an extended defence of his practice in *Tono-
Bungay*. In that novel the individual is clearly not part of a composition, a painting: the frame gets into the picture in that the
representative figures, George and Teddy Ponderevo, are seen
caught up in the web of economic, biological and historical pro-

cesses which make them what they are. The reference to
Trafford snared in the 'meshes' of love seems to be moving
towards such a vindication, but it is no more than a gesture.
When he does come, in this 'Digression about Novels', to refer to
Tono-Bungay, his remarks are disappointing in content and
curiously defeatist in tone. He says that it was 'an indisputable
Novel' (in the Jamesian sense; that is, a serious work of art) but
it was 'extensive rather than intensive'. It presents its characters
'only as part of a *scene*. It was planned as a social panorama in the
vein of Balzac'. He then goes on to dismiss that 'vein' as a
played-out literary tradition which has been superseded by
'competent historical and contemporary studies' (pp. 503–4).
He is referring, presumably, to his own *Outline of History*, which
had huge sales in the 1920s, and had earned him more money
than any of his previous books and established for him a world-
wide reputation as a teacher and sage. What he is saying, in
effect, is that the battlefield of The Novel is a small one and he
can afford to concede it to James: by this time he has made
bigger conquests elsewhere.

It was foolish of Wells to call *Boon* a 'waste-paper basket'. In
the 1920s he made much more responsible claims for it. Its form
belongs to the tradition of Mallock's *New Republic* (itself an anti-
aesthetic polemical work) and Peacock's discussion novels, and
it was more than 'literary badinage'. In it Wells expresses his
recognition, 'half derisive, half terrified, of the increasing
dangerousness of political and international affairs'. He adds,
intriguingly, that *Boon* was the most 'frank and intimate' of his
books. Presumably the frankness and intimacy are to do with his
feelings about literature and his own position as a writer. He
derides the 'pretentious solemnity of various contemporary
literary artists and critics' and complains that he has 'been
patronised and reproved by them to the limit of endurance'
(Atlantic, XIII, p. x). As well as James these 'literary' artists
include Conrad and (especially) Ford Madox Ford, whose dogmatism and patronisingly patrician air Wells found infuriating.
In *Boon*, Ford (here referred to as 'Hueffer'; he changed his name
to Ford in 1919) is playing Badminton with Wilkins the author
(Wells himself) and at the same time seeking to put everyone
right about literature. He contributes an exhortation 'not to
forget that Henry James knew Turgenev and that he had known
them both,' and he flatly denies that Dickens was a novelist (ch.
4). Boon, of course, is jealous of other writers' prestige. Conrad,

for instance, has been taken up *by the Americans* (*Chance* had been a runaway success in America) as a writer who has style. Wells says of Boon: 'conspicuous success, and particularly conspicuous respectable success, chilled his generosity. Conrad he could not endure. I do him no wrong in mentioning that; it is the way with most of us' (ch. 5).

The attack on the masters of form in *Boon* co-exists with a demonstration, as it were, of the open-endedness, capacity for surprise, and discursiveness that are permissible to the novel. It is a comic work, of course, but some of it is devoted to a plea for the 'seriousness' of art. I am thinking of 'Hallery's' address to the World Conference on the Mind of the Race in chapter 5. Hallery certainly expresses *one* of Wells's attitudes to literature when he says that writers are engaging in actions of such profound moral significance that they can be regarded as religious actions. Like the philosopher and the scientist, every artist becomes 'for just that instant when he is novel and authentically *true*, the Mind of the Race, the thinking divinity'. This activity is 'sacramental': the writer brings his thoughts 'as the priest brings a piece of common bread to the consecration' (ch. 5). What is one to make of this? The framing devices in *Boon* set up a series of jocular defences between the reader and Hallery's discourse: the jocular title, the use of a supposed editor, 'Reginald Bliss', who is collecting Boon's jottings, the fact that Boon himself is a joker and makes scurrilous drawings of his friends ('Bliss' among them) and of the real-life figures, Shaw, James, George Moore, Gosse and others. 'Hallery's' discourse is itself written by Boon, and 'Reginald Bliss' as editor remarks that it is hard to know how seriously to take it. For Hallery writing is a priestly activity, the mind that creates becoming, like the consecrated host, miraculously divine; and 'Bliss' then remarks that for Boon, too, this was the truth about literature. But although Boon believes this 'at the bottom of his heart' he also, and equally, chooses to deride it, decorating his manuscripts with grotesque drawings of the audience leaving during Hallery's talk. Both attitudes, piety and derision, were necessary parts of Boon's belief, 'as the gargoyle on the spire and the high altar are necessary parts of a Gothic cathedral' (ch. 5).

This seems to say that Boon/Wells is divided, indeed schizoid, and certainly leaving *Boon* as a gift to Henry James seems to be schizoid behaviour. Many of the novels of the 1920s and 1930s explore divided consciousness, and indeed the best of

Wells's 1930s novels, *The Bulpington of Blup*, grows out of the same preoccupations that produced *Boon*, since it presents a schizoid personality involved with the arts who is clearly based on Ford Madox Ford. In short, *Boon* seems to me not so much a waste-paper basket as a compost heap, full of nutritious matter which Wells would later dig back into his working life and put to better use than it is put here.

5

Wells in the modern world: *Mr Blettsworthy on Rampole Island*, *The Bulpington of Bulp*, *The Croquet Player*, dualism and education

A one-man didactic system, 1920–46

Wells had little direct experience of power. His brief involvement with the Fabian movement had ended in a quarrel and separation, and during the last year of the Great War he worked for Lord Northcliffe, Director of Enemy Propaganda, as Chairman of the 'Committee for Propaganda in Enemy Country'. Wells soon fell out with Northcliffe; characteristically, he wanted to do things his way and to use the committee to tell the world how it should reorganise itself when peace was restored. Further, he detected what he saw as a split between the conciliatory proposals that his committee was drafting in Northcliffe's name and the crude anti-German stance adopted in Northcliffe's newspapers (MacKenzies, pp. 315–17). He resigned, taking from this brief spell of government service a sense of futility, and seems at this point to have turned his back on politics and administration and returned to the earliest of his roles, that of teacher; with the difference that he was now to be a 'teacher-at-large to the human race' (MacKenzies, p. 318). Works like *Joan and Peter* and *The Undying Fire* demonstrate the prominence of the new preoccupation. *The Outline of History* (1920) is his first sustained performance in his new role. It was his testament, an 'alternative to the Bible, retelling the story of mankind in secular terms' from a Fall to the promise of a new (Wellsian) Jerusalem (ibid., p. 323). It was the first part of an encyclopaedic educational trilogy dealing with history, biology and economics respectively (the other two parts were *The Science of life* (1930), written in collaboration with his son, G. P. Wells, and Julian Huxley, and *The Work, Wealth and Happiness of Mankind* (1931)). An even bigger project – that of creating a universal encyclopaedia, a repository of world knowledge – was announced in 1936 but never begun, although many of his writings on politics and economics in the late 1930s and during the war may be seen as notes towards this grand design.

Wells never ceased to engage in some kind of political activity. In 1918 and 1919 he was a leading advocate of the establishment of a strong League of Nations; he stood unsuccessfully for parliament as a Labour candidate in 1922; he was active in the P.E.N. Club, which in the 1930s became concerned with rescuing Jewish and dissident writers from Hitler's Germany. And he sought to bring direct influence to bear on world affairs by making contact with world leaders. In 1914 he had visited Russia (he was a friend of Maxim Gorky) and developed a proprietorial interest in that country. The Bolshevik Revolution of 1917 seemed to him a happy outcome of the Great War; he made another visit in 1920 and had a meeting with Lenin which he recorded in an article called 'The Dreamer in the Kremlin'. He was attacked from both flanks for this – by Trotsky for 'bourgeois' condescension (and indeed it does seem that he had sought rather naively to convert Lenin to the view that what Soviet Russia needed was an educational élite) – and by friends at home for selling-out to the Bolsheviks (MacKenzies, pp. 326–7). In 1929 he visited Berlin and spoke in the Reichstag: his lecture was published later in the same year under the title 'The Common Sense of World Peace'. In the 1930s he took it upon himself to act as a self-appointed courier between Stalin and Roosevelt, seeking to judge whether his educational ideas were making an impact in the right quarters; how far 'these two brains' were working towards the 'socialist world state that I believe to be the only hopeful destiny for mankind' (quoted in MacKenzies, pp. 378–9). Roosevelt responded warmly to the visit, but he would seem to have made little impact on Stalin. During the 1930s the principal enemies, in Wells's view, were fascism and Catholicism: after the out-break of the Second World War his disillusionment with Russia was completed and he added communism to the list. His journalism of the Second War focused on the Catholic Church as a principal enemy of mankind; his other activities included organising the Sankey Committee for the Declaration of the Rights of Man (1940). He was awarded a Doctorate of Science (1942) but was denied a life-long coveted honour, election to the Royal Society. He always felt an outsider when confronted by academics, and this labour, of an immensely distinguished and ageing man, to write a doctoral thesis in the hope of receiving an academic distinction, is a remarkable tribute to his insecurity.

He was a one-man didactic system, exhorting the world to

save itself according to his principles. The vision of the future of mankind to which he sought to convert Stalin and Roosevelt is enshrined in his writings on 'The Open Conspiracy' in the 1920s and early 1930s. There may be a certain degree of megalomania and absurdity in all this, but it is extraordinary that one man should have done so much and spread himself so widely. *The Outline of History* (1920), the first of the publications of the teacher-at-large to the human race, is also the best. It is 'an attempt to tell, truly and clearly, in one continuous narrative, the whole story of life and mankind so far as it is known today'. Man needs to have a global overview of his own history in order to understand himself in the period of reconstruction after the Great War: 'There can be no peace [. . .] but a common peace in all the world; no prosperity but a general prosperity. *But there can be no common peace and prosperity without common historical ideas.* Without such ideas to hold them together [. . .] races and peoples are bound to drift towards conflict and destruction' (Introduction).

Wells's private life went through dizzying vicissitudes during these years. In 1923 the relationship with Rebecca West ended when she left him – in order to preserve her own individuality and devote herself to her career – and sailed for America. He soon took up with another mistress, Odette Keun, a cosmopolitan journalist working in France: she was 36, he was 58 and at the height of his powers and reputation. The sales of *The Outline of History* were enormous (over two million copies in England and America alone) and had commanded for him a wider audience than any of his previous works. It is not surprising that Odette Keun was eager to hook him. She turned out to be as tough and self-centred as Wells was: they built a house for themselves in the South of France (1926–27, MacKenzies, pp. 346–7), but there were constant quarrels and recriminations. In the middle of all this, in 1927, Wells's wife died of cancer and he went through a period of bitter remorse. The relationship with Odette Keun dragged on until 1933, when Wells finally left her (MacKenzies, p. 373). Under an agreement drawn up earlier in their relationship (an agreement typical both of Wells's generosity and, perhaps, of Odette's rapacity and shrewdness) she retained the 'usufruct' (the use for her life-time) of the house in France. For consolation Wells turned to an old friend, Moura Budberg, formerly the secretary (and mistress) of Maxim Gorky. She valued her independence too much to commit herself completely to Wells, but she provided a degree of domesticity, at least, for the remainder of the 1930s. After the collapse of the Odette Keun relationship Wells settled at Hanover Terrace, Regent's Park (where he wrote *Experiment in Autobiography*). He stayed there throughout the Second World War, despite the blitz and the V bombers (and despite invitations from Margaret Sanger to take a holiday with her in Arizona), and died there on 13 August 1946.

Wells never stopped writing, and produced a huge number of books between 1920 and his death. The books of the early 1920s include a number which indicate what Wells himself referred to as 'grave mental distress' (MacKenzies, p. 336). This distress can probably be related to the separation from Rebecca West. Typically, he would deal with stress-induced conflicts by externalising them: hence the group of novels dealing with divided personalities (ibid., p. 412). *The Secret Places of the Heart* (1922), dealing with the sexual needs and suffering of one Sir Richmond Hardy, is the most autobiographical (and the worst) of these; the others are *The Dream* (1924) and *Christina Alberta's Father* (1925). None of these three books is an artistic success, but after the separation from Rebecca West and the start of the new relationship with Odette Keun – and, however little they were now seeing each other, the death of his wife in 1927 – Wells made a fresh start, artistically, with *Mr Blettsworthy on Rampole Island* (1928). Here the practice that he had already had in writing about divided states of mind combines with themes from his earlier romances to produce a powerful indirect treatment of the Great War and its aftermath. This and *The Bulpington of Blup* (1932), another 'divided consciousness' novel, seem to me by far the best long works of this period, equalled in quality only by two short romances, *The Croquet Player* (1937) and *The Camford Visitation* (1927). Too many of the other works of fiction in the period are ambitious failures: I would include under that heading *The World of William Clissold* (1926) which is huge in scale and very ambitious in conception, but is unrewarding to read. I would also include *Men Like Gods* (1923), *Meanwhile* (1927) and, especially, *The Autocracy of Mr Parham* (1930), an excruciatingly laboured political farce which has been kindly described as an example of what happens when Wells tries to do too many things at once (MacKenzies, p. 357). In the 1930s *The Bulpington of Blup* marks an artistic recovery, and a very intelligent case has been made for other 1930s novels – especially *Brynhild* (1937) and *Apropos of Dolores* (1938) – to be considered with *The Bulpington* as

significant 'anatomies of egotism'.[1] Vigorous and literate
though the argument is, I don't finally agree with this critic;
indeed, I think if anything he damages his case for *The Bulpington*
by pressing too hard for inferior works to be considered as its
equal (discussed below).

In these years Wells was an increasingly irascible and bad-
tempered man, and one of the reasons for his anger was the
belief that he was being written off by the intelligent young.
Rebecca West, his former mistress, lumped him together with
the 'Edwardian Uncles' in her book *The Strange Necessity* (1928)[2]
and 'Geoffrey West' in his biography of 1930 regards Wells as a
genius in decline. 'Geoffrey West's' real name was G. H. Wells:
Wells suggested that he should write his biography under a different name, and it was an ironical quirk of fate that led him to
choose 'West' as his pseudonym: he did not know, of course, of
Wells's relationships with Rebecca West, nor of the existence of
Anthony West, their son. 'Geoffrey West's' biography was
written with Wells's assistance and therefore can be taken as
reflecting Wells's own view of himself in the late 1920s. The view
presented is of a *former* novelist who has now become a promul-
gator of ideas. Wells does not believe in the permanence of art:
'all art, all science, and still more certainly all writings are
experiments in statement' (West, p. 218). But for 'Geoffrey
West' a 'round dozen' of the works will secure for Wells 'the
literary immortality he seems so anxious to avoid'. His list consists of: *The Invisible Man, The War of the Worlds, The Time Machine,
A Modern Utopia, Kipps, The War in the Air, Tono-Bungay, The History
of Mr Polly, The New Machiavelli, Mr Britling Sees it Through, The
Undying Fire* and a number of the stories: 'The Star', 'The Door in
the Wall', 'The Country of the Blind', 'Under the Knife', 'The
Story of the late Mr Elvesham', 'The Man who could work
Miracles' and 'A Vision of Judgement' (p. 283). Throughout his
discussion West praised Wells's 'realism' and for that reason I
find it extraordinary that *Love and Mr Lewisham* is omitted from
his list of novels likely to survive, and that among the romances
the relatively insubstantial *Invisible Man* should be preferred to
The Island of Dr Moreau.

When he uses the word 'realism' Geoffrey West is expressing
something which is certainly central in the experience of reading
Wells. Of the romances he says, rightly, that the 'specifically
scientific basis was in fact incidental' and should not obscure his
natural gifts, the special qualities of his imagination, its 'exuber-

ant inventiveness, its visual penetration, its powerful and relentless actuality' (p. 109). In an essay on Gissing, Wells himself had said that a young man can do 'romance of all sorts, the fantastic story, the idealistic novel', but 'to see life clearly and whole' (a central Victorian ideal, phrased thus by Matthew Arnold), 'to see and represent it with absolute self-detachment, with absolute justice, above all with evenly balanced sympathy, is an ambition permitted only to a man full-grown' (quoted by 'West', p. 110). 'West' justly praises Wells's ability to set an Angel or an Invisible Man in an English village and 'to keep both familiar and unfamiliar on a single plane of reality'.

'Geoffrey West' is right to identify 'reality' as a virtue of the early works but he is also thinking narrowly in terms of sexual realism. He remarks that with a different upbringing Wells might have become like D. H. Lawrence and that that would have been a disaster for him. This tells us what an intelligent but not sharply literary mind was capable of thinking about Lawrence in 1930 (namely, that he was no more than a prurient sexual rebel) but it also points to something true about Wells. The role of sexual revolutionary was, indeed, one that he might have played to the exclusion of all others, and it makes for the erosion of comedy in his work and for an exhaustingly didactic tone.

In *The New Machiavelli* Dick Remington rages at the Victorians:

Will anyone, a hundred years from now, consent to live in the houses the Victorians built, travel by their roads or railways, value the furnishings they made to live among and esteem, except for curious or historical reasons, their prevalent art and the clipped and limited literature that satisfied their souls? (ch. 2).

It must have been difficult for the man who wrote that to accept the verdict of the brilliant young people in the 1920s that he himself belonged to that past. Rebecca West called him Edwardian, and surely she was right; that decade was undoubtedly the period of his highest achievement. But Wells was inclined to regard the Edwardian period as no more than an extension of the Victorian. In *The Soul of a Bishop* he wrote that the death of Queen Victoria was 'as if some compact and dignified paper-weight had been lifted from people's ideas, and at once they had begun to blow about anyhow [. . .]. Her son, already elderly, had followed as the selvedge follows the piece, he had passed and left the new age stripped bare' (ch. 2). If the young thought him finished as a novelist then he would demand recognition as a prophet; but this attitude laid him open to attacks like that of Virginia Woolf in 'Modern Fiction', where she praises his generosity of spirit but sees it as fatal to his writing: he has taken upon his shoulders 'the work that ought to have been discharged by Government officials' and has become blind, as a result, to the 'crudity and coarseness' of the people in his books.[3] People as different from each other as Virginia Woolf, Forster and Orwell misjudged Wells throughout these years: Orwell in 1941 saw him as holding a naive faith in the ability of science to save the world, thus following the line taken by Forster when he parodied Wells's utopias in his early story, 'The Machine Stops' (1909). Anthony West, Wells's son, was much closer to the truth when he said that his father was fundamentally pessimistic. In his view there are related tensions between Wells's early pessimism and the subsequent optimism, and between his early artistry and his later denial of art:

What happened as his powers declined from 1940 onwards was that he reverted to his original profoundly-felt beliefs about the realities of the human situation. He was by nature a pessimist, and he was doing 'violence' to his intuitions and his rational perceptions alike when he asserted in his middle period that mankind could make a better world for itself by an effort of Will (Views, p. 10).

Anthony West believes that the change from pessimism to apparent optimism in 1901 was not real, that doubt was already present in *The Food of the Gods*, and that Wells's quarrel with art was fundamentally misconceived:

He knew in his bones that the aesthetes were right, and that the writer's sole duty is to state the truth which he knows. At the close of his life, from *The Croquet Player* onwards, he was trying to recapture the spirit in which he had written *The Island of Dr Moreau*, and what haunted him, and made him exceedingly unhappy, was a tragic sense that he had returned to the real source of what could have been his strength too late (Views, p. 23).

In a passage in *The Bulpington of Blup* Wells attributes to Theodore Bulpington a view of literary history which he knew was widely shared. Theodore is describing the literary situation immediately after the Great War: 'The old reputations stood up over us now like great empty hulls that had served their purpose, Hardy, Barrie, Conrad, Kipling, Galsworthy, Bennett, Wells, Shaw, Maugham and so forth; they had all said what they had to say; they were finished [. . .]. They were pre-war. They ought to have gone onto the bonfires of Armistice Day' (*The Bulpington of Blup*, ch. 8).

Orwell in 'Wells, Hitler and the World State' wrote that Wells was fixed in an Edwardian antithesis between 'science and reaction' which made him 'a shallow, inadequate thinker now'. Because he believed that science and superstition were in antithesis he was incapable of understanding communism or fascism. The Bolshevik revolutionaries introduced not a 'Wellsian Utopia' but a 'military despotism enlivened by witchcraft trials' and Hitler – 'all the war-lords and witch-doctors of history rolled into one' – had enlisted dark and irrational forces as well as science: 'much of what Wells has imagined and worked for is physically there in Nazi Germany' in 'the service of ideas appropriate to the Stone Age'. He complained that Wells 'was, and still is, quite incapable of understanding that nationalism, religious bigotry and feudal loyalty are far more powerful forces than what he himself would describe as sanity'.[4]

Orwell is quite wrong. *The Croquet Player* shows clearly what *Mr Blettsworthy on Rampole Island* had already indicated– that Wells fully understood the strength of the irrational in the modern world. *The Bulpington* does indeed seem, on one level, to dramatise again the conflict between science and reaction, but an attentive reading shows that it is more complex and less polarised than that – indeed, that it resists summary.

Mr Blettsworthy on Rampole Island
and *Christina Alberta's Father*

Mr Blettsworthy on Rampole Island (1928), not much liked in its day, can be better understood now as psychological science fiction in which the fantastic events take place internally. Arnold Blettsworthy, a young Oxford graduate disillusioned after the failure of his attempt to start a bookshop (and by the dishonesty of his partner, Lyulph Graves) travels to South America on *The Golden Lion*, makes an enemy of the furiously aggressive skipper and when the ship founders is locked into a cabin and left to drown. He is rescued, but as a result of his ill-treatment becomes deranged and imagines himself on an island where the inhabitants live in a stinking gorge, the sunny plateau above made uninhabitable by giant sloths which neither breed nor die. The sloths are all female, and destroy all competing forms of life including their own young (they represent British institutions such as the Church, the Monarchy and the Empire; a good comic touch is the fact that they reproduce by parthenogenesis, and are liable to become pregnant – a condition they resent – when startled). Blettsworthy is adopted as the Sacred Lunatic of this savage tribe, its privileged oracle whose words are interpreted by the hunchback, 'Chit', the most intelligent of the savages. Ardam, the community's war-leader, persuades the tribe to attack the next village; Blettsworthy rescues Ardam's girl, Wena (presumably by using this name Wells is consciously referring to Weena in *The Time Machine*) and is wounded in the shoulder by an arrow. He wakes to find that Rampole Island has been an hallucination, part of the madness from which he has suffered for five years, and that he is in New York: 'Wena' is Rowena, a girl he rescued from suicide in the Hudson River and whom he subsequently marries, and 'Chit' is a contraction of the name of his psychiatrist, Minchett (the arrow wound is an injury received in a traffic accident). There are other 'real' equivalents for features of his hallucination, the most important being that Ardam's attack on the next village is a reflection in Blettsworthy's fantasy of the outbreak of the Great War in Europe in 1914. Here (and in *The Bulpington of Blup*) Wells picks up a motif from Rebecca West's *The Return of the Soldier* (1918), in which a shell-shocked soldier is cured only to be sent back into mortal danger. Blettsworthy volunteers for the British army and fights in the trenches as a private: he discovers that the army is all Ardam and that war-torn Europe is all Rampole Island:

'The fair and kindly civilized world I dreamt of in my youth was a childish fairyland. In this gorge we must live hatefully, driven by ignoble stresses, and in this gorge we shall presently die' (ch. 4).

The Island of Dr Moreau and Rose Macaulay's *Orphan Island* (1924) are Swiftian satires which can be seen as antecedents of this novel, but its clearest literary precursors are to be found in Conrad. Wells signals this in the dialogue in which (following his uncle's death and his foolish speculation with his bookshop) Arnold Blettsworthy is advised by the family solicitor to take a voyage round the world; it will be 'very beneficial' and he might write about it: ' "Like Conrad" I said. "Why not?" asked Mr Ferndyke, betraying no elation that I nibbled at his hook, and making no cavil about the probability of my writing like Conrad' (ch. 1). Like Conrad's Lord Jim, Blettsworthy spends his formative years in a vicarage and his uncle, like Jim's father, preaches a placid, conservative Christianity which is suited to the late-Victorian class-bound English countryside but useless on the high seas or among savages. The brutality of the skipper and the hostility of the officers on *The Golden Lion* recall the opening chapters of *Lord Jim* while the dark, malodorous solidarity of the forecastle and the burial at sea of a boy whom the skipper has tortured to death resemble the scenes among the crewmen and the funeral of James Wait from *The Nigger of the Narcissus*; the storm immediately following the burial recalls those in *The Nigger*, 'Typhoon' and 'Youth', and the cannibalism of the Rampole Islanders echoes (more distantly) the presence of this theme in *Heart of Darkness* (and perhaps also in 'Falk'). The cook producing soup and repeating this 'miracle of warmth' with coffee at the height of the storm recalls the same detail in *The Nigger*, and the skipper's defiance of the weather reminds me of both Allistoun (from *The Nigger*) and MacWhirr from 'Typhoon'; the skipper's 'desperate and exasperated struggle against an obdurate universe for the asserting of his own imperfectly apprehended will, became manifest only as he battered himself towards ultimate defeat' (ch. 2). The sea makes a noise like 'ten thousand little kettle drums' (ch. 2) which is almost a quotation from *Lord Jim*: 'the sea hissed "like twenty thousand kettles" ' remarks Jim in chapter 10 of that novel. And the behaviour of the water in Blettsworthy's cabin on *The Golden Lion* resembles the disorderliness of the sea in 'Typhoon' (and MacWhirr's deadpan response to it): 'Frothy water came into the cabin like a lost dog in search of its master', and 'a pair of boots departed in the custody of a wave and never returned' (ch. 2; MacWhirr's shoes gambol 'playfully over eath other like puppies' from end to end of his cabin).

Another source is Voltaire's *Candide* (the subject of the novel's dedication). In his late-Victorian childhood Blettsworthy believes that things are fundamentally 'all right' (recalling Candide's culpable innocence). Uncle Rupert, the easygoing broad-church clergyman, is perhaps an equivalent of Voltaire's Pangloss, the optimistic pedagogue; Uncle Rupert's Christianity is so ill-defined that it will embrace Darwin and Huxley – 'sound Christians both' – and he believes that man is fundamentally good unless 'pressed or vexed or deluded or starved or startled or scared' (a good list). He can take 'socialism', as understood by upper-class late-Victorians, as a 'wholesome corrective' to hardness among manufacturers and businessmen: he lends Blettsworthy Ruskin's *Unto This Last* and Morris's *News from Nowhere* (Wells seldom misses an opportunity to take a slap at these two, particularly Ruskin). They confirm Arnold Blettsworthy's ignorant innocence: 'I agreed enthusiastically with the spirit of these books, and I looked forward with a quiet assurance to a time when everyone would understand and agree' (ch. 1).

On his first voyage the narrative is at pains to distance Blettsworthy's experience from conventional sea-literature (though not from Conrad): the sea is not 'open', all that is 'open' in the world is 'the roads and paths in a land of kindly people,' and the sea, by contrast, is a prison. Water and air are the 'enormous and invisible walls of your still unrealised incarceration' (ch. 2). When left to die on the drifting ship Blettsworthy tests and loses his Christianity, invoking one of Wells's favourite books, Winwood Reade's *The Martyrdom of Man*: life is 'harsh reality' and all religions are 'illusions' unfolded 'like veils' to obscure it (ch. 2). This disillusionment leads to the best part of the book: its sustained treatment of Blettsworthy's divided consciousness. Anticipations of the method have been present in short pieces like 'The Plattner Story' and 'The Remarkable Case of Davidson's Eyes'; in the latter story a young scientist's eyes convince him that he is on an uninhabited Antipodean island while he is in fact in civilised London (from *The Stolen Bacillus*, 1895). While imprisoned in the fetid gorge on Rampole Island, Blettsworthy describes a 'sort of transparency' in the rocks, which at times appear to be 'pierced by phantom windows' and inscriptions in 'letters of fire' (the office-blocks and illuminated advertisements of modern New York), and he hears passing trams and a river-boat's hooter (ch. 2). With the Great War, dream and reality change places. On the way to the trenches Blettsworthy encounters the skipper of *The Golden Lion*, who had earlier left him for dead. There is an endearing absence of recrimination in this encounter: they are like 'old acquaintances who had met by chance'. The skipper has found a war-job suited to his murderous instincts; he hunts and destroys German submarines. His untamed aggression is a demonstration to Blettsworthy that Rampole Island has 'swallowed the world' (ch. 3). In post-war England, married and settled with his family, Blettsworthy still feels the Rampole Island 'reality' threatening to break through, the shadow of the gorge lying across his spirit and the whiff of Megatheria in the London air. Conversations with his old friend and dishonest former partner Lyulph Graves (now another wounded war-veteran) keep Rampole Island present in his mind; and an intriguing and persuasive feature of his psychological state is that Blettsworthy *needs* to keep alive his sense of the reality of Rampole Island. It is for him a wholesome corrective to the false sense of security offered by civilisation.

In the final chapters Graves and Blettsworthy fall into a recognisable pattern: they represent polarised aspects of Wells himself. Graves is a political optimist, half-seriously planning a book called 'The Prospectus of Mankind' (a recall of *Mankind in the Making?*) while Blettsworthy believes that the Megatheria – the obstructive and obsolescent institutions – will never die, and that man will never get out of the stinking gorge in which he has chosen to make his life. Man is a 'coward, perpetually stultifying himself,' void of objectives among the 'ruins of Victorian liberalism' (ch. 3). The executions of the American radicals Sacco and Vanzetti upset Blettsworthy (they had greatly upset Wells) and he sees the two men on Rampole Island being led to the Reproof (the club used to kill malefactors): 'so far from forgetting Rampole Island, it is this sensible world that sometimes threatens to vanish out of my consciousness' (ch. 3). *Mr Blettsworthy on Rampole Island* is a worthy descendant of the romances of the 1890s, and as well as inheriting their energy and darkness it has a good deal of fine comedy. There is the behaviour of Mrs Slaughter, who addresses Blettsworthy 'with a rich motherliness that made me happy to be an orphan' (ch. 1) and the blinkered good nature of Uncle Rupert confronted by the facts of violence and aggression in the world: he remarks of a murderer whose case is reported in the newspaper, 'I suppose he ought to be hanged (These are excellent kippers . . .)' (ch. 1). And there is the affectionate treatment of the false securities of Victorian England – Queen Victoria as a deity, a cottage loaf with a crown on – and the odd jocular title. It is not as powerful as *The Island of Dr Moreau* but it is in a sense richer, encompassing as it does an affectionate but ultimately damning picture of late-Victorian and Edwardian England followed by a taxing Conradian sea-voyage, a sustained and vividly conveyed hallucination, and an account of the Great War and its aftermath. The madness of modern Europe is expressed by Blettsworthy's madness: in the bankrupt and exhausted condition of the post-war world a divided consciousness is the appropriate state for the representative intelligent man.

Christina Alberta's Father (1925) has a similar theme – the individual consciousness responding to the disordered outside world by withdrawing into insanity. This novel has been praised by some (notably Hammond, p. 197) for the fullness of its characterisations, especially those of Edward Albert Preemby – who believes himself to be Sargon, King of Kings (Wells uses his material on the Sumerian-Akkadian Empire in chapter 16 of *The Outline of History*; Sargon was the semi-legendary creator of this empire, *c.* 2,750 BC) – and of Christina Alberta herself. Personally I am unable to see these virtues; the novel seems to be exhaustingly jocular in tone, full of comic effects which don't quite come off and encumbered with a heavily creaking plot. The moment at which Christina Alberta discovers that Edward Albert is not her father, and that she is the natural daughter of the eminent psychiatrist who happens to be treating Edward Albert, is over-contrived even for an avowedly comic work. But there is a good deal of interest in the theme: to withdraw into a condition of madness and dualism is a reasonable response to the boredom of lower-middle-class life (in 'real' life Edward Albert runs a laundry) and it is the duty of the individual to seek fulfilment for himself. As Preemby puts it on his death-bed: 'When I called myself Sargon King of Kings and proposed to rule all the world I was [. . .] symbolizing.' One may note that at the end of *Mr Blettsworthy on Rampole Island* Arnold Blettsworthy makes it quite clear that Rampole Island is a *mythical* expression of the nature of the real world. Preemby urges men to find what is in effect a romantic solution to the frustrating intractability of circumstance by releasing their inner impulses: 'Of course, everybody is really Sargon King of Kings, and everybody ought to take hold of all the world and save it and rule it' (bk. 3, ch. 3). Mr Polly's discovery, that if life is unsatisfactory it can be changed by an act of will, is taken a stage further.

Education, 'The Open Conspiracy' and *The Croquet Player*

In 1941 Wells fell out with Orwell. In response to Orwell's claim that he believed that ' "science can solve all the ills that man is heir to" Wells wrote an angry note insisting that "I don't say that at all. Read my early works, you shit" ' (MacKenzies, pp. 430–1). Yet the writing on education in the years 1920–45 does seem to express the notion that science can solve all the ills that man is heir to – that the Giant inheritors at the end of *The Food of the Gods* (1904) will put right the wrongs of civilisation, that the sighted man in 'The Country of the Blind' (1904) is the scientist, or visionary, on whom the intellectual pygmies (or, in this case, those suffering from sensory deprivation) will turn in envious rage. In a number of novels and romances – *Men Like Gods* (1923), *The Dream* (1924), *The World of William Clissold* (1926*), The Autocracy of Mr Parham* (1930) and *The Camford Visitation* (1936) are the ones that I shall refer to here – he develops the notion that education must be totally reformed, and that society will be constructed by the 'Open Conspiracy' of a right-minded élite; a conspiracy to which educational reform is the key.

A thread binding all these works together is Wells's systematic attack on the ancient universities and the obstructiveness of the class-ridden conventions that in his view sustained them. The assault begins during the Great War with asides about the fatuity of dons in *Mr Britling* and a good deal of blistering scorn in a book called *What is Coming? A Forecast of Things after the War* (1916). Here Wells notes that in wartime conditions Oxford and Cambridge were virtually closing down – running short courses and catering mainly for foreign students – and he predicts that the new generation of undergraduates, veterans from the war, will demand a different kind of education. He asks whether the universities will resume on the old lines:

I hope with all my heart that they will not. I hope that the Oxford and Cambridge unphilosophical classics and Little-go Greek for everybody, don's mathematics, bad French, ignorance of all Europe except Switzerland, forensic exercises in the Union Debating Society, and cant about the Gothic, the Oxford and Cambridge that turned boys full of life and hope and infinite possibility into barristers, politicians, monolingual diplomatists, bishops, schoolmasters, company directors and remittance men, are even now dead (ch. 7).

The theme was anticipated in a comic form in *Bealby: A Holiday* (1915). This work is no more serious than *The Wheels of Chance* but it does contain a satirical attack on English upper-class education in the figure of a young Captain Douglas, who is too intelligent for Eton and Sandhurst and *reads books* – not 'official biographies about other fellows' fathers' (a nice touch from an outsider about the closed world of Etonians) but 'Philosophy, social philosophy, scientific stuff, all that rot. *The sort of stuff they read in mechanics' institutes*' (ch. 4).

With *Men Like Gods* (1923) Wells returns to the preoccupations of *A Modern Utopia* (1905) with which it is explicitly compared in the preface. The Samurai, the Arnoldian élite who ran things in the earlier book have been replaced by the universal aristocracy advocated in *The Research Magnificent* (1915). From the retrospect of the 1920s *The Research Magnificent* can be seen as a pivotal novel which closes the sequence of giant-(or 'god'-)against-common-humanity novels, and initiates a sequence of giant-as-legislator-for-mankind novels. In *Men Like Gods* 'all the people are Samurai'. Wells's belief in a 'scientific reorganisation of society based on a broader conception of education' has strengthened so that he need no longer admit the 'necessary survival of inferior types'. An essential feature of *Men Like Gods* is that these new Utopians all live in a state of total nudity, emphasising the sexual sanity of this civilisation, its freedom from sexual guilt, and the final triumph of political well-being over sexual individualism. The nudity guarantees the 'uncompromising frankness' which is to be the 'soul' of this new world; a state in which the individual escapes from the 'passionately egotistical beast in our inheritance'. Those who prefer the conditions of early twentieth-century society – clothing, sexual concealment, inherited taboos – are summarily dealt with: 'Of course the present life is rich in interest for such people [. . .] just as a rat-infested drain is richer in interest for a dog than a library or a laboratory' (Atlantic, XXVIII, pp. ix–x). This theme is also expressed in *The Secret Places of the Heart* and *Christina Alberta's Father*. In *The Secret Places of the Heart* (1922) a Wells figure, 'Sir Richmond Hardy', complains to a psychiatrist about the disruptive pressures of his sexuality: Mother Nature is a 'fumbling old fool' driving man into 'indignity and dishonour'. In *Christina Alberta's Father* (1925) Christina Alberta declares her intention of enjoying sex without marriage, and of avoiding children ('a swarm of hidden dwarfs' is how she sees her unborn babies, bk. 3, ch. 4). Her true father, the psychiatrist Devizes, commends her egotism but remarks that it is only a necessary stage of self-assertion, like the screaming of a healthy baby, and that before long she will work for the common interest and dispense with sex altogether (ibid.).

Utopia in *Men Like Gods* has come into existence for Malthusian reasons. Overcrowding in the last 'Age of Confusion' (the early twentieth century) was the 'fundamental evil out of which all the others that afflicted the race arose' and led to a universal war which was necessarily followed by a 'deliberate change in Utopian thought', an educational process creating an improved species. A somewhat chilling feature of this society is that those who are personally unfitted to its hygienic beauty have not survived. 'The idle strains, the people of lethargic dispositions or weak imagination, have mostly died out; the melancholic type has taken its dismissal and gone [. . .]. Spiteful and malignant characters are disappearing'. The eugenics practised in *A Modern Utopia* have been perfected (ch. 5). There is no central administration: the attitudes of each individual within the state ensure that there is no need of one. The closing lines of this chapter, 'The Governance and History of Utopia', is the key to the whole system: *'Our education is our government'*.

Wells would like to believe that the historical convulsions that have resulted in this beneficent order might have been bloodless, but his sense of history prevents him from making such a claim. At an early stage in Utopia's history a kind of Marxist revolution has taken place: 'extensive private property was socially a nuisance' and the 'irresponsible rich [. . .] had to go, for the good of the race'. They resist, of course, the 'coming of the universal scientific state, the educational state' for five centuries: 'the fight against it was the fight of greedy, passionate, prejudiced and self-seeking men against the crystallisation into concrete realities of this new idea of association for service'. The narrative rather glosses over the fact that what it is describing are five hundred years of bloody civil war, and puts it as though it were a civilised process conducted by committees: 'Point after point was won [. . .]. No date could be fixed for the change. A time came when Utopia perceived that it was day' (ch. 5). This is clearly a 'prig' book and too much of its length is devoted to solemn exposition of the world state that is thought desirable, but it does have humour as well. Among the men plunged into Utopia are 'Cecil Burleigh', who is Balfour, 'Rupert Catskill', who is Churchill – violent, irascible, masterful, fatally determined to declare war against the Utopians – and 'Freddy Mush' as Eddie Marsh, Churchill's private secretary, an elegant homosexual who edited the *Georgian Poetry* anthologies. Freddy Mush is introduced in these terms: 'Taste. Good taste. He is awfully clever at finding out young poets and all that sort of literary thing [. . .]. If there is a literary academy, they say, he's certain to be in it. He's dreadfully critical and sarcastic' (ch. 1).

Details like this go some way to redeem *Men Like Gods*, but it remains a somewhat dull and undistinguished romance, especially when compared with its successor, *The Dream* (1924). Here Wells recovers the density and particularity that characterise the early chapters of *Tono-Bungay*. Sarnac, living some

2,000 years in the future, recalls his early twentieth-century life as Harry Mortimer Smith. He is brought up by a struggling shopkeeper and lifted into the middle-class profession of journalist because his sister becomes the mistress of 'Newberry', owner of one of the popular magazines published after the Great War (he is based on the Harmsworth brothers, Northcliffe and Rothermere; Wells had worked for Lord Northcliffe during the war). Smith's father is an ignorant, imaginative, defeated small shopkeeper. Wells's feelings about his own father, on whom this man is modelled, surface momentarily as Smith describes his father's death in a motor accident: 'I thought of his endless edifying discourses about flowers and hillsides and distant stars [. . .]. Life had treated him badly. He had never had a dog's chance' (ch. 4). After the father's death the Smiths move to London to live in lodgings in Pimlico with one Matilda Good. (Like the shabby–genteel suburbs in *Tono-Bungay*, these houses have been built for middle-class families but have never been lived in by them.) The odd shape of the book makes good dramatic sense; Sarnac devotes rather too much of his narrative to Matilda Good and her shabby, dirty household of displaced persons because he is reluctant to come to the painful story of his marriage. Harry Mortimer Smith marries Hetty Marcus just before he goes off to fight in the Great War. She has a child by another man, and Harry divorces her, marries a cold prude in her stead, and after further complications shoots the father of Hetty's child. As my brief summary indicates, this plot is a somewhat over-schematic illustration of Wells's belief that sexual jealousy is an atavistic evil which must be bred out of modern man. Confusion over sexual matters was the worst evil of the 'Age of Confusion': 'Our passions were fevers. We were only beginning to learn the art of being human' (ch. 6).

An important part of the experience of reading *The Dream* is the distance that the narrative device – Sarnac recalling his life as Harry Mortimer Smith – imposes on the events. Sarnac compels the reader to look back at Edwardian Wells through the wrong end of a telescope. Having survived the War and the weird mystical phase of which *God the Invisible King* and *The Soul of a Bishop* were the major fruits, Wells can see the late-Victorian and Edwardian world as an abominable past, still infected by a religion which bred over-population, dirt, disease and dishonesty. The Smith family – 'my mother had been unable to avoid having six babies and four of us were alive' – live above and below their shop, as did the Wells family. The only person to escape this 'troglodyte' existence is the beautiful Fanny who chooses to become a rich man's mistress: one recalls that in reality Wells's elder sister, also called Fanny, escaped by dying of appendicitis when she was nine. Wells's mother never ceased to mourn her precious 'Possy', the prettiest and best behaved of her children and her only girl.

A major theme of *The Dream*, as of all these books, is the role of education. School for ordinary children in Victorian England was conducted by exhausted teachers whom Sarnac in retrospect sees as 'holy saints', battling with overcrowded classrooms and inadequate equipment. Sarnac's audience – the people of the year 4,000 – are astonished by the 'supreme wickedness of hindering the growth of a human mind', and Sarnac replies: 'It was not merely that their minds were starved and poisoned. Their minds were stamped upon and mutilated. The world was so pitiless and confused, so dirty and diseased because it was cowed and dared not learn of remedies' (ch. 4). One of Sarnac's audience asks about worship in this past: 'Their sound of church-bells and of congregations singing. Wasn't there a certain beauty in that?' Sarnac's reply – Wells's too, of course – is that Christianity was a disease, its churches 'abnormal and unserviceable growths' which were also often beautiful (ch. 2).

The World of William Clissold: A Novel at a New Angle (1926) is an inordinately long and portentous work. To dismiss it is wrong – a writer as intelligent as Wells would scarcely have written a thousand pages about nothing at all – but the experience of reading it is unrewarding. In a way it revisits the themes and ambitions of *Tono-Bungay*; it is another 'Condition of England' novel, written by a narrator who declares on the opening page that he is limited, and qualified by another narrator – Clissold's brother, who edits the manuscripts after Clissold's sudden death – who sets a frame round the story and tells us that Clissold was an impatient man who overstates but that he was substantially right in his views. These devices seem designed to emphasise that the book is 'fiction', but, for all that, much of it is direct homily – an extended statement of Wells's views about civilisation and the changes it needs. In volume III, where Clissold declares that what mankind needs for its salvation is the 'Open Conspiracy' of the intelligent and the forward looking, the Arnoldian scorn and reforming zeal become explicit. The function of the Open Conspiracy is not 'to overthrow existing governments by insurrectionary attacks, but to supersede them by disregard'. Its purpose is to 'consolidate and keep alive and develop the living powers in the world today by an illumination, a propaganda, a literature, a culture, an education and the consciously evoked expectation of a new society' (bk. 3). Wells's next book, *The Open Conspiracy* (1928), sets out a programme of sweeping change with bloodless committee-man's clarity: education is to be the key to the coming changes: 'Necessarily, for a time, the Open Conspiracy children would become a social élite' (ch. xv). In *Clissold*, by contrast, the recommendations for educational change are incisive, not to say lacerating. Perhaps because the text is still notionally the work of Clissold (of a dramatised figure who is 'not Wells') the attack on educators is ferocious and draws blood: 'We have bred our governing class mentally as the backward Essex farmer bred his pigs, from the individuals that were no good for the open market' (bk. 5). Schoolmasters are 'a class of refugees from the novelties and strains and adventures of life'; they are the useless upper-middle-class boys of whom it is said, 'He's got a second class. His people have no money. His games are pretty fair. He'll have to go into a school'. The result is that the mentality of the public school is the mentality of 'residual men' (ibid.). Dons are no better; they must be done away with to make room for efficient technical education: 'We must be prepared to cut out this three or four year holiday at Oxford or Cambridge [. . .] from the lives of the young men we hope to see playing leading parts in the affairs of the world. It is too grave a loss of time at a critical period; it establishes the defensive attitude too firmly in the face of the forcible needs of life' (bk. 5).

The behaviour of Mr Parham in *The Autocracy of Mr Parham: His Remarkable Adventures in the Changing World* (1930), with his cocooned arrogance and patronising fastidiousness, is donnishness at its most appalling. To gratify his power-lust he seeks to make use of Sir Bussy Woodcock (based on Beaverbrook and Churchill) but Sir Bussy is too vulgar and aggressive to be used. He has no understanding of the civilisation that Mr Parham stands for. He had gone into advertising at the age of fourteen because there was 'no *go* in the other stuff'; 'the other "stuff", if you please, was Wordsworth, the Reformation, Vegetable Morphology and Economic History as interpreted by fastidious and obscurely satirical young gentlemen from the elder universities' (the university Extension Lecturers whose lectures Sir Bussy had ceased to attend, ch. 1). What is Wells's attitude to this? If he has the deepest contempt for Mr Parham, he also, clearly, has considerable contempt for Sir Bussy, the primitive egotist who is a more comprehensive threat to good social order and honest decency than was that rather similar charlatan and entrepreneur, Teddy Ponderevo. His loyalties seem divided, as they often are, between these two figures. Mr Parham, as 'Lord Paramount', seeks to lead a fascist movement of national regeneration against Bolshevism; he is an inept leader and his principal aides, Sir Bussy and Camelford, the scientist, seize world control (by taking possession of Gas L, the ultimate secret weapon) and frustrate Lord Paramount and his gorilla-like general, Gerson. In Low's caricature Gerson resembles Mussolini (Low's illustrations to *Mr Parham* are consistently wittier than Wells's text).

The irresponsibility of educational establishments and the presence of primitive forces in the modern world are handled much more elegantly in two short and neglected fantasies of the 1930s, *The Camford Visitation* (1937) and *The Croquet Player* (1936). *The Camford Visitation* continues the attack on dons. In the dining-room of Holy Innocents College (All Souls) the Fellows are listening as the Master deplores the growth of London University as the 'dictatorship of the half-educated'. A disembodied Voice interrupts him to ask 'very clearly and distinctly: "Half-educated? Now how can you measure education and divide it into halves and quarters? What do you *mean* by education? . . . " ' (ch. 1). Mr Trumber, whose subject is English Literature, is very much disturbed by this question. Trumber is a disciple of T. S. Eliot, whom Wells detested: in his penultimate book, *The Happy Turning* (1945) Wells declared that Eliot's poetry was 'jingling vulgarity', 'void of the mysterious exaltation of beauty'. Trumber, following Eliot, has rediscovered the Metaphysical poets and has learnt to be rude about Milton. Like Freddy Mush in *Men Like Gods* he 'dealt in taste and judgement', but he is more up-to-date than Freddy: 'He taught how T. S. Eliot was really *it* and why Rupert Brooke wasn't' (ch. 2).

One of the problems that Wells set himself in the thirties was that of writing about the factors that were changing the world. *The Holy Terror* (1939) is a study of the psychology of Hitler in the person of a boy called Rudolph Whitlow who begins rather like Wells himself – a screaming egotist of a child who demands everything for himself and throws dangerous missiles at mealtimes (Wells once threw a fork at one of his brothers; the fork stuck into his brother's face, narrowly missing an eye). Whitlow is in a way a development of Mr Parham: he passes examinations with ease and goes to 'Camford' and 'in the stabler past' might have become a don, but instead becomes a fascist dictator. The passages on Camford in *The Holy Terror* need to be read in conjunction with *The Camford Visitation*: Whitlow would have been a 'formidably malicious, secretly vicious, conservative don, the sort of don who is feared and propitiated during his lifetime and forgotten gladly almost before he is dead'. Camford itself is a medieval institution which has nothing to say to the modern world. Since 'the Catholic scheme of salvation had fallen into disuse' nothing in Camford 'except for a few dreaming spires' had pointed in any direction at all (ch. 2). It is the inertia and bankruptcy of the old order that allows political disasters like the rise to power of Whitlow/Hitler to take place. *The Camford Visitation* urges the educational establishment to resume its neglected responsibilities if it wishes to avert a political catastrophe and *The Holy Terror* shows the kind of catastrophe that Wells has in mind.

In the group of works that I have been discussing – *Men Like Gods*, *The Dream*, *William Clissold*, *Mr Parham* and *The Camford Visitation* – the belief is expressed that education can save mankind. *The Croquet Player* (1936) takes a different direction. It is a parable about the condition of Europe in the wake of the Spanish Civil War: the violence that has erupted in Spain and in the fascist dictatorships forces man to recognise the kind of animal that he is. The narrator, George Frobisher, is as effeminate young man – 'what the Americans call a sissy' with 'soft hands and an ineffective will' – who lives with his aunt and devotes his life to playing croquet, of which he is a master. He encounters a doctor, Finchatton, who is recovering (in his own view) from a nervous breakdown: he is taking a rest from his practice in a district of England called 'Cainsmarsh' (which exists only in his imagination; it is a distorted version of his experiences in Ely). Finchatton has come to believe that man's ape-like ancestor is returning to the modern world; instances of brutality in his practice (a dog beaten to death, a crazed clergyman who attacks his wife) have supported this belief. The psychiatrist, a much stronger personality called Norbert, knows that Finchatton's 'experiences' in mythical Cainsmarsh are reflections of the political realities of the modern world. Man's ape-like ancestors *are* returning, not in remote English villages but in seats of power throughout Europe: Hitler and Mussolini are the Old Men of the Neanderthal tribes described in chapter 9 of *The Outline of History*; their political appeal is based on primitive atavistic cravings. Norbert declares that man is still what he was: 'bestial, envious, malicious, greedy', and when unmasked he is the 'same fearing, snarling, fighting beast he was a hundred thousand years ago [. . .]. The brute has been marking time and dreaming of a progress it has failed to make.' Modern man is 'just a cave-man, more or less trained' (ch. 4).

If Orwell had read *The Croquet Player* he would not have been able to write 'Wells, Hitler and the World State' (1941), where he suggests that Wells's middle-class faith in science blinds him to the reality of the modern world in which 'Creatures out of the Dark Ages have come marching into the present'. The terrifying presence of primitive drives in modern men is precisely *The Croquet Player*'s theme. The idea has occurred before, in *The Island of Dr Moreau* and *Mr Blettsworthy on Rampole Island* especially, but here it is treated with a striking degree of elegance and clarity. George Frobisher is a type that Wells detests but he is characterised with unwavering firmness and assurance; it is one of the best instances of Wells's capacity for artistic detachment, comparable with the characterisation of Theodore Bulpington (discussed below), another unsympathetic figure who is fully explored from within. The brevity of the romance forces Wells to write with uncharacteristic economy and to restrain the editorialising impulse that swamps so many of the long books. The limited, selfish, food-loving George is impervious to the terrors of the modern world. He seldom reads the newspapers, he is only dimly aware of the political disorders that Norbert refers to, and for him the 'Frame of the present', the illusory world of civilisation and its assurances, has not been broken. Norbert sees George's imperviousness as a form of moral strength and appeals to him to become a 'giant' (a recall of the theme of *The Food of the Gods*) and a fellow-architect of a 'harder, stronger civilization' which must be bound 'like steel round the world' if the world is to be saved. But George will have none of this; his intelligence accepts that what Norbert tells him is true, but his imperviousness is shown to be not strength but the bottomless frivolity of the abdicating upper-middle class. He goes off to play another game of croquet: 'This may, as you say, be the sunset of civilisation. I'm sorry, but I can't help it this morning. I have other engagements' (ch. 4). The fantasy is hard, elegant and unyieldingly pessimistic. Those who 'care for civiliz-ation' will, on the whole, refuse to join the giants. It pulls together, condenses and focuses preoccupations that had been written about extensively elsewhere, so that its success is partly the result of perfected technique. The irresponsibility of the ruling class in *The Bulpington of Bulp* and the presence of savage violence in the modern world (treated mythically) in *Mr Blettsworthy on Rampole Island* yield the structural polarity of *The Croquet Player* – on the one hand George Frobisher's effete self-sufficiency, on the other Norbert's passionate desire to bring man to an understanding of his own nature. It counters the 'Open Conspiracy' with a drier, more intellectual version of the apocalyptic pessimism of the 1890s romances. It is one of the best works in the whole of Wells's canon, and yet it remains extraordinarily little known.

The Bulpington of Blup

The Bulpington of Blup (1932) can be seen, from one point of view, as a more considered and much more carefully constructed treatment of the literary issues raised in *Boon*. In *Boon* and elsewhere, as I have argued in chapter 4, Wells could have made more than he did of his intellectual case against Henry James. Reputable modern critics have turned against James in a manner that Wells would have approved of. Scholes and Kellogg in *The Nature of Narrative* see James's devotion to the form of the novel as restrictive and limiting; they remark that the unity of 'point of view', a principle implicit throughout James's prefaces and codified by his disciple, Percy Lubbock, is unlikely to sur-vive the work of Proust and Joyce just as the dramatic unities of the French classical critics could not survive the prestige of Shakespeare: 'Criticism can never reduce art to rules. Its aim should be not to enact legislation for artists but to promote understanding of works of art.'[5] James, in their view, can be seen making 'the least' of the methods of both Joyce and Proust, sac-rificing 'huge areas of life to his desire for neatness' (Scholes and Kellogg, p. 271). This is exactly the view of James that Wells himself takes and he would have been both gratified and sur-prised, I would guess, to find two of James's countrymen at the heart of academic life agreeing with him; at the time of his quarrel with James his antagonism was fuelled by, among other things, the conviction that James had the support of the academics and that he, Wells, did not. After James's death Wells continued to fight against James's view of the novel. The prefaces to the Atlantic Edition, published in the 1920s, give him a peculiarly Jamesian revenge, since the Atlantic Edition confers on Wells's own work precisely the kind of 'processional dignity' that he had mocked in James's New York edition.But in *The Bulpington of Blup* James's place, as the focus of Wells's aggression and the representative of all that Wells dislikes in literature and the arts, has been taken by Ford Madox Ford.

At one time Wells and Ford had been very close: in the early days of their friendship Ford had been an enthusiastic admirer of Wells, speaking of him in the 1890s as a 'genius' and as 'the Dean of our Profession' (MacKenzies, pp. 116, 143). But the latter hyperbole perhaps masks a twinge of envy – Ford was never free from literary envy – and serious trouble broke out over the publication of *Tono-Bungay* in *The English Review*, the literary periodical which Ford launched in 1908. *The English Review* was highly prestigious but Ford's management of it was disastrous, and it soon became apparent to Wells that *Tono-Bungay* – which was, after all, his best novel to date, and he knew it – would not make him any money from its serial publication. When he took this up with Ford, Ford's response was to write a ludicrously pompous and high-handed letter to Wells's wife, accusing Wells of behaving 'treacherously'. The consequent breach was never healed. Ford's vanity was seriously piqued by the quarrel and he chose to create an insulting caricature of Wells in his pseudonymous satire, *The New Humpty Dumpty* (1912).[6]

Here Wells appears as 'Mr Pett', a journalist who is working for the brotherhood of man, 'bringing the whole world to one standard' (p. 18), and like Wells has a squeaky voice and speaks in a cockney accent, 'High and shrill with [...] impish malice' (p. 191). He displays what was undeniably another of Wells's traits, naive vanity: he 'intensely disliked that anyone other than himself should lecture an assembly in which he was present' (p. 74) and he is aggressively conceited about his working-class origins: he complacently observes that he has no 'spark of generosity' because he comes from 'the lower classes' (p. 427). This last touch is deeply unjust: Wells may have been inclined to congratulate himself on his upward social mobility but he was never mean. Indeed, he displayed considerable generosity to

Ford himself, helping him financially for old time's sake after Ford had lost all his savings in the Wall Street crash in 1929 (MacKenzies, p. 330). Wells could reasonably have felt that he owed himself a little revenge, and he duly took it by casting Ford as the central figure in *The Bulpington of Blup*, Theodore Bulpington.

This novel is a distinguished achievement which pulls together a number of important themes. It stresses the irresponsibility of anti-scientific aestheticism in an increasingly chaotic world, so that it ties in with the educational ideas present in the works discussed above (pp. 135–45), and it also looks back to the divided personalities in his novels of the 1920s: Edward Albert Preemby, who imagines himself to be Sargon King of Kings, and Mr Blettsworthy, who inhabits a dream world in which the violence of the real world is reflected in mythical forms. Wells must have enjoyed writing this: 'Raymond [Theodore Bulpington's father] had been reviewing a book by "those two very promising young men", Conrad and Hueffer [Ford]' (ch. 2). This book is *The Inheritors* (1902), a decidedly feeble romance – largely Ford's – in which a new species of human being makes its presence felt in London. *The Inheritors* has an obvious debt to Grant Allen's *The British Barbarians* (1893) and to Wells's own romances of the 1890s (as does Ford's equally feeble *Mr Apollo*). Wells takes pleasure in drawing attention to what is certainly one of Ford's (and Conrad's) worst books, published during the Edwardian decade when he, Wells, had been clearly in the ascendant. He rightly saw the impulse of *The Inheritors* as anti-scientific (Wells re-wrote *The Inheritors* from a pro-scientific viewpoint when he wrote *Star-Begotten: A Biological Fantasia* (1937), in which Martians peaceably invade the planet by causing genetic change in human beings). *The Inheritors*, as described by Raymond Bulpington, presents a new species of man 'without pity or scruples'; they are 'just the kind of people science was producing. And they were different – different. They saw life with a kind of cold inhuman clearness' (ch. 2). *The Bulpington of Blup* can be seen as an extended rebuke to the authors of *The Inheritors*. The saviours of the race, in Wells's view, are to be figures like Teddy Broxted, the young scientist who has the courage to be a conscientious objector during the Great War, and his sister Margaret (with whom Theodore Bulpington is in love); the older species are cowards, conservatives and parasites, like Theodore himself.

As an officer in the Great War Theodore panics and runs away from the front; this is diagnosed as 'shell-shock' or 'war-neurosis' by a young Medical Officer, whose clemency saves Theodore from being shot for cowardice:

The treatment of such cases as Theodore's varied with the M.O. concerned. Sometimes the diagnosis led straight to the bleak and sorrowful firing party at dawn. But there were understanding and merciful men among these M.O.s, there were some who never once passed a man on to such a fate, and it was Theodore's luck to encounter a doctor of that new school (ch. 7).

Ford had a nervous breakdown between 1904 and 1906 and was always psychologically unstable. He had volunteered for the army in 1915 – an act of real courage – but suffered physical and psychological collapse during the war. By the time of his demobilisation in 1919 he had gone through a pattern of experience familiar to many literary men who became soldiers, a progression from patriotism to disillusionment. In his *Parade's End* tetralogy (1924–28), especially in the two inner novels, *No More Parades* and *A Man Could Stand Up* – , he dramatises Christopher Tietjens' experience in the war as a matter of extreme emotional and psychological torment. Ford lost his memory in 1916 on the Somme after being concussed by the blast from an exploding shell and had to be hospitalised; later he developed a bronchial disorder which he attributed to gas. He wrote a number of letters to C. F. G. Masterman hoping that Masterman's influence would find him a home-based alternative to his military job.[7]

Wells closely follows these details in his story of Theodore Bulpington, who claims (falsely) to have been stunned by a near-miss, claims also to have been affected by poison-gas and appeals to an influential relation, Sir Lucien Brood, to get him out of active service. It is an intriguing detail that Ford was reading Stephen Crane's *The Red Badge of Courage* (1896) on the Somme in 1916 (Mizener, *Saddest Story*, p. 288) since that also seems to have been a source for Wells's novel. In Crane's short novel Henry Fleming, a young private in the American Civil War, runs from his first battle and receives the 'red badge' – his first wound – when struck on the head with the butt of a rifle by a fellow-yankee. This steadies him and dispels his panic, and he returns to the battle with 'a quiet manhood, non-assertive, but of sturdy and strong blood'.

The portrait of Theodore benefits from the fact that he is based on someone of whom Wells was once fond, and whom he has known over many years. Theodore stands for everything Wells detests; such as upper-classishness, 'taste' and the Pre-Raphaelite and aesthetic impulse to return to a world order based on a kind of medieval monarchy. Yet his consciousness is explored in such detail, and Wells writes about him so well, that he becomes, like George Eliot's Rosamond Vincy or Gwendolen Harleth, a figure who is fully and exhaustively known before he is adversely judged. The psychology of his adolescence, for instance, is faithfully and carefully dramatised. He is in a divided state about sex because his parents have not prepared him for wet dreams and the furtive conversation of other adolescents: 'The Bulpington of Blup had no use for the squalid [. . .]. The Bulpington of Blup was the sublimating genius. He went through the air while Theodore stumbled in the mire. He vanished whenever Theodore wallowed' (ch. 3). 'The Bulpington' is an aristocratic other self that the middle-class Theodore has invented, just as Ford Madox Hueffer, later Ford, invented, in Wells's unkind recollection, a 'system' of 'assumed personas and dramatized selves'; 'what he is really or if he is really, nobody knows now and he least of all' (Autobiography, II, p. 617).

As a schoolboy Theodore makes friends with Teddy Broxted, son of Professor Broxted of Kingsway College (a disciple of Huxley, and a figure clearly based on Wells's recollection of his student days at the Normal School of Science), who is collecting specimens on the beach in order to examine them through his microscope. Theodore is introduced to the use of the microscope and is allowed by the novel to make an imaginative generalisation which Wells himself would clearly regard as true, and which illumines and extends the reader's apprehension of the novel's themes. Looking at microbes through the instrument, Theodore has a 'flash of vision' in which he sees 'the whole world magnified in texture and teeming with unfamiliar particles', and he imparts this vision to Teddy. For a moment the two boys share in a numinous insight: 'it hung over both their minds that the world about them was a mere summary of the material multitudinousness of reality, each apparent thing in it like the back of the binding of a volume in a limitless encyclopaedia', and that there is an 'abyss beneath the apparent universe' (ch. 2). In Theodore's young manhood Wells again displays his capacity for artistic objectivity by giving this cowardly anti-hero a moment of 'Wordsworthian ecstasy'. Theodore watches a sunset over the sea and is granted an intuitive vision: 'The universe was transfigured – as though it smiled, as though it opened itself out to him, as though it took him into complete communion with itself. The scene was no longer a scene. It was a Being [. . .]. Time ceased. He felt a silence beneath all sounds; he apprehended a beauty that transcends experience.' This Wordsworthian moment is pointed up by a brief commentary which detaches it from Theodore's bogus other-self, the Bulpington: it is Theodore's 'reality' which had 'nothing to do with the Bulpington of Blup and [. . .] the Bulpington of Blup had never any use for it. There it stayed in Theodore's mind generally quite overlooked but never completely forgotten. It was like a hidden particle of fire that might glow again and very brightly before it was altogether extinguished' (ch. 3).

On the surface, Theodore in his Edwardian boyhood is an objectionable aesthete. The world exists 'for Art'; the function of art is to interpret. In 1915 Henry James had protested 'It is art that *makes* life, makes interest, makes importance' (James/Wells, p. 267), and Wells here caricatures that doctrine:

'Interpretation,' expanded Theodore, quoting Raymond [Theodore's father] quoting Henry James; '*rendering*, giving it a form – the only thing that matters' (ch. 3).

As the young Ford Madox Ford had been, Theodore is a gifted dilettante who might turn his hand to anything: painting, criticism, writing. Teddy Broxted argues that Theodore ought to be 'training' to become a writer, as a pianist does his daily practice. Theodore holds that that is unnecessary: writing just 'comes'. Clearly Theodore's view here is not James's. One may note that Henry James *did* practise like a pianist. The quarrel with Henry James is receding as the characterisation of Theodore develops, and as Wells interests himself in the task of dramatising the split in Theodore's personality. It is not Theodore who evasively claims that writing 'comes' but his other self, the Bulpington, which 'so soon as his mind was released from the checking action of speech with the Broxteds' is released and floats off into a reverie in which he becomes 'a Leonardo, a Michelangelo, a world leader'.

As Theodore matures so his considerable intelligence falsifies the world by drawing across it his 'loose versatile Scheme of Values'. In his vocabulary the Fabians are 'bourgeois' (Wells had little sympathy with the Fabians, of course, but we may be certain that he had less with Theodore's superficial

insolence) and so are 'science' (represented by the Broxteds),
'Florentine art, and the Royal Academy and most portraiture';
with rhetorical gestures of this kind he protects himself from
'drudgery and veracity' (ch. 3). The narrator's commentary
ensures that by the middle of this chapter the polarities of the
novel are clear: the Broxteds stand for truth, realism and sanity,
Theodore as 'The Bulpington' for 'versatile, unverifiable and
reassuring' fictions. The Broxteds are 'prigs' – the use of this
word is a firm assurance (if any further assurance is needed) that
they are clear-minded Wellsian serious thinkers – who seek to
strip away Theodore's Bluppish illusions, but it takes experience (the death of his father, the outbreak of the war) to achieve
that. His sensations after his father's death are acutely
registered: he tries to imagine himself dead but finds it impossible and his Bluppish self comes to the rescue. 'Of *course* he was
immortal! [. . .]. He did not want immortality for everybody. He
wanted it for himself' (ch. 5). Theodore is 'Christian' in an
aesthetic Anglo-Catholic way; in his bereavement the stages
whereby genuine egotism cocoons itself in self-deception are
charted and religion is exposed as a childish myth with which the
egotist characteristically consoles himself. His Christianity is a
response to ceremony and decoration (Ford Madox Ford used to
call himself a Catholic when it suited him); Theodore has opted
for Anglicanism rather than the Catholicism of his model simply
because St Paul's is handsomer than pictures that he has seen of
St Peter's and the Anglican God is in any case a gentleman, 'a
God with *tact*' (ch. 5).

The outbreak of the Great War, and the test that it brings to
Theodore's manhood, yields much better writing than we find
on the same topic in *Mr Britling Sees it Through*; Wells has
benefited from his knowledge of such novels about the war as
Rebecca West's *The Return of the Soldier* and Ford's own Tietjens
novels (and he had probably re-read *The Red Badge of Courage*).
Wells stresses, as he has done before in *Mr Britling*, the civilised
world's 'astonishment' at the outbreak of war in August 1914,
together with its failure to understand the scale of the war.
British troops sing on the way to Belgium; American tourists
motor about on the frontier and are reluctant to get out of the
way. There is ubiquitous 'maladjustment' to the realities of war.
Responding to 'gently rippling water' and 'weather-mellowed
stonework' Theodore participates in the national patriotic
illusion that '*My* England' has a latent reservoir of inherited

strength, and that its country houses and its gentle landscape are the symbolic custodians of the national virtues. Teddy Broxted, by contrast, refuses to fight, predicts that the English in their unpreparedness will be defeated, and courageously opposes the war as 'the most deadly and stupendous Bore that ever confronted the spirit of man'. Teddy represents, of course, Wells's own intellectual position during the thirties: the way forward is through education and the Open Conspiracy, the 'informal co-operation of an invisible circle of enlightened people' assisted by the advance of science (ch. 6), but this is blocked by patriotism, religion, belief in kingship and the other atavistic beliefs which continue to have such a disastrous hold on the mind of 'civilised' men (and to which Theodore weakly subscribes) – the polarities of *The Croquet Player* are anticipated here. War demonstrates the ascendancy of the irrational, the triumph of untruth; man is an ape with 'one gift' to help him in his 'hideous battle with fact', the gift of lying: he is 'the one animal that can make a fire and keep off the beasts of the night. He is the one animal that can make a falsehood and keep off the beasts of despair' (ch. 9). Yet, paradoxically, Theodore in his cowardly panic in the trenches is less deluded, less of a liar, than at any other time. The narrative voice presents this with great delicacy. Terror has enabled him:

to strip himself and his world bare, to see plainly the incoherence of his lusts and sentimental phases, to admit his fear of pain and his reluctance for endeavour, to own up to his endless insufficiencies.

But this clarity cannot last. He returns from the war a liar and a braggart, 'a war hero returning to civil life. He had served and suffered. The Bulpington of Blup had played his part' (ch. 8), and spends ten futile years in literary Paris, pursuing distinction of a conservative kind with a 'brilliantly aggressive' literary periodical which attacks the values of science and industry (the resemblances to Ford as he was in the 1920s are cruelly close) before settling in genteel retirement in Dorset where he becomes a systematic praiser of his own past.

The Bulpington of Blup stands out from Wells's work of the 1930s as a major novel in which Wells recovers, to a considerable extent, the virtues that he displayed in the Edwardian period; structural coherence, dramatic energy, comedy, and the ability to link the study of an individual figure to large public concerns. And it adds to those virtues a new objectivity; it explores exhaustively, and with great sensitivity, the consciousness of a figure who is to be repudiated and condemned by the novel's dramatic organisation. The younger Wells was incapable of such artistic detachment: it required, I would argue, the failure of confidence that he displays in the 1920s and the experience of writing about divided, depressed and alienated personalities in the fictions of those years to prepare him for this achievement.

In his study of Wells's later novels Robert Bloom has made equally strong claims for *Brynhild* (1937) and *Apropos of Dolores* (1938).[1] Although these books are indeed interesting and the things he says about them are often persuasive, my own view is that they are nothing like as good as *The Bulpington* and that the attempt to claim parity of virtue for them weakens the case for that novel. *Apropos of Dolores* is the slighter of the two; a lively piece of literary revenge, systematically ridiculing and reviling Wells's former mistress, Odette Keun, it seems to be not more than a channel for Wells's vexed and aggressive feelings towards this woman, although it does have some good comic dialogue. *Brynhild* is more ambitious, and Bloom claims that it is an attempt to write a novel 'as James understood the form' (p. 86). By careful selection he succeeds in making the novel look a good deal more coherent and dramatically responsible than it really is: one has only to read it through to see that it is loosely constructed and that much of it is badly written. Comparison with a tightly organised work like *Love and Mr Lewisham* immediately shows up the patchiness and awkward contrivances of *Brynhild*. The people, admittedly, are 'Jamesian' in that they are intelligent, literary and self-conscious. Brynhild Palace's sensuality detaches her from her writer husband, Rowland, who is immersed in vanity and self-preoccupation, and propels her into an affair with a Lawrence-like writer who has sprung from the working class (and writes under the ludicrous pseudonym of Alfred Bunter). She has a child by Bunter and several children by her husband; she settles down to a double life with her husband and her lover, and at the end of the novel she is planning to work for education and world peace 'so that they don't kill or starve my children or leave them alive with nothing sensible to do' (ch. 12). The novel ends with a curious image which seems to claim for the whole text a subtle symbolic pattern:

In New Zealand [. . .] the decorations on a beam or a pillar may be expanded by an understanding imagination into the most complete and interesting of patterns, and so it is with this book. It is a novel in the Maori style, a presentation of imaginative indications ('Envoi').

I am unable to see this pattern. If Wells had re-written the novel he might have been capable of giving it the system of 'imaginative indications' (with its strong suggestion of James's 'figure in the carpet') that this passage suggests is present; but as it stands the novel does no more than gesture towards the notion that subtlety is a literary virtue. With its ludicrously melodramatic subplot (it emerges that 'Alfred Bunter' is not only a successful working-class novelist but also a murderer on the run) and its rather too easy acceptance of sexual freedom devoid of anxiety, it simply does not have the tightness and tension that Wells seems to be claiming for it.

Conclusion

In the late 1930s Wells was suffering from a sense of failure in both his private and his public lives. Moura Budberg, whom he had first met in Russia in 1914, settled with him in London in 1934 but steadfastly refused to marry him despite his persistent pleading. In his public life the disappointment was, quite simply, that the world had not listened to his ideas. In a sympathetic memoir, C. P. Snow remarks on Wells's near-desperation in these years. Wells's work in the thirties, he says, became overbearingly didactic because he was hoping in vain to recapture his earlier audiences, to reclaim for his work as a teacher the prestige that he had forfeited as a novelist, and to compensate himself for the contempt levelled at him by the gifted young. In 1938 Wells abruptly asked, one evening in Cambridge, 'Ever thought of suicide, Snow?', and then confessed that he had been considering suicide himself since he had reached the age of seventy (he was then seventy-two).[1] It is perhaps to be expected that a fighting temperament, propelled by neurotic energy, should express itself in alternating extremes of hope and despair. Dualism, as I have indicated, is a constant feature of Wells's work. Pessimistic and optimistic ideas co-exist throughout: on the one hand is the belief that man is a degenerating species who invents gods to compensate himself for his own weaknesses and is doomed by the laws of entropy, and on the other is the hope that man can transform his future by the exercise of his will and the right understanding of his own history. G. P. Wells wrote in 1968 that he saw two motifs running like threads through the whole of his father's work, 'his belief in the immensity of human opportunities, and his dread that mankind may fail to take them'.[2]

The optimism of *The Outline of History* is summed up in its final chapter: religion and education, the forces which have traditionally restrained the violent impulses in man, became divorced from each other in the nineteenth century, and it was this divorce that permitted the disaster of the Great War. The hope for mankind is that education should become once more 'religious' in the sense that it will establish in the next generation a spirit of 'devotion', 'universal service' and a 'complete escape from the self'. If this can be achieved, then a 'United States of the Old World' (comprising Europe and Asia) will come into being to balance the United States of America, and world unity will be established. The leading features of the universally aristocratic society advocated in the 'Open Conspiracy' writings of the 1920s and 1930s are anticipated here: there will be 'elimination of drudgery' through the intelligent use of machines, and life will 'go with a stronger pulse, it will breathe a deeper breath' (ch. 41).

The 'religion' which will underpin this education is, of course, wholly distinct from Christianity. Apart from the aberrant phase during the Great War in which he invented a kind of Wellsian God to whom suffering humanity might turn, Wells resisted deism (and Christianity in particular) throughout his career. With its vigorous parodies of the Commandments and the Creeds, *The Island of Dr Moreau*, a 'theological grotesque', is the earliest of his attacks on Christianity, anticipating what he describes in *The Happy Turning* (1945) as the 'theological jokes' of his last phase. Here he remarks that he has written 'a considerable amount of excellent blasphemy' and has published only a small proportion of it (ch. 2). One example that got into print is *All Aboard for Ararat* (1940) in which God the Father, a dishevelled old gentleman newly escaped from a lunatic asylum, tries to persuade a reluctant twentieth-century Noah to man a second ark. Clearly the 'excellent blasphemies' can be related partly to his mother's early attempt to impose an evangelical training on him: he acknowledges in *The Happy Turning* that there must be 'lingering bits of belief' to produce 'the relief of laughter' (ch. 2), and in his novel-writing, of course, he drew heavily on his own childhood to illustrate his struggle with God. This was still going on in *You Can't be Too Careful* (1941); Edward Albert Tewler, in this novel, is the last of Wells's lower-middle-class anti-heroes, and the early chapters, describing Tewler's Edwardian childhood, link him closely with such figures as Lewisham and (especially) Kipps. Tewler's mother tries to smother his struggling sexual curiosity with religious teaching, but nature is against her: the adolescent Tewler masturbates and at the same time considers the illuminated text that his mother has hung on his bedroom wall, 'Thou God Seest Me.' 'Could He see through the bedclothes?' wonders Tewler, 'whatever you chanced to be doing? There was something indelicate about this relentless stare' (ch. 5).

After the publication of *The Outline of History* in 1920 his hostility became focused specifically on *Catholic* Christianity; this seems to have been a direct result of his venomous dispute with Hilaire Belloc over what Belloc saw as *The Outline of History*'s 'provincial' anti-Catholic prejudice, a prejudice which is a product of Wells's lower-middle-class 'satisfied ignorance' and inability to understand matters 'not of his own religious and social experience'.[3] Belloc's attack was arrogant, dogmatic and viciously personal: Wells was enraged and replied with *Mr Belloc Objects to the Outline of History* (1926). Belloc hit back with a pamphlet and a book; it was a vigorous public clash, and its aftermath rumbled on for several years. It prepared the way for one of Wells's most extraordinary books, *Crux Ansata* (1943: one of a series of 'Penguin Specials' on matters of topical interest in the Second World War). Here Wells begins by urging the Allies to bomb Rome in reprisal for the bombing of Canterbury in June 1942, and then goes on to revile the Catholic Church as a wholly self-seeking, repressive political institution, run by old men who have forgotten any ideals that they may once have had in the course of their life-long struggles for short-term advantages. The God of these people is a 'vain and vindictive Bogy' (ch. 16) and their life-style has turned them into monsters: a celibate priest is by definition sexually thwarted and intellectually deformed. 'We are dealing with ideas left from the Dark Ages, in the brains of beings at once puerile, perverted and malignant. Pius XII, when we strip him down to reality, shows himself as unreal and ignorant as Hitler' (ch. 21). This book was an easy target for a Catholic riposte – the editor of the *Catholic Herald* was surely right to call it 'unfair, inaccurate and libellous'[4] – but, typically, Wells neither apologised nor relented. In the dream-world described in *The Happy Turning* there is a holy water stoup containing 'Truth'; with it Wells says that he can sprinkle 'The Holy Catholic Church, or whatever ugly menace to mankind happens to be upon my heels' which will then explode 'with a slightly unpleasant odour' and vanish (ch. 4).

In spite of the rancour and inaccuracy of his attack on *The Outline of History* Belloc was right on one point, which was that Wells's attitude to Christianity is that of a late-Victorian scientist; it is permissible to see the Wells of 1920–46 as the pupil of

Huxley who keeps the Victorian conflict between religion and science going well into the twentieth century. His blasphemy was not just a joke, nor merely part of his rebellious temperament's drive to destroy all existing systems and conventions; it was a real intellectual position. His last two books, *The Happy Turning* and *Mind at the End of its Tether*, continue to defend this position. They are very different from each other in tone, and it is a curious fact, and a further instance of his dualism, that he was composing them at the same time: G. P. Wells recalls seeing the two typescripts, neither quite complete, in his father's study late in 1944.[5] The optimism of his utopias (including *A Modern Utopia* and *The Dream*) finds its last expression in *The Happy Turning*, while the darkness of *The Island of Dr Moreau*, *Mr Blettsworthy on Rampole Island* and *The Croquet Player* returns in an extreme form in *Mind at the End of its Tether* (1945). In this short book – the last of Wells's life – there are two somewhat contradictory propositions: one is that an 'Antagonist', an 'unknown implacable', has turned against man and is intent on extinguishing him as a species, while the other is that in Darwinian terms man is now in his final decline: he must 'go steeply up or down and the odds seem to be all in favour of his going down and out', to give way to 'some other animal better adapted' to the changing circumstances of life on earth. By contrast with the hysteria of *Mind at the End of its Tether* the tone of *The Happy Turning* is strikingly cheerful; Edwardian Wells is back on form, buoyant, cocky and pleased with himself. In a chapter called 'Jesus of Nazareth Discusses his Failure' a deeply misunderstood Jesus, whose 'scorn and contempt for Christianity go beyond my extremest vocabulary', warns Wells against stupid and over-zealous followers: '*Never* have disciples [. . .] it was my greatest mistake' (ch. 5). In his own words, blasphemous jokes depend on 'lingering bits of belief' for their effect (ch. 2), and the obvious enjoyment with which Wells writes *The Happy Turning* seems to depend on the latent presence of the God whose existence he gleefully denies. The same is true of his chosen epitaph; Wells is quoted by Sir Ernest Barker as saying that his last words would be 'God damn you all: I told you so'.[6] It is an interesting choice of phrase from a man who so vigorously resisted the notion that a deity might be in control of human affairs.

The Happy Turning restates a view of the writer's duty with which one has become familiar from *Boon*, *The Bulpington of Blup*, the quarrel with James and the autobiography: the written word is not art but a vehicle for communication, it must 'talk about what things are, what life is' and present 'the work of the human mind in telling and enforcing a view'. Used thus, writing can yield 'real' literature which is clearly distinguishable from the 'sham' literature of those who cultivate 'beauty' (this sham literature includes Tennyson, Morris, Blake, Byron and T. S. Eliot). Literariness – all that claims to be high, distinguished, cultivated, ascendant – gets its last come-uppance: 'There can be no classical novels or romances. The strictly circumstantial ones last longest. Fielding's *Voyage to Lisbon* will outlive *Tom Jones*.' I have said above (ch. 4) that Wells lost the quarrel with Henry James on tactics: that he was in possession of a defensible alternative to James's view of the novelist's art but failed to defend it responsibly. In an introduction to *Babes in the Darkling Wood* (1940), which is the last of his discussion novels, Wells recalls his early differences from James, Conrad and Ford and his resentment of their claim to practise '*The* Novel', but he still does not defend his own novels beyond saying that they were 'spontaneous' and that a novel can be 'any sort of honest treatment of the realities of human behaviour in narrative form'. This introduction is a serious, formal essay on 'the novel of ideas', but after the opening paragraphs it abandons the quarrel with James – once more leaving James in possession of the field by default – in order to defend the discussion, or dialogue, novel; it is a sad reflection on his own judgement that the author of *Love and Mr Lewisham*, *Kipps* and *Tono-Bungay* should still in 1940 have been urging people to read *Joan and Peter* and *The Undying Fire*. *The Happy Turning* makes no attempt to conduct an argument; it simply attacks the familiar literary targets in a familiar way, but one can at least admire the fact that the cheek and iconoclasm which fuelled his quarrel with James continue to animate this little book written when he was nearly eighty.

If one stands back from Wells it is not, of course, upon the advocate of an Open Conspiracy, the teacher who urges man to understand his own history or the Victorian scientist struggling with God that one's attention is focused, but upon the writer. The scientific romances of the 1890s and the realist novels of the Edwardian period are major achievements with which *Mr Britling Sees it Through* and *Mr Blettsworthy on Rampole Island* will bear honourable comparison, and from the over-production of his last twenty years *The Bulpington of Blup* and *The Croquet Player* stand out as works of permanent interest. *The Bulpington of Blup*, in my

CONCLUSION

own view, is a subtle and sophisticated work of art which marks an advance on the methods of his Edwardian books and ought to be among the group of Wells's novels and romances which establish his claim to be regarded as one of the great twentieth-century writers.

Notes

1. The romances of the 1890s

1 C. T. Watts, ed., *Joseph Conrad's Letters to Cunninghame Graham* (Cambridge University Press, 1969) pp. 56–7.
2 V. S. Pritchett, *The Living Novel* (Chatto and Windus, 1966) p. 119.
3 This may well have been inspired by T. H. Huxley's 'Prolegomena to Evolution and Ethics' (1894) where he writes that human decision enables man to make gardens out of jungles, and altruism out of the instinct to survive. Gratitude and tenderness, along with humour and conscience, are signs of this essentially human, self-willed improvement.

2. The Edwardian achievement, I

1 See Robert P. Weeks, 'Disentanglement as a Theme in H. G. Wells's Fiction', in Views, pp. 25–31.
2 H. G. Wells, 'Jude the Obscure', *The Saturday Review*, LXXXI, 8, February 1896, p. 154.

3. The Edwardian achievement, II

1 Wells is, of course, against the modernist aesthetic: he renounces it (for instance in his correspondence with Henry James) just as it begins to get a real footing in English literary life, and for this reason, to Modernists like Virginia Woolf and D. H. Lawrence, he became in the 1920s a representative figure of the Old Guard. I discuss Wells's quarrel with Henry James in chapter 4.
2 In his autobiography Wells notes that he was on good personal terms with Grant Allen, and adds: 'I do not think I have ever made a fair acknowledgement of a certain mental indebtedness to him. Better thirty-five years late than never' (Autobiography, II, p. 546).
3 W. W. Robson, *Modern English Literature* (Oxford University Press, 1970), p. 12.
4 Polly's indigestion is one of the many disorders affecting that ill-adjusted animal, urban man. In *The Biology of the Human Race* (vol. 9 of *The Science of Life*), a good deal of space is given to the evils of modern man's eating habits. Man is born with the instincts of 'an ape-

man living from hand to mouth', and in the civilised state his impulse 'to gorge and fatten' has become dangerous (ch. 3). In Mr Polly, Wells presents a victim of a civilisation which has produced women who can't cook, men who have no outlet for their aggressions, and meals which are eaten for social or ceremonial rather than nutritional reasons.

4. The decade of struggle

1   Richard Ellmann notes that 'The Edwardians were looking for ways to express their conviction that we can be religious about life itself [. . .] The capitalised word for the Edwardian is not "God" but "Life" ' ('Two faces of Edward', *Golden Codgers* (Oxford University Press, 1973), p. 120).

2   Conrad had gained his first literary recognition through Wells's enthusiastic review of *Almayer's Folly* (*The Saturday Review*, 15 June 1895, xxix, p. 797).

3   Alfred Habegger, in *Gender, Fantasy and Realism in American Literature* (Columbia University Press, 1982), takes a similarly hostile view of James. In a chapter called 'The Gentleman of Shalott: Henry James and American Masculinity' he speaks of James as an inadequate male, 'so detached, so uninitiated, so alone [. . .] that all human associations remained secret societies from his point of view. He never learnt the things boys took for granted, never caught on to the language men actually spoke' (p. 255). His work reflects his 'deep and humiliating anguish at his failure ever to become a proper man' (p. 267).

5. Wells in the modern world

1   Robert Bloom, *Anatomies of Egotism: A Reading of the Last Novels of H. G. Wells* (University of Nebraska Press, 1977).

2   Rebecca West, 'Uncle Bennett', *The Strange Necessity* (Jonathan Cape, 1928), pp. 199–213; pp. 199–200 are devoted to 'Uncle Wells'. Wells had already been riled by Rebecca West's admiration for Henry James and was further irritated by the fact that the title essay, 'The Strange Necessity', expressed great admiration for James Joyce.

3   Virginia Woolf, 'Modern Fiction', *Collected Essays*, Vol. II (Hogarth, 1966), p. 105.

4   George Orwell, 'Wells, Hitler and the World State', *Collected Essays*, Vol. II (Secker and Warburg, 1968), pp. 139–45.

5   R. Scholes and R. Kellogg, *The Nature of Narrative* (Oxford University Press, 1966), p. 272.

6   'Daniel Chaucer' (Ford Madox Ford), *The New Humpty Dumpty* (John Lane, the Bodley Head, 1912).

7 Arthur Mizener, *The Saddest Story: A Biography of Ford Madox Ford* (Bodley Head, 1974), pp. 281–3, 291–3.

Conclusion

1 C. P. Snow, *Variety of Men* (Macmillan, 1967), p. 61.
2 G. P. Wells, ed., *The Last Books of H. G. Wells* (H. G. Wells Society, 1968), Introduction, p. 11.
3 Hilaire Belloc, *A Companion to Mr Wells's Outline of History* (Sheed and Ward, 1926), pp. 4–6.
4 Michael de la Bedoyere, *Was it Worth it Wells?* (Paternoster, 1944), p. 450.
5 G. P. Wells, ed., *The Last Books of H. G. Wells* (H. G. Wells Society, 1968), Introduction, p. 9.
6 Ernest Barker, *Age and Youth* (Oxford University Press, 1953), p. 108.

Chronology (including major publications)

Some of the relationships with women described in *H. G. Wells in Love* (edited by G. P. Wells: Faber, 1984) – for example those with Violet Hunt in the Edwardian period and with Antonina Vallentin in 1929 – are not listed in this chronology.

1866 Born in Bromley, Kent, 21 September. Third son of Joseph Wells, a former gardener and professional cricketer turned shopkeeper, and Sarah Wells, a former lady's maid.

1873 Goes to school at Morley's Academy, Bromley.

1877 Joseph Wells is injured and is thereafter unable to support his family.

1880 Sarah Wells leaves her husband to work as a housekeeper at Up Park, Sussex. H. G. Wells, aged fourteen, is apprenticed to a draper.

1881 During a brief apprenticeship to a chemist Wells is sent to Midhurst Grammar School, where his talent is recognised by the headmaster, Horace Byatt.

1881–83 Apprenticed to a draper in Southsea.

1883 Aged seventeen, returns to Midhurst Grammar School to be trained as a teacher by Byatt. Wins a scholarship to the Normal School of Science in South London (now Imperial College).

1884–87 Studies at the Normal School of Science. For the first year he studies biology under T. H. Huxley.

1887 Leaves the Normal School with mediocre qualifications and teaches at Holt Academy, North Wales, where he sustains a serious kidney injury. Also suffers lung haemorrhages and is thought to be tubercular. Convalesces at Up Park. Joseph Wells sells the shop in Bromley and moves to a cottage in Nyewoods, Sussex.

1888 'The Chronic Argonauts' (first version of *The Time Machine*) published in *The Science Schools Journal* (student magazine). Poor health persists; stays in Stoke-on-Trent, Staffordshire, to recuperate; here he conceives an unwritten 'industrial' novel (of which 'The Cone' is a product). Returns to London: supports himself by teaching, and studies for the London B.Sc. (external).

1889 Tutors for the University Correspondence College.

1890 Takes the B.Sc. with first class honours in zoology. Continues as a salaried tutor for the Correspondence College.

1891   *The Fortnightly Review* (edited by Frank Harris) accepts 'The Rediscovery of the Unique'; Wells starts his second career, that of journalist. Marries his cousin, Isabel Wells, and moves to Haldon Road, Wandsworth.

1892   Wells attracted to one of his students, Amy Catherine Robbins ('Jane').

1893   *Textbook of Biology.*
        Honours Physiography (with R. A. Gregory).
Sarah Wells is dismissed from Up Park and joins Joseph Wells at Nyewoods. Renewed lung haemorrhages force Wells to give up teaching; henceforth lives entirely by writing. Publishes a large number of short jocular pieces in *The Pall Mall Gazette* and places articles with a number of other magazines.

1894 (Spring)   Leaves his wife for 'Jane'; they move into lodgings in Mornington Place.

1895 (January)   Divorce from Isabel Wells.
        Select Conversations with an Uncle.
        The Time Machine published and is an immediate success.
        The Wonderful Visit.
        The Stolen Bacillus (15 short stories).
Reviews fiction for Frank Harris's *The Saturday Review* (until 1897); evolves a theory of realism through this work. Makes friends with G. B. Shaw. (October) Marriage to 'Jane'; the Wellses move to a villa in Maybury Road, Woking (the setting for *The War of the Worlds*).

1896   *The Island of Dr Moreau.*
        The Wheels of Chance.
Wells an established success; J. B. Pinker becomes his literary agent. Moves from Woking to 'Heatherlea', Worcester Park. (November) First meeting with George Gissing, who becomes a close friend. During the Worcester Park period, 1896–98, he encourages Dorothy Richardson (who had been at school with 'Jane') to persist with writing the *roman fleuve* which was eventually to become *Pilgrimage*: the relationship leads to a brief affair. Wells and his wife were to appear as 'Hypo and Alma Wilson' in the fourth novel of the *Pilgrimage* sequence, *The Tunnel* (1919).

1897   *The Plattner Story: And Others* (17 stories).
        The Invisible Man.
        Certain Personal Matters (humorous essays).
        Thirty Strange Stories (previous collections plus 3 new stories).
First correspondence with Arnold Bennett, who becomes the most loyal of Wells's friends.

1898   *The War of the Worlds.*
Illness precipitates a move from London to Seaford, and then to a rented cottage in Sandgate, near Folkestone. Persistent anxiety over his damaged kidney. Establishes friendships with Joseph Conrad, Ford Madox Ford (Hueffer) and Henry James.

1899   *When the Sleeper Wakes.*

Tales of Space and Time (five stories, including 'The Man Who Could Work Miracles' and 'The Star').

Friendship with Stephen Crane.

1900   *Love and Mr Lewisham.*

Builds 'Spade House', Sandgate. (June) Death of Stephen Crane. (December) The Wellses move into Spade House.

1901   *The First Men in the Moon.*

Anticipations.

(July) Birth of G. P. Wells.

1902   *The Discovery of the Future.*

The Sea Lady.

Wells is taken up by Beatrice and Sidney Webb, prominent members of the Fabian Society (which included E. Nesbit, her husband Hubert Bland, and G. B. Shaw).

1903 (February)   Wells joins the Fabian Society.

Mankind in the Making.

Twelve Stories and a Dream (includes 'A Dream of Armageddon' and 'The New Accelerator').

(October) Birth of Frank Wells. (Christmas) Wells goes to the deathbed of George Gissing in France.

1903–04   Dramatises *The Wheels of Chance* as *Hoopdriver's Holiday* (published 1964).

1904   *The Food of the Gods.*

1905   *A Modern Utopia.*

Kipps.

(June) Death of Sarah Wells. Growing disagreement with the 'Old Gang' (which included Shaw, the Webbs, Hubert Bland and Pember Reeves) of the Fabian Society. (Winter, 1905–06) Visit to America; meets Maxim Gorky.

1906   *In the Days of the Comet.*

The Future in America.

Faults of the Fabians (pamphlet).

Socialism and the Family.

Reconstruction of the Fabian Society (pamphlet).

First encounters with Rosamund Bland (daughter of Hubert) and with Amber Reeves (daughter of Pember). Wells's struggle for mastery of the Fabian Society ends in defeat (mainly at the hands of Shaw) on 14 December.

1907   A number of socialist publications (including *This Misery of Boots*).

1908   *New Worlds for Old.*

The War in the Air.

First and Last Things.

Developing relationship with Amber Reeves.

1909 *Tono-Bungay.*
Ann Veronica.
Quarrel with Ford Madox Ford (Hueffer) over the serialisation of *Tono-Bungay* leads to a permanent breach. *Ann Veronica* is virulently attacked on moral grounds by St Loe Strachey in the *Spectator*. Amber Reeves, expecting a child by Wells, is married (in July) to G. R. B. White, but the relationship with Wells continues. Spade House is sold: the Wellses move to 17 Church Row, Hampstead. (31 December) Birth of Amber Reeves's daughter.

1910 *The History of Mr Polly.*
(Spring) End of relationship with Amber Reeves. (June) Death of Joseph Wells. Wells's friendships with Shaw, the Webbs and other former associates severely strained by the Amber Reeves affair; he feels himself under attack from all sides.

1911 *The New Machiavelli.*
The Country of the Blind: and Other Stories (33 stories).
The Door in the Wall (8 stories).

(1911–12) Relationship with Elizabeth von Arnim.

1912 *Marriage.*
Meets Rebecca West, who had written an adverse review of *Marriage*. The Wellses move from Hampstead to the Rectory, Little Easton (later 'Easton Glebe'), Essex, leased from Lady Warwick (H.G. also has a flat in London from this date).

1913 *Little Wars.*
The Passionate Friends.
Developing relationship with Rebecca West. Growing disagreement with Henry James over the art of the novel. Publishes pamphlets on war (later included in *An Englishman Looks at the World*) and an attack on Lloyd George.

1914 *An Englishman Looks at the World* (26 essays).
The World Set Free (anticipates the invention of the atomic bomb; predicts a post-nuclear utopia).
The Wife of Sir Isaac Harman.
The War that will End War (collection of articles written after the outbreak of war in August).
(January) Visit to Russia: renews contact with Maxim Gorky, meets Marie von Benckendorff (later Moura Budberg). (April) Henry James's articles in *The Times Literary Supplement*, 'The Younger Generation', arouse Wells's animosity. (August) Anthony West, son of H. G. Wells and Rebecca West, born on the day war is declared.

1915 *The Peace of the World* (articles on war).
Boon (precipitates final breach with Henry James).
Bealby.
The Research Magnificent.

1916 *What is Coming* (scheme for post-war reconstruction).

Mr Britling Sees it Through.
The Elements of Reconstruction (pamphlet).
(February) Death of Henry James. (August) Wells tours the battlefields in France and Northern Italy.
1917 *War and the Future* (an account of his visit to the war fronts of August 1916).
God the Invisible King.
The Soul of a Bishop.
(March) Revolution in Russia welcomed by Wells. Serves on the 'Research Committee' for the League of Nations (with Gilbert Murray, Leonard Woolf, Ernest Barker and others); campaigns vigorously for a League of Nations 1917–19.
1918 *In the Fourth Year* (advocating a League of Nations).
Joan and Peter.
British Nationalism and the League of Nations (pamphlet).
(May) Wells is invited by Lord Northcliffe to organise propaganda warfare directed at German civilians and armed forces for the Ministry of Information; (late June) breach with Northcliffe leads to Wells's resignation. Wells plans a major work which will furnish mankind with 'salvation by history' (becomes *The Outline of History*). Recruits Gilbert Murray, Ernest Barker and other League of Nations associates to advise on this project.
1919 *The Undying Fire.*
(Spring) Resigns from the 'Research Committee' but continues to publish pamphlets and articles advocating a League of Nations.
1920 *The Outline of History* (outstrips all Wells's previous sales and establishes his new role as world teacher).
(Summer) Meets Margaret Sanger. (September) Visits Russia with G. P. Wells; renews contact with Maxim Gorky and Moura Budberg (now Gorky's secretary), has an interview with Lenin. This visit is the subject of *Russia in the Shadows*. (December) Is attacked in the press by Winston Churchill for being a 'pro-Bolshevik'.
1921 *The Salvaging of Civilisation.*
Articles and lectures on the teaching of history (sequels to the *Outline*). Autumn; visits Washington to report on the World Conference for Disarmament (for the *New York World* and the *Daily Mail*), renews contact with Margaret Sanger. (November) Stands unsuccessfully for parliament as Labour member for London University.
1922 *Washington and the Hope of Peace* (collected articles on the Washington Conference).
The Secret Places of the Heart.
A Short History of the World.
Stands unsuccessfully for parliament (again) as a Labour candidate in the general election. (Summer) Death of F. W. Sanderson, headmaster of Oundle (to which Wells had sent his sons).
1923 *Men Like Gods.*

(October) End of relationship with Rebecca West, who sails with Anthony for America.

1924 *The Story of a Great Schoolmaster* (memoir of F. W. Sanderson).
The Dream.
A Year of Prophesying (55 articles).

Publication of the 'Atlantic' edition of Wells's works, which includes his prefaces to each volume and a general introduction. (Autumn) Attends a League of Nations assembly in Geneva and meets (by arrangement) Odette Keun.

1925 *Christina Alberta's Father.*
A Forecast of the World's Affairs.

(**1925–32**, spends part of each year in the South of France with Odette Keun; these visits become progressively shorter after the death of 'Jane' in 1927.)

1926 *The World of William Clissold.*
Mr Belloc Objects to the Outline of History.

Public quarrel with Hilaire Belloc over the alleged anti-Catholicism of *The Outline of History*, following a new edition of *The Outline* (*Mr Belloc Objects* is part of this quarrel). Builds 'Lou Pidou', Grasse, for himself and Odette Keun. Conceives the second volume of his 'new bible' (becomes *The Science of Life*; the *Outline* being the first volume of a projected trilogy).

1927 *Meanwhile.*

(A 'collected' volume of his short stories and a number of writings on the inadequacy of current peace movements published during this year.) (April–October) Wells is in England during 'Jane's' final illness. (April) G. P. Wells marries Marjorie Craig, Wells's secretary. (October) Death of 'Jane' Wells from cancer, the day before Frank Wells's marriage to Peggy Gibbons.

1928 *The Way the World is Going* (collection of essays).
The Open Conspiracy.
Mr Blettsworthy on Rampole Island.
The Book of Catherine Wells published as a tribute to 'Jane' Wells; a collection of her writings with an introduction by H. G. Wells.

Plans for a third volume of the 'new bible', *The Science of Wealth* (this becomes *The Work, Wealth and Happiness of Mankind*).

1929 *The King who was a King* (novel in the form of a film script, based on an abandoned film scenario).
The Adventures of Tommy (children's book).
Imperialism and the Open Conspiracy (pamphlet).

(April) Gives an address in the Reichstag in Berlin, later published as *The Common Sense of World Peace*. Renews contact with Moura Budberg in Berlin. Difficulties with H. P. Vowles, one of the collaborators on the projected *Science of Wealth*. Takes a flat in Chiltern Court, London (a block in which Arnold Bennett also has a flat).

1930 *The Autocracy of Mr Parham.*

The Science of Life (with Julian Huxley and G. P. Wells).

The Way to World Peace (pamphlet).

Gives up the lease of Easton Glebe and makes Chiltern Court his home in England. Difficulties with Vowles lead to a quarrel with the Society of Authors (Wells publishes two privately-printed pamphlets presenting his side of the quarrel). Moura Budberg, having left Maxim Gorky, is now living in London. 'Geoffrey West' publishes a biography of Wells.

1931 *The Work, Wealth and Happiness of Mankind* (third part of the 'new bible' or education trilogy, of which the previous parts were *Outline* and *The Science of Life*; this third part was earlier planned as *The Science of Wealth*).

The Open Conspiracy revised as *What are we to do with our Lives?* during this year.

(March) Death of Arnold Bennett. (September) Death of Isabel Wells. Partly in response to 'Geoffrey West's' book, Wells starts work on his autobiography.

1932 *After Democracy* (a collection of topical articles).

The Bulpington of Blup.

What Should Be Done Now? (pamphlet).

Relations with Odette Keun difficult throughout this year.

1933 *The Shape of Things to Come.*

(Spring) Final quarrel with Odette Keun. Under an earlier agreement she has the 'usufruct' of Lou Pidou; she insists on her rights, and he has to cede possession of the house to her for her lifetime. Developing relationship with Moura Budberg, with whom Wells spends much of the rest of the year. Becomes chairman of the international P.E.N. clubs.

1934 *Experiment in Autobiography* (vols. I and II).

Odette Keun attacks Wells in two reviews of the autobiography. (May) Visit to Roosevelt in Washington. (July) Visit to Stalin in Moscow. Public quarrel with Shaw over Wells's attitude to Stalin (recorded in *Stalin–Wells Talk*, report and discussion, published by the *New Statesman* as a pamphlet). Moves to 13 Hanover Terrace and establishes a settled relationship with Moura Budberg, but she refuses to marry him.

1935 Wells publishes an account of his meeting with Roosevelt in *The New America*, and collaborates with Alexander Korda on a film version of 'The Shape of Things to Come' (the scenario published as *Things to Come*; the film completed in 1936).

1936 *The Anatomy of Frustration.*

The Croquet Player (written under the stimulus of the Spanish Civil War).

(October) Seventieth birthday celebration organised by the P.E.N. club. Plans a 'World Encyclopaedia' (outlined in a lecture in November).

1937 *Star-Begotten.*

Brynhild.

The Camford Visitation.

Lecture to the Education Section of the British Association for the Advancement of Science on 'The Informative Content of Education' (elaboration of his plan for a World Encyclopaedia).

1938 *The Brothers.*

World Brain (articles and lectures).

Apropos of Dolores (takes literary revenge on Odette Keun).

(October) Orson Welles's radio adaptation of *The War of the Worlds* causes panic in America. (Winter, 1938–39) Short stay in Australia as a visiting lecturer.

1939 *The Holy Terror.*

Travels of a Republican Radical.

The Fate of Homo Sapiens.

The New World Order.

Wells in Stockholm to speak to the P.E.N. club when Hitler invades Poland. Predicts that the new war will mark the end of nationalism.

1940 *The Rights of Man* (in support of the Sankey Declaration).

Babes in the Darkling Wood.

The Common Sense of War and Peace.

All Aboard for Ararat.

Other publications (articles and pamphlets) on world peace and reconstruction during this year. Wells defies the bombing of London and stays at Hanover Terrace for the duration of the war.

1941 *Guide to the New World* (on post-war reconstruction)

You Can't be Too Careful.

1942 *The Outlook for Homo Sapiens.*

Science and the World Mind (pamphlet).

Phoenix: A Summary of the Inescapable Conditions of World Organization.

Writes a number of pamphlets on reconstruction and a D.Sc. thesis on 'The Quality of Illusion in the Continuity of Individual Life'. In poor health for much of this year.

1043 *Crux Ansata.*

(April) Death of Beatrice Webb. Wells is awarded the D.Sc. and hopes to be elected an F.R.S., but this honour is withheld despite the efforts of his friend Sir Richard Gregory.

1944 *'42 to '44* (collection of essays and his D.Sc. thesis).

V bombs attack London; Wells declines an invitation from Margaret Sanger to take a holiday in Arizona; stays at Hanover Terrace.

1945 *The Happy Turning.*

Mind at the End of its Tether.

(August) Atomic bombing of Japan stimulates Wells to write a new film script (unfinished; *Things to Come* brought up to date with the reality of atomic weapons).

1946 (13 August) Dies at Hanover Terrace.

Index

H. G. Wells's works are listed under their titles

INDEX

INDEX

The King's Pudding

Retold by Mairi Mackinnon

Illustrated by Nathalie Ragondet

Reading consultant: Alison Kelly
University of Roehampton

Little Deer lived in a **dangerous** jungle.

SNAP!

One morning, he went
to the river to drink.

Suddenly, something
caught his eye.

Little Deer looked
around quickly.

"Oh no, I can't possibly be
your breakfast," he said.

"I'm guarding the
King's pudding."

"The King's pudding?"
asked Tiger.

Little Deer pointed to a brownish cake on the ground.

It's the most delicious thing you ever tasted.

"No one else is
allowed to go near it."

10

"You mean I can't even
try it?" asked Tiger.

11

"Oh no," said Little Deer.
"The King would be
furious."

"You could pretend you didn't see me," said Tiger.

"I know!" said Little Deer. "I could pretend you chased me away."

And Little Deer ran away,
as fast as he could.

15

Tiger closed his eyes
and licked the pudding.

Bleurgh!

It was just a heap of mud.

"Little Deer, wait until I catch you!" he growled.

But Little Deer was safe, far, far away.

17

In the middle of the day,
Little Deer went to the
river to drink.

Suddenly, something
caught his eye.

19

"Tiger!" gasped
Little Deer.

"Lunch!"
growled Tiger.

Little Deer looked around.
"Oh no, I can't possibly be
your lunch."

21

"I'm guarding the King's belt."

"The King's belt?" asked Tiger.

Little Deer pointed to a
bright loop hanging over
a branch.

23

"No one else is allowed
to touch it."

"You mean I can't even
try it on?" asked Tiger.

25

"Oh no," said Little Deer.
"The King would be
furious."

"The King won't know,"
said Tiger. "I won't tell."

"But someone else might see," said Little Deer.

And Little Deer ran away,
as fast as he could.

29

Tiger draped the belt around his waist. He pulled it tight.

Yowww!

The belt hissed. It was a snake, a very angry snake.

"Little Deer, wait until I
catch you!" growled Tiger.

But Little Deer was safe,
far, far away.

That evening, Little Deer
went to the river to drink.

Suddenly, something
caught his eye.

"Tiger!" gasped
Little Deer.

"Dinner!"
growled Tiger.

Little Deer looked around.
"Oh no, I can't possibly be
your dinner."

"I'm guarding the King's drum."

"The King's drum?" asked Tiger.

Little Deer pointed to a
dark shape hanging from
a tree.

37

"No one else is allowed
to touch it."

38

"You mean I can't even
tap it?" asked Tiger.

"Oh no," said Little Deer.
"The King would be furious."

39

"You could say you didn't
see me," said Tiger.

40

"That's no good,"
said Little Deer.

"I need to be far, far away,
so I can't even hear you."

41

And Little Deer ran
away, as fast as he could.

Tiger patted the shape.
Wasps poured out of their
nest, buzzing angrily.

Ow! Ow!!
Ow-ow-ow!!!

They stung poor Tiger
again and again.

"Little Deer!" roared
Tiger. "I give up!"

"My mouth is full of mud."

"My tummy is full of snake bites..."

"...and my paws are full of wasp stings."

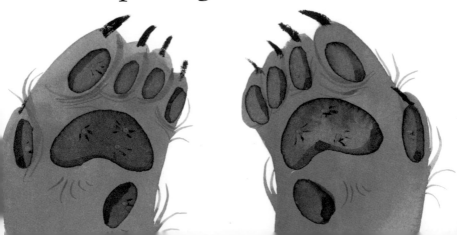

"I promise I will never try to eat you again!"

Far, far away, Little
Deer heard Tiger's roar
and smiled.

47

The King's Pudding is a story
from Indonesia. Little Deer is a tiny
mouse deer, between 20-30cm
(about 8-12 inches) tall.

Designed by Caroline Spatz
Series designer: Russell Punter
Series editor: Lesley Sims

First published in 2012 by Usborne Publishing Ltd., Usborne House,
83-85 Saffron Hill, London EC1N 8RT, England. www.usborne.com
Copyright © 2012 Usborne Publishing Ltd.

USBORNE FIRST READING
Level Four

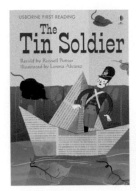

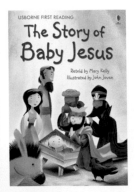

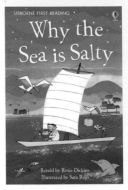

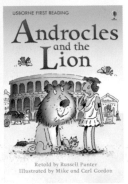

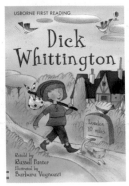